CRAFT BEER WORLD

CRAFT BEER WORLD

A GUIDE TO OVER **350** OF THE FINEST BEERS KNOWN TO MAN

MARK DREDGE

About the author

Mark Dredge is an award-winning beer writer and runs the popular blog Pencil & Spoon where he writes about anything ale-related—from food and beer pairings to the world's best places to try new and exciting drinks. He won awards from the British Guild of Beer Writers in 2009, 2010, and 2011, his work has featured in leading publications across the globe, and he's an international beer judge.

Published in 2013 by Dog 'n' Bone Books
An imprint of Ryland Peters & Small Ltd

20–21 Jockey's Fields   519 Broadway, 5th Floor
London WC1R 4BW   New York, NY 10012

www.rylandpeters.com

10 9 8 7 6

A CIP catalog record for this book is available from the Library of Congress and the British Library.

ISBN: 978 0 957140 99 8

Printed in China

Editor: Caroline West
Designer: Mark Latter
Motif illustration: Anna Galkina
Picture credits: p161 ESB Postiljon by BeerSweden; p107 Tilquin © Gueuzerie Tilquin; p107 barrels by MikeDonk/Brewbokeh; p177 Brasserie St Helene Black Mamba © www.atelierdesign.be; p86 Tara Boulba and p93 Jambe de Bois © Katherine Longley

For digital editions, visit www.cicobooks.com/apps.php

CONTENTS

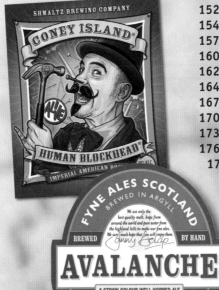

INTRODUCTION

I have "There's a story at the bottom of this bottle" tattooed on my left arm. Those nine words encapsulate what I love most about beer. Every beer has a story made up of numerous interlinking stories: the story of how it's brewed; why it's brewed; and the people who brewed it. It's also about the ingredients that were used and the story behind them: how they were produced and where they originated. Combine those ingredients to create a beer style, and that style then has its own history, whether it has been developed over time or is an innovative introduction.

Then there's the story of you, the drinker, who, getting to the bottom of the bottle, are more refreshed and relaxed, and also now involved by adding your own narrative to the beer's story—that might be how the beer made you feel, where you had it, or who you drank it with. Whatever it is, attaching your story to the beers you drink gives them so much more meaning. Just think about the best beer you've ever had: I bet you can remember the moment you drank the beer better than the way it actually tasted.

Trying to cover the whole world of craft beer has shown me just how exciting, innovative, and inspiring the brewing community is. It's also shown how history plays a big role in the present. What I've come to regard as the most interesting fact about beer is how it's always changing and always has been changing. The story of India Pale Ale is one of the most often repeated, but we know the story as a soundbite of a snapshot taken at one particular moment. We don't see the whole

evolving biography. Look at it on a larger screen and there are so many changes as it evolves every decade or so to suit new tastes. And that's still happening: think about American IPAs in 1993, then think about them in 2003, and then again in 2013. And it's happening with every beer style on the bar; beers evolve with the flavors and inspiration of the time, although style names tend to stay the same.

It's that evolution which makes beer exciting and sets the premise for this book: what are the most interesting and best-tasting beers brewed in the world right now? At the same time, though it's great to see all the new stuff, it's also important to know what happened before because this very often provides the context or inspiration for new developments, and there are so many classic

beers that we shouldn't overlook while spending a lot of time searching for new tastes. History, too, whether it's being made, followed, or providing inspiration, is always there and always important. Beer is continuously progressing and updating itself—and that's exciting.

Craft Beer World celebrates the stories of beers made around the world. It celebrates how they are made, where, why, and by whom. It also celebrates the drinking moment and how beer plays a role in our lives. This is a snapshot of the world of craft beer. It shows a small part of what's happening—too small, in fact, as I'm only sorry I couldn't get another 350 beers in—and there's so much more to be discovered: so many new beers, so many classics to revisit, so many new breweries to drink at, and so many more stories to be told.

WHAT IS CRAFT BEER?

Craft beer is many things and can't easily be distilled into a dictionary definition. It's not just about good beer or beer brewed on a small scale; it's not just about passion, innovation, creativity, integrity, or extremities of flavor. For me, it's a knowing, thoughtful way of brewing and drinking, which is concerned with flavor, variety, ingredients, and story.

The Brewers Association in America defines craft beer as small, independent, and traditional. Small means producing less than six million barrels of beer a year (that's a lot of beer). Independent means that less than 25 per cent of the brewery is owned or controlled by "an alcoholic industry member who is not himself a craft brewer." And traditional means brewing beers with just malt or adjuncts that add, rather than lighten, flavor. It's not an entirely helpful breakdown and means that some breweries such as Goose Island, in Chicago, don't count as "craft" because they are owned by AB-InBev (who also own Budweiser and many other brands). Goose Island is definitely a craft brewery, in the same way that Blue Moon should definitely count as a craft beer, even if it is part of MillerCoors—another one of the world's biggest brewing companies. It counts because it gets people drinking different beers, and works as a transition of tastes.

DEFINING CRAFT BEER

We probably all know what is craft beer and what isn't craft beer, and the choice we make when we get to the bar represents that. Here are just a few of my thoughts on the subject:

CRAFT BEER IS...

... about *great* beer (but not all of it is good).

... made by *small* breweries (although some of those once-small breweries are now very big).

... about intangibles, including passion, flavor, *freedom,* and *knowledge,* but also takes account of successful business practices.

... about provenance but also uses *ingredients* from around the world.

... forward-thinking and *innovative* while also drawing on *history* and *tradition*.

... an idea, a *marketing* term, a community.

... an *educated* and *conscious* choice.

CRAFT BEER—RAISING ITS PROFILE

In the United Kingdom some people insist on using inverted commas around the term "craft beer," which suggests it should invite a level of skepticism. The Campaign for Real Ale (CAMRA), which is the consumer mouthpiece for real ale, doesn't yet have a useful approach to "craft beer" and looks upon it as threateningly alien. The trouble is that CAMRA regard "craft beer" as kegged beer (CAMRA are only about real ale, so keg products aren't part of what they support). However, this isn't strictly correct, as almost all of the cask beers produced in the United Kingdom might be defined as craft. This then creates its own issue: is every small brewery a craft brewery? Surely there must be some kind of qualifying quality? Should the term "craft" be reserved for only the better or more interesting breweries? If so, to whom is the craft-beer doorman granting or denying access?

Around the world, the label "craft" has been inherited from America. Other words are used, too, including "microbrewery," once common but now largely replaced by "craft," and "nanobrewery," which is used to describe very small breweries. "Brewpubs" make and sell beer on site, while "gypsy brewers" don't own a physical brewery, but use other brewers' equipment instead. But it's all craft beer. It's all beer.

Beer is an industry—a community—that is different from others in that it provides an affordable, consumable luxury. If you want to drink one of the best beers in the world, then you are unlikely to spend more than an hour's salary on it (an hour of your salary is affordable and worth working for). Beer is also mass-produced, mass-marketed, readily available, and consumed *en masse*, unlike anything else except fast food. We all know what a Big Mac tastes like in the same way that we all know what Budweiser tastes like. We also know that if we want a hamburger,

there are many alternatives to a Big Mac, ranging from worse to way better. Beer is the same.

However, beer has a blind spot—it isn't in the public consciousness in the same way as fast food: some people just don't know that amazing alternatives to macro brews exist, or they don't trust themselves to make the right choices on the other side of the beer aisle. In America, the craft beer industry hollered and high-fived as it passed 5 per cent of the market for the first time in 2011, but this means that 19 out of every 20 beers drunk isn't a craft beer.

AND SO TO THE FUTURE...

But there's good news. Craft beers are growing in number and total volume sold around the world, while macrobreweries are losing volume. New craft breweries are opening with such regularity that it's impossible to keep up. Drinkers are starting to learn about beers and demanding more delicious drinks: beers with provenance and flavor, something different. This is a kick-on from an increasing awareness about what we eat. That's why we need a term such as "craft beer." It's there to label what we drink as different. In five or ten years' time it'll be an outdated term, and we'll look back on the last decade and laugh about when we called it "craft," but, while we've still got people out there to convert, we need a name for our team: Craft Beer United works for me.

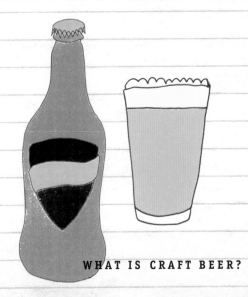

HOW IS BEER MADE?

Making beer is, in theory, a simple process: mix grain and hot water in a mash tun, separate them, and then dump the spent grain; move the liquid (now called wort) into a kettle, boil, add hops, and transfer to a fermentation tank; add yeast, let it ferment, and leave to condition before packaging (with or without filtering first); and then drink.

Making beer is, in reality, a very complicated thing. Breweries use different systems and processes, and every single ingredient or production choice will affect the final drink. The following pages look at the key ingredients as well as at how beer is made.

WATER

Don't underestimate the importance of water: it is the main constituent of beer, and you need good water to make good beer. Because water provides the base for the beer, it has to be of great quality. Small differences in water composition can result in big differences in flavor. Soft water, for example, gives beer a soft, clean body and is especially good in lighter beer styles, such as Helles and Pilsner, while hard water gives a dryness that emphasizes hop and malt bitterness, so is good for IPAs and Stouts. Great brewing towns (such as Pilsen, in the Czech Republic, with its soft water; Burton-on-Trent, in England, with its hard water; and Bend, in Oregon, with its fresh mountain water) have grown—and continue to grow—around the best water sources.

All breweries treat their water in some way. Some breweries have a treatment plant to control the water, while others simply add different salts and minerals to the brew. This is to balance the water composition to suit the beers they make and to ensure that the brewing water (known as liquor) is always consistent.

GRAIN

The combination of water and grain creates the rough outline of the beer before the defining details are provided by the hops and yeast. Malted barley is the most common brewing grain but it is not the only cereal used: wheat, oats, and rye add texture and flavor to beer, while rice and maize tend to lighten flavor (and are generally only used in macrobrewing).

Grain provides the sugars needed to make alcohol, so if you want a lot of alcohol, then you need a lot of grain. It also provides body and color, and the brewer produces the foundation for the beer by combining different types of grain. For example, pale malt, Munich malt, crystal malt, and chocolate malt might give you a good Brown Ale base: replace the Munich malt with roasted barley, and you get a Stout; lose all the dark malt and increase the pale, and you've got an IPA.

Before it can be used in a brew, the barley has to be malted. There's a little pearl of sweetness inside each grain that holds the starches, which are converted into sugars (these are later turned into alcohol by the yeast). As barley has a hard outer husk, it needs to germinate first, meaning it's soaked in water so that the rootlets can crack through the shell. At this point, the germination process is stopped, the grains are dried in a kiln, and then roasted to different levels—the longer they are roasted, the darker they'll become. Think of it like toast: it starts sweet and bready, gets caramelized and sweeter in the middle, and then, if you leave the bread in the toaster for too long, it becomes black, brittle, and bitter with no remaining sweetness.

Different malts undergo different processes to change their starch and sugar content. Crystal malt, for example, is germinated, then immediately heated to convert the starch to sugar, emulating the mashing process, and then roasted, with the end result being crystallized sugars that are unfermentable, giving a caramel-like sweetness and depth to the beer it goes into. Some barley is just roasted (not malted) and this will be black and bitter. As well as malted barley, other grains produce different beer qualities: oats give a smooth richness to the body; wheat helps head-retention and gives texture; and rye adds a nutty, spicy depth of flavor.

The grains are milled or crushed and then go into the mash tun where the process of mashing with hot water (the saccharification sweet spot is around 67°C or 153°F, though different enzymatic activity happens at different temperatures) converts the starches in the malt into fermentable sugars. The mash is like a big, malty porridge as the color and sweetness is sucked out of the grain and taken up by the water, making it taste like a delicious sweet tea now called wort (rhymes with pert). From the mash tun, it's all transferred to the lauter tun where the wort is separated from the grain and sparged (or sprayed) with hot water to get as much goodness from the grain as possible. Then it's into the kettle—not all breweries have a lauter tun, in which case the separation happens in the mash tun as the wort transfers to the next tank.

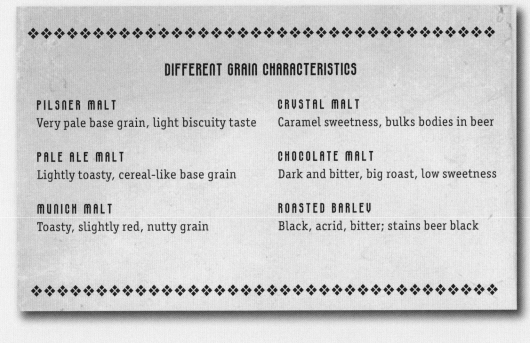

DIFFERENT GRAIN CHARACTERISTICS

PILSNER MALT
Very pale base grain, light biscuity taste

CRYSTAL MALT
Caramel sweetness, bulks bodies in beer

PALE ALE MALT
Lightly toasty, cereal-like base grain

CHOCOLATE MALT
Dark and bitter, big roast, low sweetness

MUNICH MALT
Toasty, slightly red, nutty grain

ROASTED BARLEY
Black, acrid, bitter; stains beer black

HOPS

Hops bring beer to life, providing bitterness, flavor, and aroma. They are the fireworks of beer, the face-slap, the laughter, or the delicate kiss. They are also the A-list ingredient, which has catapulted craft-brewing around the world, thanks to the amazing qualities it gives to beer.

Hops have been used as beer's bittering agent for hundreds of years, but things only really exciting in the 1970s and 1980s when American hops were used by pioneering American craft brewers. Not only were these brewers now making beers other than light lagers, they were also using ingredients with huge flavor profiles and hops bursting onto the tongue with citrus pith and juice, bitterness, and a floral freshness. It was beer's color-cinema moment.

Grown around the world, hops are varietal with each variety having a different flavor profile ranging from delicate to brutal, where they can be aromatic, citrusy, spicy, tropical, herbal, earthy, grassy, piney, or floral.

With the base block of the beer created in the mash tun, the hops (plus the yeast) are then used to define the beer style: the same malt bill can be hopped in two different ways to create two different beers: Porter vs. Black IPA; Tripel vs. Belgian IPA; Scotch Ale vs. Barley Wine. Like spices in food, hops generally work best in combinations rather than solo—"try my delicious, single-spiced curry made with just cumin!" should give you the idea—although there are some fantastic beers that only use one variety.

Hops are used as flowers, pellets, and oils. Flowers are harvested, dried, and pressed together; pellets are flowers that have been blitzed up, squashed together, and cut into small blocks; oils come in a pourable form. (Oils were once a craft beer no-no, but are now accepted, particularly in very hoppy beers where they give the bitterness and aroma that would be difficult to achieve with just flowers or pellets.) Some brewers only use flowers, while others stick to pellets; a mix of both is common.

As the wort reaches the kettle, it is brought to a rolling boil. That's when the first hops are added. Boiling sterilizes the beer. It also allows hop bitterness to get in. Hops contain acids and oils, and the alpha acids in hops (which give beer its bitterness) need to be boiled to isomerize into water-soluble iso-alpha acids. Hop oils are volatile, so boiling them for extended amounts of time drives off the flavor and aroma qualities. For this reason, early hop additions give bitterness, while middle and late additions give flavor and aroma. Hops can be added after fermentation (a process known as dry-hopping) to produce extra aroma and flavor. Crafty brewers are finding endless ways to get more hops into their beer, including adding them in the mash tun.

Hops rule the craft-beer world and IPA is king. More than any other style, IPA represents what craft beer is all about, with big flavors and aromas. It's screaming, "Look at me! I'm different to all those look-alikes on the beer shelves." American hops started it and they continue to be in huge demand. US hop farmers, alongside Australian and New Zealand farmers, are the New World hop growers; Europe is the Old World of hop growing with the classic varieties, while new varieties are constantly being developed and cross-bred to give new and different flavor profiles.

YEAST (AND TEMPERATURE)

You don't get beer without yeast. These micro-organisms are looked after well in the brewhouse because good yeast means good beer. There are a lot of different commercial yeast strains (check out www.whitelabs.com). Some are neutral in flavor, some leave a fruity taste behind, some are used for funky flavors and sourness, some are specific strains belonging to breweries, and some are style-defining strains.

There are "top-fermenting" yeasts and "bottom-fermenting" yeasts. If "Beer" is at the top of the family tree, then it branches down into "Ale" and "Lager". Ale is made with top-fermenting yeast, which works quickly to ferment the wort in three to six days at warm temperatures of 18–24°C (65–75°F), rising to the top of the tank to form a thick, sticky foam before dropping back into suspension. Top-fermenting yeast contributes some fruity flavors to beer. Lager, on the other hand, is made with bottom-fermenting yeast, which works slowly, fermenting all the sugars in five to ten days at cool temperatures of 8–14°C (46–57°F) before falling to the bottom of the tank. Lager yeast is clean with little flavor added to the beer.

The yeast goes into the fermentation tanks and eats the sugars created during the mash, producing booze and bubbles as by-products. As yeast is sensitive, control over temperature is important and the two work together. For example, if you try to ferment lager yeast at ale temperatures (higher than usual), you'll typically get a range of unusual and unwanted aromas (esters). If you try to ferment ale at lager temperatures (lower than usual), it works slowly or not at all—although some examples exist that go against these general temperature rules, Steam beer being one.

Some beers are defined by their base malt (e.g. Bock and Scotch Ales); some are defined by the hops used (e.g. all types of IPA); and some are defined by the yeast and the qualities it brings (e.g. Wit, Saison, and Wild Ales). Hefeweizen is a good example of yeast being the key component to give aroma, texture, and flavor. Unfiltered, the beer still contains all the yeast, and the aromas that swirl out of the vase glass are of bananas, bubble gum, cloves, and vanilla. These aromas are known as esters, which are primarily formed by the yeast during fermentation. Typical ester aromas include banana, pear, apple, rose, honey, and a solvent-like whiff. Esters are appropriate in some beers, but not in others, where they could be a sign of a lack of control in the brewery.

A lot of beer's potential off-flavors come from yeast. For this reason, careful control over yeast and temperature is key in the brewhouse.

FRUIT, SPICES, AND OTHER INGREDIENTS

After using water, grain, hops, and yeast, brewers can then add whatever else they want. Fruit is common, including cherries, raspberries, blueberries, strawberries, grapes, oranges, apricots, raisins, and pumpkin. The fruit can be used fresh, frozen, or cooked and either as syrup or peel. Any type of herb or spice can also go in to give depth or flavor; often seen are ground coriander, ginger, chili, pepper, curaçao, and hard herbs such as thyme, lavender, and rosemary. Coffee is one of the most common ingredients, particularly in stouts. Honey, nuts, vanilla, and chocolate are also popular. Some of the more unconventional ingredients include nettles (a relative of hops), bacon, tea, peanut butter, spruce, and many more. Some ingredients are added to the mash tun, some go in like late or dry hops, some are added during fermentation, some during conditioning, and some are blended in late in the process.

BARRELS

An extra element in beer-making is the use of a barrel to impart flavor. The beer is added to barrels that either once held something else such as whisky, bourbon, or wine, or to "virgin" unused barrels.

If it previously held a spirit, then the beer picks up the "ghost" of what was originally in the barrel, plus some wood character and texture. It can add incredible complexity to a beer, but can also be horribly overpowering. Bourbon barrels are the most commonly used and, combined with the barrel, add vanilla, coconut, toffee, spice, and bourbon-like flavors. Wine barrels add a fruity sharpness to beers, which can also be spiked with wild yeast and bacteria to mimic the sour Lambic style of Belgium. Barrels are generally saved for the special, strong beers, and some of them are extraordinary; the best balance barrel character with depth in the beer.

TIME (AND TEMPERATURE)

Not a physical ingredient, time nevertheless is a key element in beer-making. Good beer takes time to make. Some beers need weeks to mature; some need months; others only peak after a few years in the bottle. Temperature plays an important role in this process, and after fermentation the beers are chilled and undergo a conditioning period. Think of beer maturation or conditioning time as you would the cooking time for a delicious chili: if you've added all the ingredients and cooked it for 20 minutes, then it'll taste like a chili, but it won't be great. If you let it cook for another two hours at a steady temperature, all the flavors will come together magnificently. You can't make good beer (or chili) in a hurry. Beer needs cool temperatures to mature properly: too warm and it warps in weird ways, or the aging processes are sped up like a sun-wrinkled tan-aholic.

FILTERING, CENTRIFUGE, FINING, AND PASTEURIZING

Some beers leave the brewery hazy and unfiltered (i.e. with the yeast still present) and many drinkers are happy with a pint they can't see through—craft beer has taught us that beer you can watch TV through isn't necessarily a signifier of quality. Unfortunately, there are still too many drinkers who see cloudiness as a fault—but it's only a fault if it tastes bad. Still, there are some styles, or places, where clear beer is required. The yeast in the beer can be filtered out, spun through a centrifuge to kick it out, or pulled to the bottom of a tank or cask by a fining agent. There are good and bad ways of clearing beer and, inevitably, the process means some flavor or character will be lost (although this isn't always a bad thing, as some styles demand the sharp, clean finish of a filtered beer).

Pasteurization is a different process and is rare in craft-brewing. This is what the big breweries use to increase the shelf-life of their cans and bottles, and involves putting the beer through an intense heat-treatment to kill any possible bacteria, although this does come at the cost of flavor.

BREWERS

Beer doesn't get made without brewers. They create the recipes, control every stage of production, and define what the beer becomes based on the ingredients used and the processes the beer goes through. Brewers can transform the four ingredients of beer-making in an astonishing variety of ways. The mark of a great beer is the skill of the brewers who make it.

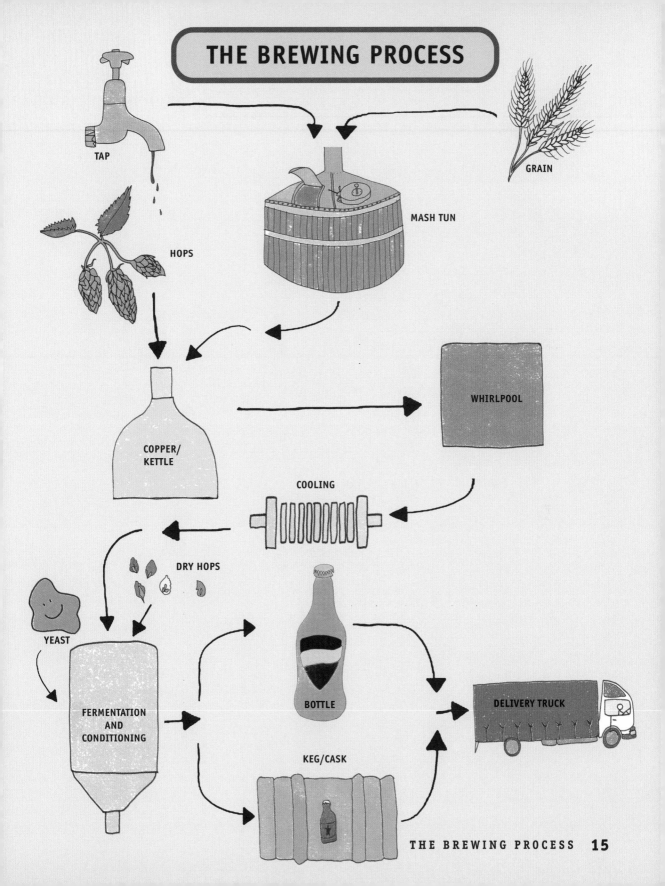

THE BREWING PROCESS

TAP

GRAIN

MASH TUN

HOPS

WHIRLPOOL

COPPER/
KETTLE

COOLING

DRY HOPS

YEAST

FERMENTATION
AND
CONDITIONING

BOTTLE

KEG/CASK

DELIVERY TRUCK

WORLD OF HOPS

Hops are varietal and perennial plants that grow around the world in a band between 30 and 52 degrees latitude in both the northern and southern hemispheres.

Being varietal, one type of hop can be grown in North America, England, and Australia, and it will taste different in each place it is cultivated. Hops provide beer's terroir—its "sense of place" and link to the ground. You will also find that each region has hops that share flavor profiles and have influenced the beers brewed there.

OLD WORLD
VS.
NEW WORLD

Great Britain and Central Europe
vs.
USA, Australia, and New Zealand

Earthy, woodland fruit, herbal, and floral
vs.
Citrus, tropical fruit, floral, pine

Classic beer styles
vs.
Modern beer styles

HOP-GROWING REGIONS

TOP 10 HOP PRODUCERS
BY VOLUME IN 2011

GERMANY
USA
CHINA
CZECH REPUBLIC
SLOVENIA
POLAND
UK
AUSTRALIA
SOUTH AFRICA
SPAIN

Source:
http://www.usahops.org/graphics/File/Stat%20Pack/2011%20Stat%20Pack.pdf

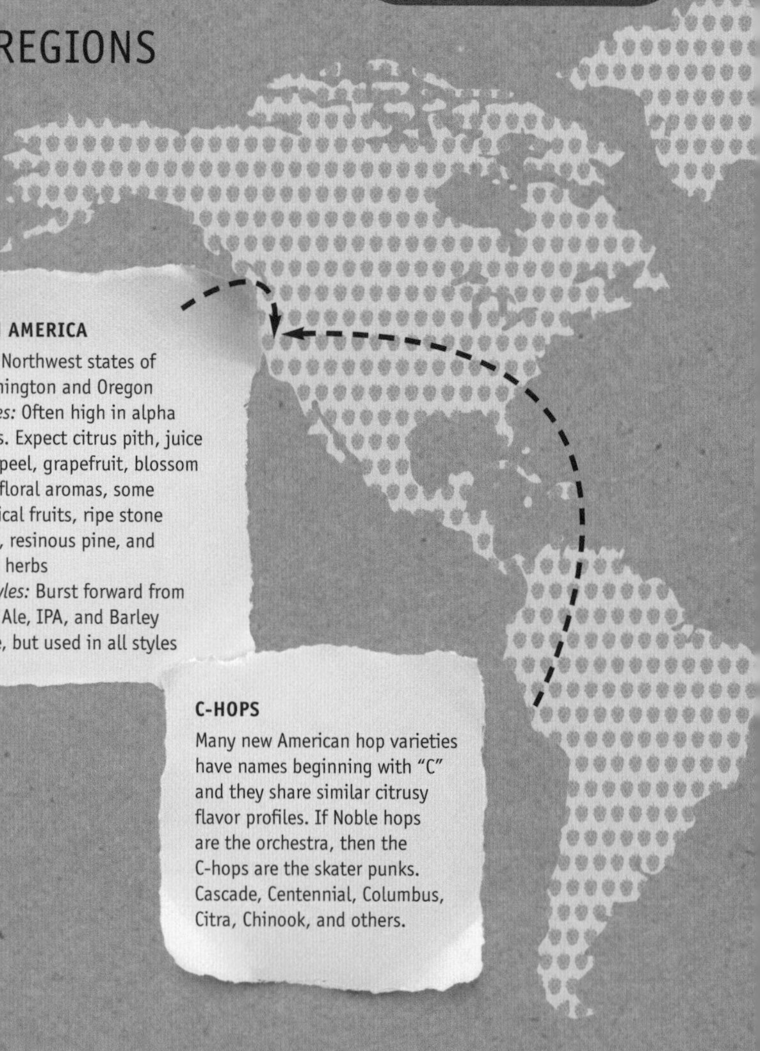

NORTH AMERICA

Grown: Northwest states of Washington and Oregon
Qualities: Often high in alpha acids. Expect citrus pith, juice and peel, grapefruit, blossom and floral aromas, some tropical fruits, ripe stone fruit, resinous pine, and hard herbs
Beer styles: Burst forward from Pale Ale, IPA, and Barley Wine, but used in all styles

C-HOPS

Many new American hop varieties have names beginning with "C" and they share similar citrusy flavor profiles. If Noble hops are the orchestra, then the C-hops are the skater punks. Cascade, Centennial, Columbus, Citra, Chinook, and others.

GREAT BRITAIN

Grown: Mainly Southeast and central England

Qualities: Earthy, spicy, floral, hedgerow and orchard fruit, capable of both delicacy and potent roughness

Beer styles: Best Bitter, English Pale and Golden Ale, Mild, Stout, and Porter

CENTRAL EUROPE

Grown: Predominantly Germany, Czech Republic, Poland, and Slovenia

Qualities: Mainly aroma varieties; they are low in alpha acid. Expect grassy, clean, elegant, lemony, herbal flavors, with some stone fruit when used in bigger volumes

Beer styles: Pilsner, Helles, dark lager, Bock

HOP TYPES

Amarillo	USA	Peaches, apricots, oranges, grapefruit
Cascade	USA	Sharp grapefruit and floral
Centennial	USA	Orange pith, juice and blossom, pine
Citra	USA	Bitter-spiked mango, tropical, sharp citrus
Simcoe	USA	Resinous pine, grapefruit, bitter orange peel
Sorachi Ace	USA	From Japan, grown in USA; lemongrass, bubblegum
Saaz	CZ	Delicately grassy, floral, clean citrus botanicals
Styrian Golding	SL	Slovenian, super aromatic, peppery, spicy, fragrant
Hallertauer	GER	Peppery, grassy, floral, hard herbs, pithy
Fuggle	UK	Like the English countryside: earthy, woody, floral
Bramling Cross	UK	Like an English forest: berries, orchard fruit, wood
Golding	UK	Tangy, floral, peppery, mildly earthy
Nelson Sauvin	NZ	Grape, gooseberry, mango, passion fruit
Motueka	NZ	Juicy tropical and exotic fruit, sweet berries
Galaxy	AUS	Mango, pineapple, passion fruit, citrus, floral

NOBLE HOPS

The classic European lager hops, elevated to brewing nobility because of their heritage and widespread importance. The names come from the region they are grown in: Hallertauer, Tettnang, and Spalt from Germany; Saaz from the Czech Republic.

SOUTH PACIFIC

Grown: South Australia and Tasmania; New Zealand

Qualities: Juicy tropical fruit, lychee, mango, passion fruit, plus gooseberry and grapes

Beer styles: Pale Ales, IPAs, and modernizing classic styles

UNDERSTANDING BEER: A HELPFUL GLOSSARY

Like getting into a new sport for the first time and hearing of birdies, off-sides, or batting averages, beer can be hard to understand because its language is filled with terms, abbreviations, and scientific stuff. Here are all the words you'll need to know.

ABV Alcohol-by-volume. This is the total percentage in your drink that is alcohol. Beer can range from less than 1 per cent to around 25 per cent through fermentation. Beers have been made to over 50% ABV but this requires fractional distillation to get it so high: the beer is frozen and, as water freezes at a higher temperature than alcohol, the brewer can take out chunks of ice, leaving just the alcohol behind. This is found in Eisbocks, as well as extreme beers. It's illegal in some countries, including the United States.

ALE A very broad range of beers brewed with a top-fermenting yeast (as opposed to a bottom-fermenting yeast for lagers). Ales commonly have a fruitiness imparted by the yeast. Styles range from lager-like Kölschs and hazy Hefeweizens, through best bitters and porters, to IPAs and up to huge Imperial Stouts and Barley Wines.

ALPHA ACID This is where hop's bitterness comes from. Alpha acids need to be isomerized in order to give their bitterness to beer; isomerization takes place as a result of extended boiling in the wort. When hops arrive at a brewery, they have a percentage figure attached that represents the total weight of the hop that is acid content. The alpha-acid range in hops can vary from under 3 per cent to over 20 per cent. Low-alpha varieties, such as Noble hops, are generally favored for their aromas; high- or super-alpha hops produce a lot of bitterness but also usually come with big, aroma-giving profiles. Low-alpha hops can give the same level of bitterness as high alphas, but brewers need to use a lot more of them.

ATTENUATION A measure of the percentage of sugars that the yeast consumes during fermentation. A highly attenuated beer will be dry and have little sweetness. *See also* Gravity.

BEER Alcoholic drink made from fermented grain. The best drink in the world.

BEER GEEK I am a beer geek. I'm obsessed with the details of beer as well as the taste. I get excited about things like hops, brewing processes, new beer releases, beer history, and beer labels. It's far better to be a beer geek than a beer snob—beer snobs aren't cool.

BODY Light, heavy, thin, full: this is the weight of the beer in the mouth. It comes from a combination of the grain base, whether it's filtered or not, and is dependent on the residual sugar left in the beer.

BOTTLE-CONDITIONED BEER Beer that undergoes a secondary fermentation in the bottle. A priming sugar (or just residual sugar left in the beer) and yeast are added to the bottle and this starts a slow, gradual conditioning process that also produces carbonation. British and Belgian beers are often bottle-conditioned. Some bottle-conditioned beers will last for decades as they mature. When you pour them, make sure you leave the sediment in the bottle (unless you want it yeast-and-all).

BREWPUB A pub that makes its own beer and sells it on site. Visit these to drink fresh beer where it was made.

BU:GU A way to consider balance in beer. It's the measure of bitterness (BU) against the relative sweetness of the gravity (GU). Knowing IBU is interesting, but it doesn't explain the balance between malt and hop—for example, a beer of 5.0% ABV with 50 IBUs would taste very different if it's very sweet or very dry, with the sweet version hiding the bitterness and the dry version emphasizing it. BU:GU isn't used widely outside of brewhouses yet, but as drinkers become more interested in technical details, this could be a stat they want to see.

COLLABORATION BREWS Beers made by two or more different companies. This may involve breweries coming together or perhaps a brewery and a restaurant. It's like two of your favorite artists recording a song together, resulting in beers that are often creative, one-off specials. They demonstrate the sharing spirit of the craft-beer community.

COLOR Anything from very pale blonde to the blackest black. Measured on two different scales: Standard Reference Method (SRM) and European Brewery Convention (EBC). A pale lager will be as low as 1 SRM or 2 EBC. American IPA ranges from 6–14 SRM or 12–28 EBC. The darkest Stout will be 70 SRM or 138 EBC. All others will fall in the middle. Talking about SRM or EBC is generally reserved for geeks who love too much technical information; most of us just say gold, red, brown, or black.

CONTRACT BREWING This is when one brewery produces beer for another. This might be because a brewery can't cope with the volume, needs to make its beer somewhere else so it can be packaged there, or exists only in name (rather than physical kit) and so contracts out its brewing. *See also* Gypsy brewer.

DEGREES PLATO A way of measuring the alcohol content in beer. It's drinker-facing in central Europe and brewer-facing around the world. For example, when you order a beer in the Czech Republic, it might say 10° on the tap or menu, whereas in other parts of the world the ABV would be given instead. However, platos are a measurement brewers use when determining the alcohol content of their beer. It's incredibly complicated to work out unless you're a brewmaster. What you need to know when ordering beer is: 12° is about 5.0% ABV.

DRY-HOPPING Adding hops to beer after fermentation, whether in the tank or cask. This gives extra aroma and flavor to a beer. Try this at home by putting hops in cool water and see how much aroma the water picks up. Taste it as well—it will have taken up some bitterness.

ESTERS These come out of beer as aromas that are created during the higher temperatures of fermentation when alcohol and organic acids react with each other. They are often fruity aromas but can be potently harsh and veer toward nail polish remover. Expect banana, pear, apple, rose, honey, solvent. Sometimes these are brewing faults and other times they are desirable—it depends on the beer style and the volume at which they are present.

FINISH A word we've borrowed from wine to indicate how the flavor ends in the mouth and then hangs around. It could be short or long; dry, bitter, sweet, or sharp; or combinations of these.

GRAVITY Original gravity (OG) and final gravity (FG). Gravity is the weight of the wort relative to the weight of the water, and it's the brewer's measure of sugars in the beer. OG is the sweetness after it's left the mash tun, and FG is after it's finished fermenting. The OG is a guide to what level of alcohol can be expected in the finished beer, and the FG will tell you how sweet or dry the finished beer is, depending on how it has been attenuated. 1.000 means no sugar. An OG of 1.050 might give a beer around 5.0% ABV, and an FG of 1.005 will be dry and not sweet (while an FG of 1.030 will be sweet and sticky on the lips).

GYPSY BREWER A brewer without a bricks-and-mortar brewery. He will travel around and use spare capacity in other breweries. This is similar to contract brewing, although the gypsy brewer will often use a number of different breweries.

HOP OIL Where alpha acids give bitterness, hop oil gives aroma. Oils are more delicate than acids, so don't like the boiling process. To get the most aroma out of them, they work best late in the brewing process—at the end of the boil in the kettle or as dry hops after fermentation.

IBU International Bittering Units. Also known as EBU (European Bittering Units) or just BU. This is the measure of bitterness in a beer and represents the parts-per-million of dissolved iso-alpha acids in the beer. Each beer style will have an appropriate IBU level. A light lager might be 10 IBU, Pilsner will be between 25 and 40 IBU, Stout might be around 50 IBU, and Double IPAs and Barley Wines can hit 100 IBU. Some beers boast even higher bitterness levels, though smart scientists debate how much bitterness the human tongue can actually handle before it can't detect any more.

ISO-ALPHA ACID This comes from the alpha acids present in hops. An extended boil converts these into water-soluble iso-alpha acids that then give bitterness to beer.

KETTLE Also known as the copper. This is where the wort is boiled and the hops are added. Brewers also drink a lot of tea and coffee, so the other type of kettle is an important part of the brewhouse set-up.

LAGER Beer made using a bottom-fermenting yeast. Often has delicate yeast profiles. The yeast works slowly at cooler temperatures (compared to ale yeast). The range of lager styles is very broad, from light lagers through to intense Eisbocks. The name comes from the process of lagering (or storing) beer in cold places for it to mature.

LAGERING The maturation process of a lager. After fermentation the temperature will be dropped to 0°C (32°F) for an extended period of time. This is to allow the flavors to mature. Some will get a few weeks; others will need a few months.

LAUTERING The process of separating the grain from the wort before the wort moves into the kettle.

MACRO BEER Beer made by big, multinational brewing companies. Some people dislike these companies because of their size, and the beers for their lack of flavor. Personally, I'm happy to drink macro beer; if nothing else, it reminds me why I love craft beers. Many of these breweries have fascinating histories that are worth reading about—they aren't just enormous beer factories that arrived overnight. Macrobreweries are now making craft brands, some of which are incredibly successful—notably Blue Moon, made under the MolsonCoors arm. It's also interesting to note the craft breweries that have been bought by macrobreweries or have distribution deals with them. The distinction between micro/craft and macro isn't as simple as it used to be.

MASH TUN Where the malt meets water and gets mashed together to extract sweetness and color from the grain.

MOUTHFEEL How the beer feels in the mouth. Another way of describing the body, although mouthfeel is more about sensation: prickly, delicate, creamy, sharp, dry, smooth.

NITROGEN/NITRO Nitrogen is an important nutrient for yeast and also a measure of the protein in malt. More appropriate for drinkers is seeing beers described as "nitro." This means they are pumped with nitrogen in the tank, copying a beer like Guinness, to get a full, creamy mouthfeel thanks to the small bubbles that nitrogen gives to beer (as opposed to the bigger bubbles in carbon dioxide).

PHENOLIC A spicy or smoky flavor or aroma in beer, which is sometimes regarded as a brewing fault. Spicy will mean something clove-like, whereas smoky will be more medicinal in character (rather like antiseptic or Islay whisky). This is not a smoked meat or bonfire flavor—that comes from smoked malt. Some drinkers are very sensitive to phenolic flavors, whether they love the taste or not.

PRODUCTION BREWERY A place where beer is made, packaged, and then distributed to bars or refrigerators. Most breweries are production sites, though increasingly they have a tap room on site in order to sell beer direct to customers.

RESIDUAL SUGARS The sweetness left in the beer after fermentation.

SECONDARY FERMENTATION The act of kicking-on a second fermentation. This can be done in a tank, bottle, or cask. Bottle-conditioned beers undergo a secondary fermentation, as do real ales, where the process gives the light carbonation. Generally, it's a slow, gentle process that is necessary to produce carbonation and allow the beer to mature.

TAP ROOM Many breweries now have a tap room. Visit them, and drink the beer at its freshest.

TRAPPIST BREWERY Monastic beer. To qualify (and very few do), the beer must be made within the walls of a monastery by monks—or under their supervision—where the brewing is not intended for profit-making purposes. Some Trappist breweries are very big (e.g. La Trappe, Chimay) and others are very small (e.g. Westvleteren). An "Abbey beer" will be an interpretation of a Trappist beer.

UNFILTERED Beer that hasn't had the yeast filtered out of it. These beers are generally hazy and have more flavor and texture than their filtered counterparts. The haze may be cleared using a fining agent, which pulls all the particles left in the beer to the bottom of the container. In the United Kingdom, the most common fining agent in cask ale is isinglass (which is made from the dried swim bladders of fish).

WILD YEAST AND BACTERIA If these get into a beer unintentionally, they can turn the brew sour. However, some brewers deliberately add wild yeast and bacteria to get wild flavors and sourness. A good beer made with wild yeast will be sharp, without a vinegary quality, and clean-tasting—try Lambic and Gueuze to see how the best taste. Brettanomyces (shortened to brett) is a common wild yeast and pediococcus and lactobacillus are common bacteria. The wild yeast adds funky flavor, and the bacteria give the sourness. They can work together or separately to change the flavor of beer.

WORT The sweet, malty liquid that leaves the mash tun. Hopped wort is what leaves the kettle before being transferred to the fermentation tank. Wort makes a very good breakfast drink, especially if you're hungover from the night before.

WHEN BEER GOES BAD

Not every beer is good. While some just won't be to your taste, others are technically faulty. Interestingly, tasters are very individual when it comes to detecting off-characters: some may not be able to detect diacetyl (buttered popcorn), for example; others may be very sensitive and find it stomach-turning; while others can smell and taste it and also like it.

These flavor characteristics will also change depending on the quantities at which they are present in the beer. At low levels, they might be pleasant, but at high levels, they may be revolting. Here is some information on the different tastes and what may cause them.

BUTTER, BUTTERED POPCORN, BUTTERSCOTCH, FATTY MOUTHFEEL
What? Diacetyl
Why? A natural by-product of fermentation. If it's in your beer, then it could mean the beer was hurried out of the brewery. It can also mean infected yeast.
Appropriate? In very small amounts in some lagers, Porters, and Stouts.

SWEETCORN, STEWED VEGETABLES, TOMATOES
What? Dimethyl sulfide (DMS)
Why? Comes from the grain (most often pale malt). It hasn't had a vigorous-enough boil in the kettle, or fermentation has been slow.
Appropriate? In very small amounts in some lagers. (Interesting fact: DMS is what truffle-hunting dogs are trained to sniff out.)

PAPER, CARDBOARD, STALE, SHERRY
What? Oxidized
Why? Oxygen is not good for beer. If it tastes like this, then you're drinking old, stale beer.
Appropriate? Never in fresh beer but can be an integral part of aged beers and contribute to their character.

SMOKY, ISLAY WHISKY, BAND-AIDS, DISINFECTANT
What? Chlorophenol
Why? Could be from a reaction between the phenolic acid naturally found in malt and either the chlorine content in the water or a cleaning solution used in the brewery.
Appropriate? No. And it's not to be confused with the flavors produced by a smoked malt or a Belgian yeast, giving a phenolic, clove-like spiciness.

"SKUNKY," ROTTING VEGETABLES, GARLIC
What? Light-struck
Why? Sunlight and beer don't work together (unless it's a hot day and you're drinking a cold pint). The UV rays break down hop molecules, causing a reaction with the sulphur in the beer and producing some of the same stinky chemicals as a skunk.
Appropriate? Never. Avoid beer in clear or green bottles, and keep beer out of sunlight.

EGGS OR BURNT MATCHES
What? Sulphur
Why? Could be from the water ("Burton Snatch" gives Burton-on-Trent's beers their famous whiff of sulphur) or from yeast. It could also be a sign of infection or of a young beer.
Appropriate? In small amounts. Some beers have a delicate, sweet, sulphury aroma that can be nice—some drinkers are very sensitive to sulphur.

BANANAS, PEAR DROPS, APPLES, ROSES

What? Esters, including isoamyl acetate (bananas and pear drops), ethyl caprylate and caproate (apples and apples/aniseed), ethyl acetate (solvent), and phenylethyl acetate (honey, roses)

Why? Fruity aromas given out by the yeast during fermentation.

Appropriate? Yes, in certain styles and in low volumes—appropriateness is down to the detectable levels. Expect isoamyl acetate in Hefeweizens, but it can be a fault in other styles.

SOY SAUCE, BURNT TIRES, MARMITE

What? Autolyzed yeast

Why? Yeast that has died and ruptured its beer-spoiling guts into your beer.

Appropriate? In some aged beers it's acceptable in small volumes; otherwise it's not.

APPLE SKIN AND JUICE, CIDER, PAINT IN HIGH VOLUMES

What? Acetaldehyde

Why? Natural by-product of fermentation. If present, then it's because the beer is "green," usually due to haste in the brewery, or the yeast is of poor quality. If it flips into being "cidery," then it's got to an extreme level.

Appropriate? No. Though can be acceptable at very low levels

SOUR MILK, VINEGAR, LEMON JUICE

What? A bad thing. Sour beer, unless intentional, isn't good.

Why? Souring bacteria in your beer.

Appropriate? It makes some wild ales what they are. Otherwise, it's only good for the drain.

BABY SICK

What? Butyric acid

Why? Bacterial spoilage. Not very common but horrible if you get it.

Appropriate? No. Never. Do you want to drink a beer that smells of vomit?

BOOZY, ALCOHOLIC, NAIL POLISH REMOVER

What? Fusel alcohol, solvent, ethyl acetate

Why? From esters in the beer. Low volumes can come across as fruity but it can sting the eyes in high volumes.

Appropriate? Small amounts are okay. It can be present in strong beers (though it isn't always pleasant).

CHEESY, SWEATY SOCKS

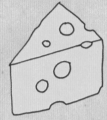

What? Isovaleric acid or old hops

Why? Could be a bacterial infection or a sign of using old, oxidized hops, which give a cheesy flavor.

Appropriate? No. Never is a beer that smells like socks going to be delicious.

MY BEER IS CLOUDY...

Why? Could be many things: an unfiltered beer with yeast still in it, a "chill haze" from being served cold, a "hop haze" from a very hoppy beer, or an infected beer.

Appropriate? Just because it's cloudy doesn't mean it's bad. If it tastes bad, then it is bad; otherwise it's fine.

SERVING BEER

The vessel you choose to drink from can play a big role in the perception and experience of the beer you pour. I was dubious of this idea—surely, it's the beer that matters, not the glass—until I sat down and tried the same beers in different glasses: some made the beer hide, others over-emphasized things, some made the beer feel more delicate or less refined. Choosing a specific size and shape of glass can really enhance your appreciation of a beer's defining characteristics.

DIFFERENT BEER GLASSES

Here are the basic glasses that every beer cupboard should have:

1. PILSNER: Tall and thin so the bubbles stream into the tight foam. For Pilsners and pale lagers, as the name suggests, this style of glass sends the delicate aroma right to your nose.

2. WEISSBIER VASE: Vase-like shape for Hefeweizens where the foam is concentrated at the top of the glass like a fragrant pillow. Shaped so that you can see the beautiful haziness in the body and get the full impact of the estery aroma.

3. SHAKER: A chunky all-rounder best with American styles—American Wheats, Pale Ales, Reds, Browns, and IPAs—where you get the hop hit in the aroma without intensifying it too much.

4. TULIP: An elegant glass best for Belgian beers—Wits, Saisons, Triples, and Wild ales— or styles where you can swirl, sniff, and focus the aromas in the tapered rim while ogling the beautiful colors and carbonation.

5. BOWL: For those big beers such as Imperial Stouts and Barley Wines that demand more attention. Think of them like fine spirits as they roll around your glass. You want to send the intensified aromas swirling out as you sip.

6. PINT: Nonic, tulip, straight-sided, or a dimpled mug, these are for those low-ABV, session-style beers—Bitter, Pale Ale, Stout, Porter. Czech lager often comes in a round dimpled mug topped with three-fingers of tight foam. It's a glass for drinking from, not thinking from.

7. GOBLET: Squat and round, and used for strong, dark Belgian beers (Dubbels and Quads) where the often-high carbonation is quickly softened. There's something majestic and special about drinking from a goblet, especially when in a Belgian café.

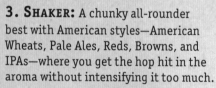

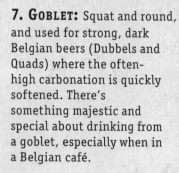

GLASSES I have a collection of favorite glasses that I use all the time. If you like drinking from one glass only, that's fine—most of the time I pick between three: Shaker, Tulip, and Bowl. But there is some science behind choosing a beer glass, and you'll find that the shape and size of the glassware can change your appreciation of flavor.

KEG The most popular dispenser for craft beer around the world. The beer is carbonated and pushed through the tap with a nudge of gas. Kegged beer is served cool or cold.

CASK The British tradition of cask-conditioned beers is one that is gaining popularity around the world. Typically, unfiltered beer is added to the cask without carbonation. A solution of yeast and a priming sugar are included and a secondary fermentation takes place inside the cask, which produces a delicate carbonation (and also slowly develops the flavor). Proper cask beer will be delivered to the pub and left to settle and condition for a few days before serving; good beer needs a good cellarman who knows when to put it on tap. Cask beers are pulled by arm-work from the cellar to the pint glass or served by gravity dispensers on the bar. Ideally, beer in casks should be drunk fast; otherwise, oxygen gets into the casks and can stale the beer.

BOTTLE Go to a beer store and you'll see an enormous variety of bottle shapes and sizes. Bottles are good because it means drinkers can take them home and put them in the refrigerator. They can also be branded, which passes on information or attitude to the drinker. Avoid beer in clear or green bottles because the beer will probably be light-struck, which isn't tasty.

CAN There are many benefits to canned beer: light, stackable, low oxygen levels, and no risk of being light-struck. Cans also don't smash and they get colder quicker than bottles. Increasing numbers of craft breweries are now canning their beers.

TANK There's no better way to drink beer than from the tank—ideally, the tank it was made in. Brewpubs around the world are now connecting bar taps directly to the tanks to serve the beer. It doesn't get much fresher than that.

GROWLER Go to your local brewery, grab a growler, fill it with fresh draft beer, take it home, drink it, go back to the brewery, refill it, and repeat happily forever. Growlers are reusable containers (typically up to 2 liters/3$\frac{1}{2}$ pints/4 US pints in volume) for drinking brewery-fresh beer at home.

❖❖❖❖❖❖❖❖❖❖❖❖❖❖❖❖❖❖

A WORD ON TEMPERATURE...

If you get your beer too cold, this will hide some of the flavor and aroma. Personally, I like my beer cold. If it's too cold, it'll warm up; if it's too warm, it's not going to get colder. Each style of beer has an ideal serving temperature: for some, such as lagers, it'll be colder than for others, such as Imperial Stouts. I say: drink beer at whatever temperature you enjoy it the most.

❖❖❖❖❖❖❖❖❖❖❖❖❖❖❖❖❖❖

BEER AND FOOD

The beauty of bringing beer and food together lies in their ability to take each other in exciting new directions. Whether food on fine white tablecloths or with paper napkins, the range of flavors, strengths, textures, and tastes in beer gives it the versatility to go with whatever you're eating. The best way to get started is just to dive right in: make dinner, open a couple of bottles, and see how the beer and food interact—it won't always work but you'll soon find out what does.

THE SCIENCE BEHIND IT...

Beer has a lot going for it at the dining table. First, there's the malt. Eat a handful of pale malted barley and you'll taste the sweetly nutty flavor; eat chocolate malt and it's like roasted coffee. The cereal quality adds a savory taste and is very complementary to food. From the grain comes beer's body and depth, which can be clean and delicate; nutty and spicy; smooth and full-bodied; caramel-like; dark and roasted; dry or sweet; as light as tonic water; or as heavy as cream. The body, intensity, and alcohol level of the beer are a key consideration: you want beer and food with similar intensities, you want the alcohol and depth to give structure, and you need the body of the beer to provide either a comforting fullness or a crisp dryness—beer that is thin is never good with food because it gets overpowered.

Hops provide most of beer's aroma, and most of our sense of taste is connected to smell. This is where hops can make food really interesting, as zesty, spicy, fragrant, floral, tropical, citrus, earthy, and herbal aromas and flavors can link glass and plate, bridging similar or complementary flavors. Hops also provide bitterness, which can cut through heavy and rich flavors and textures, giving a little kick to the tongue to keep it interested. Just watch out for high levels of bitterness, which can be overpowering—very bitter beers are only good with salty snacks.

In most beers, the yeast contributes a neutral flavor or a delicately fruity note. It's already done the difficult job and produced the alcohol that contributes to the depth and intensity of the beer. Generally, as the alcohol content goes up, so does the flavor profile; a Helles will be light and delicate, whereas a Doppelbock will be strong, sweet, and fuller bodied. In some styles, yeast also adds to flavor and texture: perhaps it's the full body and estery aroma of Hefeweizen; the spicy, fruity Wits and their sharp finish; unfiltered beers with a full body; or Sour beers, made sharp by the yeast and bacteria, with their appetite-poking acidity and ability to cut through richness.

Carbonation also contributes and is like a refresh button for the tongue. Beer can sweep across the palate, giving little bubble-bursts of liveliness to keep the tongue from getting bored or too familiar with what it's tasting. Or, with the richness of fatty meats or sweet desserts, carbonation is able to lift flavors and lighten them.

The use of fruit, spices, alternative grains, coffee, or barrels can all also change the flavor and texture of the beer, pointing it in different directions and toward (or away from) particular types of food.

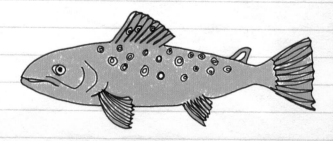

DIFFERENT APPROACHES TO PAIRING BEER AND FOOD

There are different ways to approach beer and food and each method combines the two to achieve different results. Start with the beer and find the right food to match. Here's how I do it:

BRING TOGETHER This aims to create a bridge between the food and the beer by looking for similar flavor profiles in both. It means picking out one or two aspects of the glass and plate that match each other and pull the flavors toward one another. Think about a chocolate brownie with a dark, chocolaty Stout, or marry the subtle, earthy spiciness of Saison with a peppery salad. It's about matching flavors and putting them together to enhance them.

BALANCE Full-flavored food can clash with full-on beers. Sometimes you need a pairing that mellows things out or cuts through a big flavor. Chili heat is a good example: hops kick out against the heat of chili, causing them to fight instead of play. Try smooth, chocolaty Milk Stout with chili heat and it cools everything down (in the same way that milk calms the tannins in tea). Hefeweizen, which has a full body and fruitiness plus a low bitterness, can also cool down the scorch of chili heat. It's not just about heat and any intensely flavored food needs beer to balance it: smoked, oily fish; fragrantly spiced dishes; sharp, tomato-based dishes; strong cheeses; very salty foods. With these big flavors, a delicate beer can refresh the palate and keep the experience light, instead of hitting flavor with flavor like two slugging heavyweights. Try beers with a dry or spicy finish (e.g. Wit, Pilsner, Saison), or a bitterness that can cut through fattiness (e.g. Pale Ales and IPAs), or the sharpness of Sour beer. The pairing is there to stop things getting too overpowering by balancing and controlling flavors, and not letting them fight.

BOOST Some flavors boost others in the same way that waking up to sunshine can make your day a lot happier. It's about bringing together different flavors and textures, and making them better than the sum of their parts. For example, smoked beer is like squeezing a syringe of meatiness into steak or sausages; fruity, fat-stripping IPAs cut through the richness of cheeseburgers but also match the condiment-and-cheese combo; and chocolate desserts are lifted and enlivened by sweet and sour cherry beers. The beer adds to the food (or the food adds to the beer) by becoming an extra element in the experience.

LOCAL There's an important geographical and seasonal aspect to putting food and beer together. Local beer and local cuisine often have a way of being naturally complementary: dense dumplings and pork with a full-bodied dark lager in Prague; a beef stew that's earthy, slightly sweet, and intensely savory with an ESB or a Belgian Dubbel; Asian-inspired dishes with tropical-scented Pacific Pale Ales; moules frites with a Belgian Blonde or Wit. Remember seasonal releases, too: as fall descends, drink pumpkin beer with earthy vegetables; choose spiced strong ales with festive turkey, and summer Blondes with light salads.

AVOID Some flavors just don't work together. Some beers simply don't work with certain foods: delicate Helles will be obliterated by chocolate; an Imperial Stout will smother any kind of delicate food. Acidity and bitterness crash.

Here are the most food-friendly beer styles with some suggestions for what to eat with them:

STYLE: PILSNER

Qualities: Dry, herbal, bitter, fragrant, delicate. The light, clean body, snap of herbal bitterness, and fine carbonation mean Pilsner is great for cutting through richness, but also delicate enough that it won't overpower too many dishes. It's a great "livener" to get your tongue excited for more pleasure

Bring together: Peppery bitterness of salad; shellfish, especially if it's cooked in butter with garlic; herby chicken wings; salt and pepper squid

Balance: Oily fish; sharp cheese; creamy white risotto; tapas; jerk chicken; yakitori

Boost: Fresh fried fish with a squeeze of lemon; carbonara's creaminess can be cut and lifted by a Pilsner, but it also adds a lemon and herb depth; Moroccan tagine

Local: Pork or duck and dumplings; nakládaný hermelín—"pickled" Camembert layered with chili and served with bread—Czech-style beer-snacking

Avoid: Any kind of dessert blitzes Pilsner's delicate side

STYLE: DARK LAGER

Qualities: Roasty, dry, fragrant, delicate. Subtle and often lighter to drink than the color suggests, dark lagers give a hint of dark malt flavor plus a depth of caramel, which can be very food-friendly. But watch out: you need one with body or it can taste acrid and thin with food

Bring together: Charred steak; barbecued meat and salmon; sausages; Cajun fish or white meat

Balance: Roast pork or duck; smoked fish; hamburgers; tomato-based pasta dishes; pizza; Korean; Banh mi; patatas bravas

Boost: Mexican food where the smooth chocolate depth loves the smoky, warm spice; rotisserie chicken; dark lager also wraps the sweetness of sashimi, saltiness of soy, and wow of wasabi up in

a neat little package

Local: Bratwurst and a big plate of potato salad

Avoid: Sweet or sharp dishes—they obliterate the lightness of dark lager

STYLE: KÖLSCH

Qualities:
Delicate, fruity, crisp, dry. A creaminess to the body, followed by a snap of bitterness, makes this a great beer for food. The subtle hint of fruit in the aroma is like sitting beside someone wearing a beautiful, alluring fragrance. Alongside Kölsch, Cream and Steam beers are similar in profile

Bring together: Salmon's richness loves Kölsch's smooth body; Caesar salad; asparagus tart

Balance: Roast chicken; pad Thai; pho or noodle soup; Chinese dim sum; fish kebabs; mild cheese; hot dogs with lots of onions and mustard

Boost: The sweetness of scallops, lobster, and crab can be enhanced magnificently by Kölsch; fried chicken has a buttery quality that the beer will smother in soft malt flavor; seafood tagliatelle; the saltiness of fries

Local: Pork and sauerkraut; fried potatoes

Avoid: Desserts—Kölsch is for the beginning or middle of a meal, not the end

STYLE: WIT

Qualities: Spicy, fruity, dry, herbal. Often smooth-bodied, especially in American interpretations, the sharpness of the spice and carbonation give it a dry, almost acidic, and refreshing bite, while the depth of orange and ground coriander in most Wits makes for a lively fruitiness

Bring together: Most salads love a Wit's freshness; white fish with lemon; herb-roasted chicken; chowder; lemon drizzle cake or orange Madeleines; mozzarella and basil salad

Balance: Oily fish; North African spices; falafel; oysters; calamari; mild cheese; white pizza

Boost: Wit adds an elegant lift to sushi; Thai food's balance of citrus, spice, and green leafy herbs zings with Wit; paella or seafood risotto; spaghetti con vongole

Local: Moules frites—best made with beer, best drunk with beer.

Avoid: Chocolate is no good with Wit's dry spice

Style: Hefeweizen

Qualities: Fruity, spicy, sometimes creamy, dry. The suspended-yeast fullness in the body can lie on the tongue like a soothing blanket, while the brisk carbonation pops the palate into life and can add a hint of acidity. The background of subtle malt gives depth while the estery, fruity, smoky, and spicy aroma can be a faked pass in an unexpected direction, making it work with a wide range of food. Weizenbock, Hefe's big brother, can handle bigger flavors

Bring together: Banana cake; barbecued Cajun or jerk fish, chicken, or pork where the spice and slight smoke in the beer are mirrored in the food; Weizenbock with apple pie

Balance: Mexican food, with its spice and heat, is balanced and cooled by Hefeweizen—Dunkelweizen (a dark Hefeweizen) can be even better; chicken roasted with Indian spices; the sinus dynamite of wasabi on sushi can be cooled by Hefeweizen

Boost: Thai food is given an extra element with Hefeweizen, as the beer completes all the flavors; try coconut-based curries; smoked ham; eggs are great—omelet, eggs Benedict, bacon and eggs; for dessert, have Weizenbock with roasted banana, as the toffee flavors in both are fantastic together

Local: Any kind of cooked pig part

Avoid: Acidity and sharp flavors that clash with the slight background acidity in the beer

Style: Belgian Dubbel

Qualities: Malty, fruity, nutty, sometimes dry, sometimes intense. The brisk carbonation adds lightness, the body contains plenty of dried-fruit sweetness, there's a bready depth, and a peppery festiveness to the flavors that make it good with sweet and savory dishes. It's a versatile, gymnastic kind of beer to take to the table

Bring together: French toast with blueberries; afternoon tea; figs and blue cheese; roasted eggplant (aubergine) with a sweet dressing; teriyaki

Balance: Strong cheeses; Chinese noodles; tea-smoked fish; spaghetti Bolognese; roast lamb with rosemary

Boost: Baked apples with spices; roast turkey with all the trimmings; cheese and mushroom tart

Local: Carbonnade, especially if it's cooked with Dubbel

Avoid: Any kind of curry or citrus

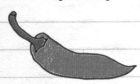

Boost: Asparagus loves Tripels, especially with a poached egg and smoked bacon; the basil, cheese, and garlic in pesto pasta sing with this style; apricot tart tastes sweeter with the nuttiness of Tripel
Local: Waterzoi—a creamy fish or chicken stew cooked with vegetables
Avoid: Chili heat; and save the Belgian chocolates for a glass of Quadruple or Kriek

STYLE: FLANDERS RED AND FLEMISH BRUIN (OLD REDS AND BROWNS)

Qualities: Intense, sharp, acetic, dry. These blood-red beers often have an iron-like tang. The acetic sharpness works like an extra addition to a dish or cuts through richness; it also gives an umami-like meatiness that's capable of enhancing flavor. There's also a depth of malt that combines with the dry, tannic, sherry-like finish and an oak woodiness
Bring together: With breakfast, replace the Bloody Mary with this style; think of a Red like the vinegar in a salad dressing; tomato bruschetta
Balance: Goats' cheese and washed-rind cheese; roast duck or venison; croque monsieur or madame
Boost: Fois gras or pâté; a Flanders Red perks up a rare steak like a squirt of ketchup; cured meats; sausages
Local: Stoemp—potatoes and vegetables mashed together and served with sausage
Avoid: Pickled food; citrus; any kind of curry

STYLE: SOUR AND FRUIT BEERS

Qualities: Intense, sharp, dry, fruity. A large bundle of beer styles combines here—Lambic, Gueuze, American sours/Wild beers, and fruit beers (including Kriek and Framboise). Where Flanders Red hits a vinegary note, these beers are closer to citrus sharpness. Some contain fruit, adding an extra element, and some of those with fruit will also be sweetened. A savory-like depth is added by barrel-aging. The effervescent carbonation combined with the sharpness and dry

STYLE: BELGIAN TRIPEL/STRONG GOLDEN BELGIAN ALE

Qualities: Spicy, dry, fragrant, crisp. Belgian Tripels have a poky carbonation capable of Hulk-like lifting and throwing power against heavy flavors. They have an earthy, spicy depth but remain surprisingly delicate, while the firm bitterness and the heft of booze make Tripel a superhero food beer. Also, think of it as Champagne's ass-kicking alter-ego. Belgian Blondes and Pale Ales are similar but toned down, although often with sharper bitterness
Bring together: Monkfish or lobster with herb butter; Caesar salad; roasted vegetables; pasta with seafood
Balance: Strong garlic flavor—the subtle, sulfurous notes in the beer and food are great together; pizza topped with anchovies, artichoke, and basil; charcuterie; Gouda or stinky washed-rind cheeses; fragrant Asian coconut dishes; cassoulet; Christmas/Thanksgiving dinner

finish makes these beers drive the appetite and demand to be drunk alongside food

Bring together: Oysters; ceviche or seafood, especially if it's with avocado; goats' cheese and Gueuze; cherry cheesecake with sweet Kriek; the rich depth of flavor of air-dried pork matches the oak profile in Lambic and Gueuze

Balance: Chocolate richness with sweetened fruit beers; fois gras or pâté with classic sours; roast duck; creamy pasta; Brie and Camembert

Boost: Salty foods such as fried chicken skin or fries; crème brulée with sweet and sour Framboise is a revelation

Local: Chips and mayo; Kriek with Belgian chocolate or waffles

Avoid: Chili heat; acidity; any food with bitterness, as it clashes with sour

STYLE: AMERICAN PALE ALE AND IPA

Qualities: Intense, fruity, bitter. Needing to carry the hops, the malt base of these beers is often big (with a caramel-like sweetness), meaning it can work really well with food. The thing to avoid is a beer that is very high in bitterness (unless it's for very salty food), as this will be like an elbow drop to the tongue. American craft lagers are similar but lighter in profile

Bring together: Fruitiness in cheddar matches the fruitiness in the hops; jerk spices match the herbal rub with citrus and pine in the beer—just watch out for too much heat; French Caribbean cuisine, especially salt fish

Balance: Steak and fries; triple-decker sandwiches; onion rings; topped nachos; creamy blue cheese; quesadillas

Boost: Cheeseburgers, where the hop fruitiness matches the cheese and condiments, and then the bitterness cuts through the fat; citrus cheesecake (if bitterness is moderate); carrot cake is delicious, especially if it's got a thick cream-cheese frosting

Local: Cheeseburgers; Mac 'n' cheese; tacos

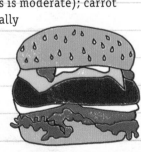

Avoid: Chocolate; tomato-based curries (think tomato and grapefruit... no thanks)

STYLE: PACIFIC PALE AND IPA

Qualities: Intense, fruity, bitter, fragrant. Similar to American Pales and IPAs, only the hop flavor is more toward tropical fruit than citrus, giving gooseberry, grape, passion fruit, mango, and pineapple instead of grapefruit, orange, and pine

Bring together: Salads of chicken or fish; Vietnamese noodles; dishes with a side of mango salad

Balance: Sushi; fish and chips; fruity cheeses; Thai coconut curries; lamb burger

Boost: Thai food where the fragrant fruitiness in the beer matches the sweetness in the dishes; Polynesian dishes
Local: Barbecued fish with fragrant salad
Avoid: Tomato-based sauces (think tomato and passion fruit… no thanks), dark chocolate, anything acidic

STYLE: AMBER, RED, AND BROWN ALES

Qualities: Toasty, fruity, bitter, roasty, nutty. A spectrum of beers combine here to give malt notes ranging from light and nutty to dark and roasty. Bitterness can be moderate or high, as can the aroma, so watch out for the intensity. These styles work well with food because they have a strong background of malt flavor and then the cut of hops. British versions are earthier while American versions are more citrusy
Bring together: Roasted red meats; barbecued meats; ham; sweet potato fries; meaty fish; satay
Balance: Fajitas; quesadillas; offal; pilau; nutty cheese; mac 'n' cheese; pizza
Boost: The earthiness of mushrooms is intensified with Brown Ales; burgers taste meatier with Red Ale's sweetness; pulled pork
Local: Sunday lunch in the United Kingdom; barbecued ribs in the United States
Avoid: Acidity; delicate dishes, which the malt will overpower

STYLE: BITTER AND ESB

Qualities: Fruity, bitter, malty, fragrant. Classic British beer styles, amber to brown in color. The balance of flavor between malt and hops shows the skill of the brewmaster. Earthy, floral, and hedgerow hops (with citrus in modern interpretations), while the malt gives toffee or toasty flavors. These are beers designed for drinking casually, so the foods follow that thinking
Bring together: Ploughman's lunch of meat, cheese, bread, and pickles; roasted meat's caramelized coating loves the sweet depths of these styles; sausages and mash with onion gravy
Balance: Salty bar snacks, such as pork scratchings; savory pies; Scotch eggs; fish and chips; a cheese sandwich

Boost: Mushroom risotto is perked up by the poke of earthy hops and malt base; there's also something interesting about Thai food with Bitters, and plenty of British pubs now have exotic dishes on the menu—the dull bitterness provides a counter to the bright Asian flavors
Local: Roast beef with all the trimmings; ploughman's lunch
Avoid: Big sweetness

STYLE: SMOKED BEER

Qualities: Intense. Smoked beer can go in a few directions: smoky like Islay whisky, smoky like bonfires, or smoky like smoked meat. Islay smoke isn't often complementary to foods, being overpowering, but the others can work very well, especially the meatier kind, which acts like a shot of meatiness into your dinner. Smoked beer is also good at softening the zing of acidity
Bring together: Roasted and barbecued meats and fish, especially with a dressed salad; smoked cheese and meat; roasted eggplant (aubergine) takes on a smoky depth—eat with hummus and fresh bread; brisket and burnt-end beans
Balance: Smoke is able to balance and calm acidity and vice-versa, so meat with a sharp side dish is often a winner—Mexican (think chipotle) with sour cream or kimchi and Korean; Japanese grilled meats
Boost: Sausages and meat taste more sausagey and meaty; chili; tomato-based pasta; fish pie; ramen noodles; try a bonfire-like smoked beer with lemon tart—unusual and delicious
Local: The Rauchbeer of Bamburg is made to go with big hunks of meat, piles of sauerkraut, and bowls of potatoes.
Avoid: Anything too delicate; most curry dishes

STYLE: MILK AND OATMEAL STOUT

Qualities: Smooth, roasty, creamy. Where Dry Stouts can bring a charred bitterness to dishes, Milk and Oatmeal Stouts introduce the dark malt flavor but also a depth of sweetness and a smooth body, making them very complementary to lots of different foods
Bring together: Roasted meats; smoked cheese; creamy desserts; yakitori, which picks up some sweet char from the grill; chocolate cake
Balance: Mexican and Caribbean heat and spice; burritos; nutty cheeses, such as Gruyère and Comté
Boost: Mexican dishes, such as chili and mole, where the chocolate flavors in the glass can match those on the plate; the dark depths are excellent with tomato-based pasta dishes and pizza; the flavor of barbecued and grilled meat is rounded out by the sweetness in the beer
Local: Drink with a full English breakfast (or oatmeal if you want the healthy option)
Avoid: Light salads (there's no place for chocolate there)

STYLE: IMPERIAL STOUT

Qualities: Smooth, roasty, creamy, rich, intense. Big beer, full of flavor, intensity, and booze. Can be roasty bitter, hop bitter, or sweet (or all three). Add some barrel-aging and you get bourbon, nutty notes, extra sweetness, and texture
Bring together: Chocolate desserts; brownies; ribs; blue cheese's salty richness
Balance: Vanilla ice cream; strong cheeses; sweeter stouts with chili con carne
Boost: Berry desserts (think about the combo of strawberry and chocolate); banoffee pie; crème brulée; peanut butter and jelly sandwiches
Local: Home is England but it moved around the world. Grab some locally made chocolate and a bottle of stout
Avoid: Delicate flavors (and drinking too much)

COOKING WITH BEER

As well as being drunk with food, beer can also be a brilliant ingredient where the depth of flavor can work wonderfully in many dishes. My personal approach is to put in beer whenever a liquid is listed in a recipe.

The beer you use is up to you, but aim for complementary flavors or beers that you hope will accentuate the qualities of the food. But here's a word of a warning: beer's bitterness is often emphasized by cooking, so using bitter beer will most likely leave you with harsh-tasting food. Some people think it's a waste to cook with beer, but I don't tend to listen to them. Here are some of my favorite beer recipes:

BEERAMISÙ Like tiramisù, but made with beer. Kick out the coffee and use an Imperial Stout instead—barrel-aged is also good, as is coffee stout. You can also mix some beer into the cream topping.

BEERY MAC 'N' CHEESE Beer and cheese love each other as the beer cuts through the richness and emphasizes the cheese's fruity side. Add a beer with toffee-like depth to a cheese sauce for Mac 'n' Cheese—IPA can also work well here. Or go in a different direction and make a cheese and beer fondue with beer bread to dip into it.

BEER BAKING Add Imperial Stout, Barley Wine, or fruit beer to the mix for cupcakes or brownies. For cookies, use Imperial Stout or strong wheat beers in the mix or crush up some pale malt and add to the dough (I've also used crushed pale malt to coat chicken to make nuggets—great with beer ketchup). Add some malty dark beer to cheese straws, cook them, and then open more beer to drink with them.

BEER BATTER Pour some cold, lively lager into batter to get a light, crisp crunch—it's the bubbles you want here. I once went to a pub and ordered fish and chips: "Which beer do you want in the batter?" the landlord asked. I could choose from any beer in the bar and they made the batter fresh—not much flavor comes through but it was a nice way to go. I once deep-fried a peanut-butter-and-jelly sandwich in a strawberry-beer batter. Only once, though. Beer is also good in pancakes. Imperial Stouts and fruit beers work best, especially if you top the pancakes with something complementary.

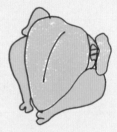

BEER-CAN CHICKEN Take a can of craft beer, pour half into a glass, and then put the half-empty beer can up a chicken's backside. Cook standing up, preferably on a barbecue with a lid. Pour some beer over the bird to marinate along with seasoning, herbs, and spices. A kick-ass way to cook chicken.

BEER JELLY At university I ate a lot of vodka jelly, which is, in some desperate way, the student equivalent of beer's "liquid bread." Mix gelatin, sugar syrup, beer, and water. Fruity beer is best. Serve in shot glasses with beer ice cream on top—it looks like mini pints.

BEER SOUP Sweet onion and Brown Ale. Delicious, especially with a cheese crouton on top.

CHERRY BEER SAUCE Fruit beer's low bitterness levels make it excellent in sauces. Add to gravy and serve with game birds.

CHILI CON CARNE Long, slow cooking is good with beer. Try adding a bottle of Imperial Stout to chili (a barrel-aged one if you can bear to pour in a whole bottle). Cook it for a few hours and taste the stout's sweet depth mixed with the fierce chili heat.

CHOCOLATE SAUCE Make a chocolate sauce. Add beer (barrel-aged stout is best). Pour over vanilla ice cream.

CONDIMENTS Make beer ketchup, barbecue sauce, mustard, chutney, or mayonnaise, or go for a beer salad dressing. Use a smoked beer in ketchup or barbecue sauce; use a malty ale in chutney or mustard; and go for sour beer or Wit in mayo. Beer can also be added to salad dressings: take oil, vinegar, and beer, and mix together—IPA can work here but fruit beer, American Wheat, Wit, or Hefeweizen are best.

HOP-FRIED CHICKEN This is my secret herb-and-spice mix for giving a bitter fruitiness to fried chicken: crush a whole hop flower, add salt, pepper, cayenne pepper, chili powder, paprika, thyme, bay, sugar, and a little flour. Cook like normal fried chicken or bake.

ICE CREAM AND SORBET Swirl beer into the mix but use Imperial Stout or fruit beer to avoid bitterness. Sharp Sour beers make excellent and refreshing sorbets. I once re-created the brewing process in my kitchen using crushed pale malt, milk, and cream to make a beautiful base for ice cream or crème brulée. Also try Imperial Stout with a scoop of ice cream for a fun beer float.

MARINADES Smoked beer can be a great marinade for meat, especially ribs or steak—somehow teasing out more meatiness.

MOULES FRITES Soften garlic and onion in a big pan, add fresh mussels, and pour in a splash of Wit or Gueuze. Finish with lemon and serve with a big pile of fries on the side.

PIZZA DOUGH OR BREAD
Add beer to the dough when you make it. Go for something malty and nutty like a Brown Ale, dark lager, or Oatmeal Stout.

RISOTTO Usually calls for a glug of wine, but try beer instead. Wit or Hefe works best, but I've made an excellent cheese risotto to which I added IPA, although I added it along with the stock and not to the dry rice.

STEWS Classic beer cooking. British Mild, ESB, Oatmeal Stout, and Bock all add great malty richness to dishes (you can take this mix and put it in a pie crust for a delicious meat and ale pie). Don't use these beers to deglaze the pan, though, as that's when bitterness butts in. Use Belgian Dubbel or Gueuze for a classic carbonnade. Coq à la Bière is chicken cooked in beer. Go for Bière de Garde or an Amber Ale, preferably French or Belgian.

WELSH RAREBIT The best cheese on toast you can make. Make a roux sauce of butter and flour, add milk and beer (something dark), strong cheese, mustard, Worcestershire sauce, pepper, and egg yolk. Pour the thick mix onto toast, and then heat under the grill until it bubbles.

ENJOYING BEER

Bad, old beer tastes like vinegar, cardboard, Marmite, or sherry, so it pays to understand which beers can be cellared or aged and which ones should be drunk fresh. Knowing this means you can be sure to enjoy all your favorite beers at their best.

CELLARING BEER

Some beers are best drunk fresh, while others age well, sometimes still being drinkable beyond 20 years in the bottle. The key is temperature: a cellar temperature of 12°C (53°F) or lower is best for a slow maturation of the beer. If you want to see how heat changes things, then leave a bottle in a warm place for a week and taste it—it'll be like it's been in your cellar for months.

The aging process is fascinating. Doing a side-by-side tasting of the same beer at different ages will show you what happens over time. One of the first changes is bitterness and hop aroma. The IBU level in the beer drops and the aroma changes, and this happens in the bottle within the first year after it's been packaged (so don't save hoppy beers—drink them fresh). Where the hops fall into the beer, the malt and yeast character pushes forward. Yeast plays a key part in the process, and the best beers to mature are those that are bottle-conditioned or unfiltered.

Not everyone has a cellar and nor can they afford huge beer fridges, so choose somewhere with a consistently cool temperature, like a garage or a closet—my beer is kept in the garage where the temperature rises and falls but does so very gradually. With beers that you know age well, buy a few bottles so that you can compare them at different ages. Maturation happens in good peaks and dull lows. Sometimes you'll open a bottle that tastes flat and uninteresting, but then you could try it again a year later and it will taste wonderful.

HERE ARE A FEW SIMPLE RULES TO FOLLOW WHEN CELLARING BEER:

❖ Cellaring is only for beers with an alcohol volume over 6.0% (unless Sour).

❖ Cellaring is best for bottle-conditioned beers.

❖ Darker beers tend to age better than light beers.

❖ Belgian Sour beers mature well.

❖ Hop-driven beers, in which you want to get the full-on hop experience, should be drunk as fresh as possible and should be refrigerated to keep their freshness.

HOW DO I KNOW WHETHER TO CELLAR A BEER?

DRINK THE FOLLOWING BEERS FRESH:
Pilsner, Helles, Kölsch, Alt
Hefeweizen, Wit
Pale Ale, all IPAs
Brown Ale, Porter, Bitter

❖

DRINK THE FOLLOWING BEERS AGED:
Barley Wine
Imperial Stout
old, strong, and vintage ale
Wild beer

BEAUTIFUL BEER

It's not just about the taste of beer—I'm a sucker for great graphic design on the beers I drink. Here are some of my favorites.

THE BEST BEERS IN THE WORLD?

The beer-rating websites ratebeer.com and beeradvocate.com—where users give scores and comments on the beers they drink—both have a list of the highest-rated beers. Compiled according to the scores given to them, they should represent the best of drinking around the world, whereby only a beer that consistently scores very highly will ever make it to the top.

See how most of these beers are strong and note that some beers are on both lists. Is this a coincidence or are they really that good?

Big-impact beers (in terms of flavor and reputation) and rarities always get to the top of these lists; it's as if the stronger the flavor of a beer, the louder someone will shout about it, regardless of whether they prefer drinking a delicious 4.0% ABV beer.

Perhaps they are self-fulfilling in that the hype of a top beer guarantees it a good score, perhaps rarity and excitement push the scores higher, or perhaps they are just brilliant beers. Maybe all three are true. One thing is certain with these beers: all are well known and all are chased by beer geeks.

RATEBEER TOP 10: 2012

1.	Westvleteren 12	10.2% ABV	Trappist beer
2.	Närke Kaggen Stormaktsporter	9.5% ABV	Barrel-aged Imperial Stout
3.	Goose Island Rare Bourbon County Stout	13.0% ABV	Barrel-aged Imperial Stout
4.	Founders Kentucky Breakfast Stout	11.2% ABV	Barrel-aged Imperial Stout
5.	Rochefort Trappistes 10	11.3% ABV	Trappist Quadruple.
6.	Bell's Hopslam	10.0% ABV	Double IPA
7.	Russian River Pliny the Younger	11.0% ABV	Double IPA
8.	Cigar City Pilot Series Passion fruit and Dragonfruit Berliner Weisse	Unknown ABV	Berliner Weisse
9.	Alesmith Speedway Stout	12.0% ABV	Imperial Stout
10.	Deschutes The Abyss	11.0% ABV	Imperial Stout

BEERADVOCATE TOP 20: 2012 (THIS LIST CAN CHANGE DAILY)

1.	Russian River Pliny the Younger	11.0% ABV	Double IPA
2.	Westvleteren 12	10.2% ABV	Trappist Quadruple
3.	Founders Canadian Breakfast Stout	10.6% ABV	Barrel-aged Imperial Stout
4.	Alchemist Heady Topper	8.0% ABV	Double IPA
5.	Three Floyds Vanilla Bean Aged Dark Lord	13.0% ABV	Imperial Stout
6.	Russian River Pliny the Elder	8.0% ABV	Double IPA
7.	Goose Island King Henry	13.4% ABV	Barley Wine
8.	Kern River Citra DIPA	8.0% ABV	Double IPA
9.	Founders Kentucky Breakfast Stout	11.2% ABV	Barrel-aged Imperial Stout
10.	Närke Kaggen Stormaktsporter	9.5% ABV	Barrel-aged Imperial Stout

FLAVOR WHEEL

What's that flavor in your beer and where's it coming from?

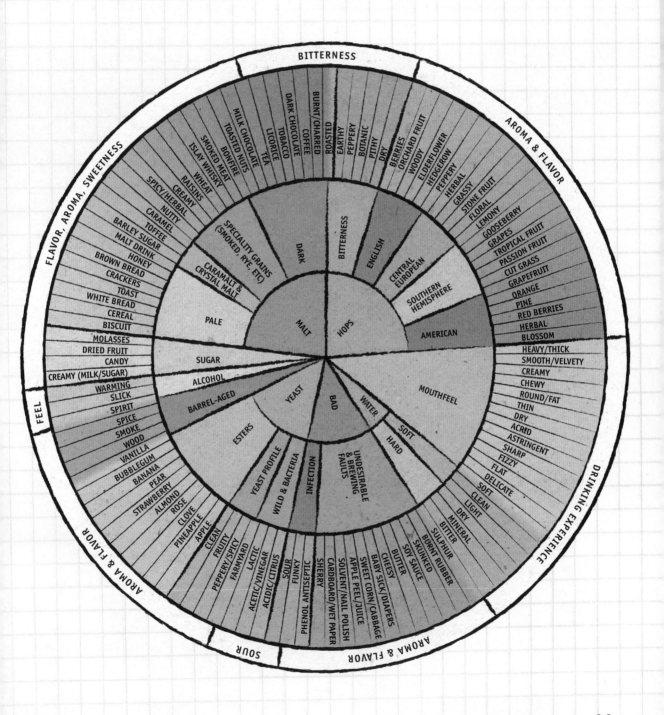

CLASSIC VS. NEW

Beer styles provide a structure, or set of rules, for brewers either to follow or break. Some styles are classics—typically those from the United Kingdom, Belgium, and Germany. Of these, a few beers in each category can be classified as quintessential examples of what the style tastes like. There are also many examples that veer away from the classic flavor profile and push it with new inspirations. Away from the classics, there's an ever-changing world of beers and styles where experimentation is changing what we drink.

HOW BEER STYLES EVOLVE

Beer styles are always evolving. IPA is a good example: starting out as India Pale Ale in the 18th century, it was brewed in England and shipped to India—a strong, well-hopped beer that, because of a long sea voyage, matured during the journey. Two hundred years later, it was lower in ABV and a shadow of the earlier seafaring beer. Then, American craft brewers took the idea of a strong, hoppy beer and, by using American hops, transformed it into a beer exploding with citrus-like hop character. Now it comes in white, black, and red, it's imperialized, or made Belgian, or spun in many other ways. The originals are gone and in their place are many new versions.

This book is about the evolution of beer. What makes beer such an exciting subject is that there's so much interesting history, so many stories, and so many classic, traditional styles that have been made for years. Now brewers are taking what's been brewed before and applying a modern attitude and approach to their beers. Thanks to this growing awareness of beer's history, brewers have brought back styles that almost became extinct, finding recipes in old brewing books, including Porter, Lambic, Berliner Weisse, and Wit, while regional beer styles—such as Kölsch, Rauchbier, and Alt—have been taken around the world. Looking more broadly at where we are now: if this book had been written in 2003, some of the styles listed here wouldn't have existed; if it's re-written in 2023, who knows what styles will be added or lost.

APPRECIATE THE OLD, EMBRACE THE NEW

When it comes to styles, beers are placed into categories depending on their characteristics. Style guidelines will list the "appropriate" range of color, ABV, IBU, and final gravity of a style, plus tasting expectations. Yet many beers labeled as a certain style fall outside these guidelines by being stronger, more bitter, darker, lighter, sweeter, hopped differently, and so on. This is how beer styles evolve and new ones are created. Knowing what a classic example of the style tastes like is important because it enables you to see how a brewer has interpreted their new version—some go for a straight-up brew to try to achieve that classic flavor, while others take the idea and flip and twist it in new directions so that it hardly resembles where it started.

New versions of beer styles are indicative of where brewing is now. Experimenting with beers and ideas is possible because drinkers are thirsty to try something new. There's always another beer, always something fresh to try, and this is what's driving beer forward. No longer do drinkers want to buy 24-packs of the same beer—they'd rather grab four six-packs or, better, four mixed sixers.

Part of the fun of loving beer is in returning to the classics; it's like recalibrating the tongue or picking up an old photograph and remembering what was happening at the moment the flash fired. It's easy to become obsessed with the new and to forget the old but, as drinkers mature, there's a drift back toward the classic flavors of beer styles. Beer styles, like fashion, food, and film, also age in different ways. While the passing of time dates some beer styles badly, it matures others magnificently. And, like other things, beer rolls in cyclical waves where it's always possible to look up over the bar and see brewing trends: first hops, then barrels, then Sour beers, then Saisons, then session beers, then...

THE PURPOSE OF THIS BOOK

This book focuses on the new and exciting examples of beer styles while also giving a high-five of thanks to where they came from. Not every style in here features a classic and that's because some styles are so new that one hasn't established itself yet. Others, normally the Old World styles, do have a classic example— these are the beers to find if you want to know definitively what the beer style tastes like, or if you want to see how brewers interpret the recipes. Not many classic beers feature here. They have been featured in other books many times before. This book is about evolution, creativity, and interpretation.

THE WORLD'S GREATEST BEERS

THE CROWN OF FOAM THAT TOPS PILSNER (PILSENER, PILS) HINTS AT THE STYLE'S ASCENSION TO BEING THE KING OF WORLD BEER. GO TO ANY BAR AND ONCE UPON A TIME THAT PALE PINT OF LAGER ORIGINATED AS A PILSNER BEFORE THE BIG AMERICAN CORPORATE BAD GUYS TOOK IT OVER AND TURNED IT INTO SOMETHING DIFFERENT. THE HAPPILY-EVER-AFTER COMES FROM THE NEW BREWERIES THAT ARE ELEVATING PILSNER BACK TO THE TOP WITH THEIR OWN TAKES ON THE STYLE. MY FIRST PROPER PILSNER, DRUNK IN PRAGUE, WAS A REVELATORY KIND OF BEER—SO FAR REMOVED FROM THE BEERS I THOUGHT REPRESENTED LAGERS. STUNNING DEPTH OF FLAVOR, REAL HOP BITE, A RICH BODY; IT IMMEDIATELY BECAME ONE OF MY FAVORITE STYLES OF BEER.

PILSNER

These clean, racily-hopped, easy-gulping brews have two homes: German Pils is typically pale gold in color, and the hops hit with a dry, herbal, rough edge; Bohemian Pilsners are a deeper gold in color with a fuller, slightly sweeter body and a cleaner, more bitter hop finish. Expect ABV to be around 5.0%. The hops used are classically aromatic Noble varieties, which give grassy, floral, pithy, and herbal qualities, though the use of New World hops is pushing Pils in delicious new directions.

PILSNER URQUELL

PLZEN, CZECH REPUBLIC
ABV: 4.4%
HOPS: SAAZ

CLASSIC

In the late 1830s, Plzeň was a town with lots of small breweries making too much bad beer, so the townsfolk decided to pool resources and start one new brewery—Burghers' Brewery. It was there, in 1842, that brewer Josef Groll made one of the first golden lagers in existence and a beer that would become known after its home town. Bottled or draft, the beer has honeyed and toasty malt, a beautiful aroma of spicy Saaz hops, and a clean, bitter finish. Go to the brewery, if you can, because you'll get to see the incredible maze of cellars (used to keep beer cool before artificial refrigeration) beneath the behemoth brewing plant and try the unfiltered and unpasteurized version of PU which will forever change what you thought you knew about lager. It might now be made by a big brewery, but don't let that put you off—this is the original Bohemian Pilsner.

Birrificio Italiano Tipopils

Lurago Marinone, Italy
ABV: 5.2%
Hops: Northern Brewer, Perle, Spalter Select

If Pilsner Urquell is the classic, then this is the modern masterpiece. Everything from the handsome haze in the golden pour to the pillow of white foam, the impossibly fresh aroma to the unbeatable balance and depth of flavor, make this a perfect Pils. The hop character lifts it above the others in its style, giving a little herbal and floral kiss before juicy, tropical fruit and orange (showing hidden beauty in the European hops) make it a full-on lip-smacker. If you can find Italiano's Extra Hop, then get it: it's lighter, hoppier, and lagered for longer—it might even be better than Tipopils, though it's only brewed a couple of times a year. You won't find a beer that's better with pizza than this, especially if the beer is on tap and the pizza is fresh from the oven.

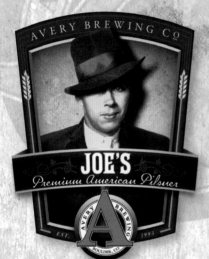

Avery Joe's Premium American Pilsner

Boulder, Colorado
ABV: 4.7%
Hops: Magnum, Hersbrücker

If I lived in Colorado, a six-pack of this would be as essential in my fridge as milk, mustard, and hot sauce. The thing about Pilsner is that it's a beer for drinking without contemplation—simple, thirst-quenching, and always there for those moments when you just need a beer. The joy of Joe's is in ripping one from the six-pack, crunching open the ring pull, and downing it with satisfied sighs. If you want to think and drink, then you'll see how the hops are really showing off, hollering: "Look at me!" as they hang on to your tonsils. Lemon pith, spritzy sherbet, floral, dry, and peppery, the Boulder brewer's bold use of hops delivers a bigger hit than you might be expecting for the style, but it's balanced by a six-pack-firm body to keep it in place.

Kout na Šumavě 12° Světlý Ležák

Kout na Šumavě, Czech Republic
ABV: 5.0%
Hops: Saaz

This is the new school of Czech lager brewing, moving traditional beers forward, while remaining true to the style. Světlý Ležák is the pale premium lager of Czech breweries (Ležák can be 11° or 12°, based on the Plato scale, and 4.4–5.0% ABV; a 10° výčepní pivo will be the lower-ABV everyday gulper). Kout's 12° is a beautiful beer with a thick foam and a smooth, deep golden body. Grassy, some citrus, floral, and hints of creamy dried apricot, the hops burst through to bring a kick of bitterness. As with most great lagers, if you can get the unfiltered version, then you are lucky: fuller bodied, slightly creamy, bready and doughy, fresher tasting with more amazing hop aroma, it shows why Pilsner is the greatest beer style in the world.

Emerson's Pilsner

Dunedin, New Zealand
ABV: 4.9%
Hops: Riwaka

New Zealand Pilsner has become its own beer style down under. Borrowing the base beer from German and Czech brewers, the Kiwi development comes with their use of hops, which concentrates on New Zealand varieties. Known for their tropical-fruit juiciness, the hops of New Zealand grow in a couple of key areas, most of which have had varieties named after them: Riwaka, Motueka, and Nelson. Many New Zealand hop varieties are bred from European varieties, so share a depth similar to Noble hops, but then add a big whack of fruitiness on top with gooseberry, grape, mango, and a lychee-likeness to Sauvignon Blanc wine. Emerson's Pilsner uses Riwaka hops to give subtle tropical fruit, the tartness of passion fruit, and the freshness of citrus zest, all of which go so well with the clean body of Pilsner malt. It's a glorious beer, especially with some locally caught and barbecued fish.

Moonlight Reality Czeck

Santa Rosa, California
ABV: 4.8%
Hops: US Perle

Imagine a list of must-visit towns for beer geeks. It's a list that ignores the big cities and instead looks at the little places that have had a big impact on the beer world. Not far north of San Francisco, Santa Rosa is one of those places, tucked in among Northern California's vineyards. People are drawn to the town because of the Russian River Brewing Co., but they stay because of Moonlight. After a day of drinking, I'm tired when I get to The Toad in the Hole, a great pub in town run by Londoner, Paul Stokeld. I order a Reality Czeck. Golden, the soft body is like a pillow for my tired tongue, but it's also the equivalent of a power-nap for the palate with its burst of zesty, floral, spicy, American-grown European hops giving a lively burst of flavor. My thirst suddenly returns just as Reality Czeck's bitterness clings onto my tonsils and calls for me to drink more.

The Crate Brewery Lager

London, England
ABV: 5.0%
Hops: Hallertauer, Cascade

Go to The Crate Brewery and you won't believe you're still in London. The big white building with its jailhouse windows sits by a narrow river. Along its edge is an inner-city outdoor gallery where you can study the bright and bold graffiti while you sip; inside, the space is sparse and industrial with brewing tanks visible through glass windows and a central bar with a pizza kitchen behind (the pizzas are fantastic—light, chewy, and charred at the edges). Crate's Golden Ale is dry and bitter, British in origin, and yet a hint of America comes through (unless that's just the Brooklyn vibe in the air), but it's the lager that's so brightly, freshly hoppy that I get a Proustian pang for Prague. It's not really a Pilsner, but not really a Helles or a Vienna either; it's a new kind of London lager—aromatic, vibrant, clean, toasty, and tasty. New lager in trendy East London.

HELL MEANS "LIGHT" IN GERMAN, AND HELLES IS THE CLASSIC GOLDEN BAVARIAN LAGER. IT'S THE SIBLING OF PILSNER AND THE OTHER HALF OF THE PALE-LAGER TAG TEAM, WHICH TOGETHER ACCOUNT FOR AROUND HALF OF THE BEER DRUNK IN GERMANY. WHERE PILSNER IS SNAPPILY BITTER, HELLES IS SOFTER AND ROUNDER WITH A LIGHTER TOUCH FROM THE HOPS. HELLES, OR HELL, IS MUNICH'S MAIN BEER AND ORIGINATED THERE AT THE END OF THE 19TH CENTURY, WITH SPATEN RELEASING THE FIRST HELLES IN 1894. IT TOOK A LITTLE WHILE FOR HELLES TO SPREAD THROUGH THE REGION—WITH SOME OF THE BIG BREWERS WANTING TO STICK TO JUST THEIR DARK DUNKELS—BUT WITH THE POPULARITY OF PALE PILSNERS AND AS GLASSES BECAME THE DRINKING VESSEL OF CHOICE, BEER GOT BETTER-LOOKING, BRIGHTER, AND PALER.

HELLES

Helles is a pale gold, medium-bodied beer with a malt character that gives fresh bread and lightly toasted malt. The hopping is traditionally delicate, giving some flavor, aroma, and a low, balanced bitterness—expect a little floral note or grassiness. Delightful because of its restrained, easy-drinking nature, the alcohol content of the beer will be 4.5–5.5% and the bitterness classically in the 20 IBUs. Helles are best drunk in 1-liter (1³/₄-pint/2-US-pint) stein glasses, but do some bicep curls in preparation because the glasses are heavy when full (although somehow dainty, light-footed waitresses manage to carry six at a time and still smile).

AUGUSTINER BRÄU LAGERBIER HELL

MUNICH, GERMANY
ABV: 5.2%

Munich has six big breweries: Löwenbräu, Hofbräu, Paulaner, Hacker-Pschorr, Spaten, and Augustiner. Between them they've been brewing for a combined total of over 3,000 years. All make a Helles, the most famous local style. Augustiner is the oldest of the Big Six with the brewery founded in 1328. Some beers belong, and taste best, in a certain place. You need to drink Augustiner Hell in the enormous beer gardens of Munich where the fresh bready depth of the beer, the subtle, refreshing caress of floral hops, and the ever-so-soft body make you never want to drink another beer again, promising faithful monogamy like a sun-struck holiday romance. Take the beer away from there and it's still very good, of course, but it loses the brilliance of drinking it in Munich surrounded by friendly faces, all lifting golden glasses to their upturned lips.

Camden Town Brewery Hells Lager

London, England
ABV: 4.6%
Hops: Perle, Hallertauer
Tradition

Not quite a Pilsner, not quite a Helles, Camden Town's Hells Lager is inspired by both styles and designed as a lager for London, where the name is a mash of Helles and Pils, not a reference to darker places. Hells takes the dry, light body of German Pilsners and mixes it with the light hopping of Helles to give a beer that is both very approachable and yet still really flavorsome. A lemony, lively, little hop aroma pokes out above a delicate Pilsner malt base before the dry, crisp finish, which has a peppery bitterness to it. It's got complexity if you look out for it, but subtlety if you don't. If you're in London, then go to the brewery, as they have a bar on site where you can get an unfiltered version of Hells, which is smoother, creamier, and has a bigger hop finish—I reckon that's Britain's best lager.

Knappstein Reserve Lager

Clare, Australia
ABV: 5.6%
Hops: Nelson Sauvin

It takes a lot of good beer to make good wine, so the remark on the famous thirst of winemakers goes, which means that it makes sense for a winery also to open a brewery and cut out the middle man. And that's what Knappstein did. They only make one beer, but then you only need one when it's this good. Inspired by Bavarian lagers, this isn't a typical Helles and instead is hopped using the outrageously fruity Nelson Sauvin from New Zealand, so called for its similarity to the gooseberry and passion fruit flavor of Sauvignon grapes. The fragrant lychee, honeyed mango, and tropical hop aromas lift out of the glass, a bready basket of pale malt wraps it together, and a pithy bitterness grips as it goes down. Reserve Lager shows the elegance and balance of a wine-drinker's sip, made for a beer-drinker's gulp.

Victory V Lager

Downington, Pennsylvania
ABV: 4.8%
Hops: Hallertauer

Victory make a great range of lagers, from Prima Pils' burst of aroma and rasping hop bitterness, up to big, bold Doppelbocks, via some single-hopped lagers showcasing classic hop varieties. With one of the founders spending time brewing in Munich before Victory was born, it's no surprise that they do such a good job with bottom-fermenting brews. V Lager is a beer that shows off the skill of the Victory brewers in packing a delicate beer with flavor without overpowering it. A dazzling gold color, it's got a bready base with subtle malt, a balancing hop flavor that gives a grassy and citrus-pith bite, and a bitterness that's light but dominates the finish, making you crave more. Philadelphia was where the first lager was brewed in America and it's where some of the best are still made, thanks to Victory.

Cisco Summer of Lager

Nantucket, Massachusetts
ABV: 5.6%
Hops: Mt Hood

This beer doesn't skimp on the lagering time: it's brewed toward the end of the year and then matured until the sun starts shining. It's based on the classic Bavarian style but is pumped up a bit, being bigger in body, darker in color (it pours an amber-gold), at the high end of the alcohol range, and loaded with hop character from the Mt Hood hop variety, which is grown in the United States but related to the Noble Hallertauer. A bready sweetness and medium body load up the middle, and the hops punch in with a grassy, floral waft and a grab of quenching, zesty bitterness as you swallow. The hopping is definitely more assertive than you'll find in other Helles but it really works here. The Cisco motto is: "Nice beer if you can get it." Being a seasonal release from a small brewery, Summer of Lager is exactly that.

Tuatara Helles

Waikanae, New Zealand
ABV: 5.0%
Hops: NZ Hallertauer,
Pacific Jade, Wai-iti

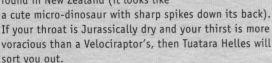

Like New Zealand Pilsner, this uses the lush fruitiness of Kiwi hop varieties to give Helles a New World flavor. This is one of those ever-reliable fridge beers, like a trusty wingman when you need something cold, quenching, and tasty. Clean, dry, and refreshing, there's a little bready malt in the middle and a great spread of hop flavor, ranging from grassy to peachy to orange pith, all from local varieties and all subtly balanced against the pale malt. Tuatara Brewing is named after an ancient reptile dating back to dinosaur days, which is now only found in New Zealand (it looks like a cute micro-dinosaur with sharp spikes down its back). If your throat is Jurassically dry and your thirst is more voracious than a Velociraptor's, then Tuatara Helles will sort you out.

Cervejaria Way Premium Lager

Pinhais, Brazil
ABV: 5.2%

In a country of pale lager, Cervejaria Way's Premium Lager lights things up like a yellow-shirted soccer player breaking through the red and green back line of global lagers. Way's Premium Lager is made with a mix of German, Czech, and American hops which give earthy, floral, and citrus flavors to counter the clean malt middle of this beer. It's different from the lackluster lagers that you need to serve ice-cold to enjoy, in that it's packed with flavor and character, and more fun than a booty-shaking samba dancer. All the Way beers are boldly packaged and their range includes a Cream Porter, an American Pale Ale and Double Pale, Belgian Dark IPA, an Irish Red, and a strong, dark lager named after the wood it's aged in—Amburana. This is Brazilian lager done Way better.

AMERICAN CRAFT LAGER

IF I COULD GO BACK IN TIME AND TASTE ANY BEER FROM HISTORY, ONE OF MY TOP FIVE PICKS WOULD BE PRE-PROHIBITION AMERICAN LAGERS. DEEP GOLD IN COLOR AND HOPPED WITH LOCAL VARIETIES ALONGSIDE GERMAN IMPORTS, THEY CHANGED IRREVOCABLY IN THE YEARS AFTER PROHIBITION. AMERICAN CRAFT LAGERS BRING BACK A FOCUS TO THIS STYLE OF BEER, ONLY USING THE CURRENT CROP OF HOPS AND DIRECTING THEM AT MODERN TASTEBUDS.

This is one of those contemporary and still-evolving beer styles that is broad and has few rules except that it needs to be made with bottom-fermenting yeast. For that reason, it's an exciting style to see develop around the world and, while I've prefixed it with "American," mostly because of the defining hops that go into it, it's also very popular in Northern Europe. Nothing like light or premium American lagers, these beers take the traditions of European lager-making along with the old American pre-Prohibition lagers and mix them with the craft-beer fireworks of New World hops.

What you can expect are gold-to-amber beers, anywhere between 4.5–6.0% ABV, often well hopped, particularly for aroma and flavor—it's Pale Ale meets pale lager. The rules are currently being written about what these lagers are and I include them here because I love the fruity burst of hops with the clean depth of good lager.

Coney Island Lager

New York, New York
ABV: 5.5%
Hops: Warrior, Amarillo, Cascade, Tettnang, Saaz, Hallertauer

Schmaltz Brewing Company splits in two directions: one goes to "The Chosen Beers," a range of Jewish-themed twists on American beer styles, while on the other side are Coney Island craft lagers made for "lager freaks and beer geeks." All are as colorful as a circus show, and the lagers Coney Island make perform new tricks: Mermaid Pilsner is a dry-hopped rye Pils; Human Blockhead is an Imperial American Bock; Sword Swallower is a conjoined twin of IPA and lager. The malt is the ringmaster that controls everything in Coney Island Lager, even if you were expecting the hops to perform the show. An amber color, richly malty but not overpowering, the Cascade dry-hop gives a great floral, pithy burst that leads into the flavor and gives more citrus for an encore at the end. Fun, bright, full of flavor—it's freaking good.

Mikkeller The American Dream

Copenhagen, Denmark
ABV: 4.6%
Hops: Nelson Sauvin, Saaz, Simcoe, Amarillo

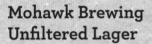

The Mikkeller Bar in Copenhagen is a beer geek's dream. There are 20 taps
with a mix of Mikkeller beers and guests, and you'll want to try everything
(especially if you look at the hefty bottle menu). Get an American Dream to start with because it'll help you
decide what to order next (because you will order something else). The American Dream is probably the
A-lister of American craft lagers and its winning smile is the big-hitting aroma. Peach, apricot, and grapefruit,
but fresher than any other beer manages, Mikkeller the hop maniac shows off his skill when adding the green
grenades into the kettle. The malt base has a fantastic, nutty subtlety and depth that can only come from the
slow, cold-conditioning of a lager, but it's the hops which you take notice of, especially the peppery pummel that
they give at the end.

Mohawk Brewing Unfiltered Lager

Taby, Sweden
ABV: 5.3%
Hops: Hallertauer, Nelson Sauvin,
Amarillo, Cascade, Citra, Centennial

"The hairstyle!" says Stefan
Gustavsson, head brewer at
Mohawk, when I ask him what
came first. "It's a big part of the
whole concept. To dare to be
different and follow your heart.
Not to be one in the crowd, but to
make a stand and make people
take notice." You definitely take
notice when you meet Stefan, his
hair like a shark's fin above a
crowded bar. And you definitely
take notice when you drink his
beer. It starts with a lager base
and is then hopped like an IPA. A
beautiful hazy gold, the aroma
fires out tangerine, sharp citrus,
mango, and herbs. The body is
smooth and has richness before
the bitterness kicks in. It's not
subtle or shy but, then again,
there's not much subtlety in a
Mohawk, is there?

Sigtuna East River Spring Lager

Arlandastad, Sweden
ABV: 5.2%
Hops:
Hallertauer,
Mittelfrüh,
Cascade

I love this label;
it brings back a
memory of the time
I tried to walk
across Brooklyn
Bridge. It was
2 a.m. and we'd
been drinking all
day. We were in
Brooklyn. Our hotel
was in Queens. We looked at a map, saw a bridge nearby,
aimed for it, assuming it was Brooklyn Bridge, even if the
walk took us west when we needed to go northeast.
Halfway across, surrounded by speeding trucks and a cage
of metal, we realized we were on the Williamsburg Bridge.
It was a long, sobering journey home from there. East
River Lager is a happier experience, thankfully. Amber to
look at, grapefruit, lime, mandarin, juicy apricot, and
some red berries hop-out, it's got a toasty, bready,
Vienna-style base and a dry, mouth-filling bitterness.

THE STORY OF LAGER

Lager doesn't have a birthday. We can't even give it a birth year. What we do know is that in the history of beer, which goes back 10,000 years, lager has gone from lurking secretly in the background to quite literally everywhere in less than 200 years.

For hundreds of years, brewers would've been making beer with yeast cells, which were both top- and bottom-fermenting, each becoming active depending on the temperature of the beer—if it was cold, then the lager yeast would go to work; if it was warm, then the ale yeast took over (while the lager yeast sweated out some off-flavors). German brewers came to realize that leaving beer in cold cellars or caves for a few months was a good thing, giving a clean depth to the drink and fewer funky flavors. That cold storage allowed the slow-working, gradually maturing lager yeast to ease through.

But brewers didn't really know about the science of yeast until toward the end of the 19th century when, finally, they started to scientifically understand the fermentation process and could peek microscopically inside their tanks. This enabled them to see the action of top- and bottom-fermenting yeast and also to isolate healthy yeast cells.

Lager's story gets interesting in the middle of the 19th century in Bohemia. Malting techniques develop and allow for paler malt, glasses begin to replace tankards as the drinking vessel of choice, meaning the appearance of beer becomes more important, and the increasing use of cold-conditioning leads to cleaner-tasting beers.

The combination of paler beer and processes that benefit bottom-fermentation saw the first golden lagers arrive. By the end of the 19th century, when the science of fermentation was better understood, lager beers could really begin to advance around the world.

The first American lager beers were brewed in Philadelphia in the 1840s before growing in popularity in Chicago and Milwaukee. Prior to this, all American beer was based on dark British ales. With a lot of central Europeans moving to America, these drinkers wanted the beer of their homeland, not the heavy, muddy Colonial ales. From the 1850s, German beers, similar to the ruddy-red Dunkel lagers, spread throughout the major cities.

The moment that changed lager forever can be attributed to Adolphus Busch who, on a trip to Bohemia, drank a golden lager. Seeing the light of inspiration, he took the recipe back with him to re-create it in America and in 1876 Budweiser was born. But to make the beer work, the brewers had to add rice or maize to the recipe; American six-row barley is higher in protein than European two-row, meaning a clumpy haze formed in the beer. By using rice, brewers could use less barley and therefore minimize haze; being pale and served in glasses, the haze wasn't as forgiving as the dark beer served in tankards. American lager is born, made different from European lagers by its use of an adjunct grain, and while it was originally popular with the immigrant populations, it soon became the beer that Americans wanted.

American lager brewing reached a heyday as the 20th century clocked in. By this stage, lager breweries had pioneered technical advances, such as artificial refrigeration and pasteurization, and grown into enormous beer factories, as well as opening up rail networks for distributing the beers. But it didn't stay good forever. Prohibition held sway for 13 years of no alcohol, and soda replaced beer on the shelves. The majority of breweries closed, although some managed to stay open by brewing "near-beer" of 0.5% ABV.

When Prohibition ended, lager came back fighting, but things soon changed again. Depression, wars, and the rationing of ingredients caused beer to get lighter. In the 1950s, a decade in which American tastebuds underwent a transformative process of homogeneity, lagers were lightened in flavor, character, and color even further.

Then came the 1970s. Say hello to Light beer. Drink it with sports. Say goodbye to yet more flavor. In under 100 years, American lager was born, hit a glorious peak, got wiped out, was reborn, and then gradually lightened until it could get no lighter and everything tasted the same. Around the world, as pale lagers spread, the same dumbing down of lager happened as flavor fell away.

But in central Europe, the home of great bottom-fermenting beers, things just kept moving forward. Styles stayed the same, quality improved, traditions were upheld, and they didn't take any notice of the rest of the world. Regional pride kept beers alive, Dunkels didn't disappear, Helles and Pilsner lived in harmony with Rauchbier and Bock, while Kölsch, Alt, and Weizen kept up the top-fermenting side of brewing. *Danke schön*, Germany.

The fight-back against blandness came from craft brewers, many of whom were inspired by European beers rather than million-dollar ad campaigns. In an America where all beer tasted alike, new brewers from the 1980s onward wanted things that tasted better, that tasted great. Flavorsome ales arrived as a big counterpoint to lager's bland dominance. Then lager returned—lager with flavor and character, beers looking back to American lager's pre-Prohibition golden years.

Now some breweries specialize in making just lager or German-style beers. Most breweries make something German in style, whether it's an ale or lager. Some of the best, most interesting lagers are made in America. And around the world, in Italy, New Zealand, Scandinavia, Britain, and South America, lager has been reinvigorated by small brewers who take classic styles and either make their own version of it or do something new with it— craft lagers, New Zealand lagers, Imperial lagers, American-hopped Doppelbocks, Japanese-hopped Helles, British-brewed lagers made with all-British ingredients. The good stuff is fighting back against the bad, and it's growing in popularity and quality all the time.

Back in Bavaria and Bohemia, the lagers are still the best in world, but now they've got some serious competition.

IMPERIAL LAGER

THIS IS LAGER, BUT BIGGER. THESE BREWS TAKE THE DELICATE, LIGHT BODIES OF PILSNER AND HELLES, AND BLOW THEM UP LIKE A BULGING BODYBUILDER. NOT SUPER-STRENGTH EURO LAGERS OR MALT LIQUORS SOLD CHEAPLY IN CANS WHERE DRINKERS WANT BANG FOR THEIR BEER BUCK, THESE ARE SERIOUS CRAFT BEERS, SOMEWHERE BETWEEN LAGER AND IPA. THE COLD-CONDITIONING IN TANK AND THE DELICATE LAGER YEAST MAKE THE BEER MORE CIVILIZED THAN THE LOUDSPEAKER OF IPA. THE DIFFERENCE BETWEEN AN IMPERIAL LAGER AND A STRONG EURO LAGER (OR EVEN A HELLERBOCK) IS THE MORE PURPOSEFUL HOPPING REGIME IN AN IMPERIAL LAGER—EXPECT BIG HOP PRESENCE, IN BITTERNESS AND AROMA.

Imperial lager is a mutant of Pilsner, Helles, or American craft lager. The alcohol goes up and the amount of hops increases, so you'll find a beer somewhere between 7.0–9.0% ABV with IBUs anything from 40–80 plus. Most often pale to amber in color, Imperial lagers are produced with a lager yeast, giving a clean depth to the malt and yeast profile and allowing the hops to play the big solo. Hops can be from anywhere in the world and give balance rather than brash bitterness, with a burst of aroma and flavor. The body could be dry and crisp or rounded and full; the malt flavor could be out on center stage or be the stage itself, holding the hops up. As a mutant beer style, it's capable of being both beautiful and brutal.

Pretty Things American Darling

Cambridge, Massachusetts
ABV: 7.0%
Hops: Saphir, Perle, Hallertauer

The more Pretty Things beers I drink, the more I cartwheel head-over-heels in love with them. Some breweries just have a special touch and it's a rare thing: there's a lightness to everything they make; a ludicrous drinkability even in the frighteningly strong beers; a fun story behind everything; a sense of light-heartedness; and they look great, too—who wouldn't pick up their bottles and go straight to the checkout? American Darling is an un-lawnmower beer that cuts a different path from other Imperial Pilsners in that it uses all-German ingredients rather than going all-American. Lagered for six weeks to give an amazing depth, it's golden like the sun, floral and grassy like your backyard, fresher than a dewy spring morning, and more delicious than the most delicious beer in Delicious Town.

PRETTY THINGS
BEER & ALE PROJECT
AMERICAN DARLING
GOOD TIME LAGER

Mikkeller Draft Bear

Copenhagen, Denmark
ABV: 8.0%
Hops: Amarillo, Cascade

Some beers make you stop and say "wow." Draft Bear is one of them. I wasn't expecting the massiveness of the aroma, the freshness, the wowing brilliance of it. It was like putting my face into a delicious bowl of juicy oranges, tangerines, mandarins, and grapefruit. I have no idea how it's possible to get so much outrageous fruitiness from hops—somehow they've made hops fruitier than fruit. I want to save this aroma and always carry it around with me in a vial like some hop junkie always in need of a hit. Taking a mouthful—WOW!—I wanted a case of the beer so I could always have some at home. More IPA than lager in flavor, there's a hint of sweetness and a clean depth of pale malt; it's addictively drinkable and outrageously orangey in so many different ways. Wow!

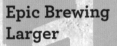

Epic Brewing Larger

Auckland,
New Zealand
ABV: 8.5%
Hops: Pacific Jade,
Kohatu, Liberty,
Tettnang, Santiam

Luke Nicholas is the guy behind Epic, a brewery without four solid walls, but one that uses tank time with other breweries. Famous for explosive IPAs, Larger turns in a different direction and blows up a lager. Pale gold in color, the beer's aroma has an elusive kind of fruitiness that I just can't work out. There's pineapple, something grassy, spicy (turmeric and thyme), and lemony—these are easy to pick out—but there's more in there: melon or grape, maybe elderflower... Mystery makes beers more interesting, I think. Larger is balanced in the extremity and drinks a lot lighter than the ABV tells you because a solid body holds all the hops in place before the slam of 70 IBUs. Have it with some freshly roasted chicken covered in thyme, lemon, and garlic, and lots of salt and pepper for an epic dinner.

Dogfish Head and Birra Del Borgo My Antonia

Milton, Delaware
ABV: 7.5%
Hops: Warrior, Simcoe, Saaz

My Antonia is the beer that started this new style of lager in a collaboration between Dogfish Head and Birra del Borgo. Both breweries made their own versions, which proved so popular that both continue to make their beers independently. You know that these beers are going to taste good before you've even opened the bottles because they are so stunning to look at. A mix of European and American hops gives a peppery, lemony background and a touch of thyme and spice before a piney, citrus-pith foreground freshness. With a body like a Belgian Tripel, the malt base is dry and clean with a knifepoint bitterness balancing between not-enough and too-much. It's "continually hopped," meaning that hops are added nonstop throughout the boil, instead of at the beginning, middle, and end like most brews. Buy both versions, if you can, to compare similarities. Serve with spaghetti carbonara.

VIENNA ✠ MÄRZEN ✠ OKTOBERFEST

THIS GERMAN LAGER TRIO SHARE A LOT OF HISTORY, BUT IT'S NOT ENTIRELY STRAIGHT FORWARD. YOU SEE, A FEW HUNDRED YEARS AGO, MÄRZEN WAS A BEER BREWED IN MARCH AND MATURED IN COOL CELLARS TO LAST THROUGH THE SUMMER WHEN IT WAS TOO WARM TO BREW. VIENNA LAGER ARRIVED THANKS TO A NEW TYPE OF INDIRECT KILNING IN THE MALTING PROCESS THAT CREATED PALE MALTS. IN 1841, A MÄRZEN-STYLE BEER, WHICH WAS INSPIRED BY THE NEW LAGERS BEING MADE IN VIENNA, WAS BREWED IN MUNICH BY SPATEN BREWERY AND INTRODUCED AT THAT YEAR'S OKTOBERFEST, THOUGH IT WASN'T UNTIL 1872 THAT SPATEN RELEASED A BEER CALLED "OKTOBERFESTBIER." VIENNA INSPIRED WHAT BECAME OKTOBERFEST, WHICH WAS ORIGINALLY A MÄRZEN. GOT IT?

The three styles are similar enough to group them together: alcohol between 5.0 and 6.0% ABV, medium-bodied, a color range of gold to red, balanced bitterness between 20 and 30 IBUs. Malt character will be toasty and clean in Oktoberfest and Märzen, becoming nuttier in Vienna. Hopping is classically low, growing grassier and more pronounced in Vienna. There is some crossover between Märzen or Vienna and American amber lagers; American hop varieties are usually the defining difference.

HACKER-PSCHORR OKTOBERFEST MÄRZEN

MUNICH, GERMANY
ABV: 5.8%
HOPS: HALLERTAUER

`CLASSIC`

The most famous beer festival in the world started in October 1810 to celebrate the marriage of Crown Prince Ludwig to Princess Therese of Bavaria. The celebration, which lasted a few days, was so good that they decided to repeat the party the following year, and so the tradition grew. Over time it lengthened into almost three weeks of fun, the dates shifted to hopefully see the late September sunshine, with the festival finishing on the first weekend in October, and it turned into the world's biggest drinking event. The first Märzen-style beer evolved over time into the deep golden brews which take over the taps and are now mass-poured into *maß* glasses. Hacker-Pschorr's Oktoberfest Märzen has some toasty cereal depth, a little caramel, bread, and some marzipan nuttiness with low and balanced hopping. Best served with 6,000 people in a massive tent.

Metropolitan Dynamo Copper Lager

Chicago, Illinois
ABV: 6.2%
Hops: Horizon, Vanguard, Mt Hood

"If malt and hops are the two poles of brewing, this beer is the gently spinning sweet spot between them." That's how the brewery eloquently describes this beer on their website. Metropolitan make a range of excellent lagers in a neat little lock-up in a leafy suburb of Chicago. Doug Hurst, head brewer, trained in Germany, which is where his love of lager and of elegant, balanced flavors comes from. Dynamo is a Vienna-styled lager made with American-grown hops of European heritage. A little lime and floral aroma peeks over the top of the glass, inviting you in; the body is bready, toasty, and rich with the alcohol level, before the hops dry it out with citrus bitterness. "The best time to enjoy Dynamo is when you're thirsty," says Metro's website. I like that.

Lakefront Brewery Riverwest Stein Lager

Milwaukee, Wisconsin
ABV: 5.7%
Hops: Willamette, Cascade

Milwaukee is the home of lager in America. In the mid- to late 1800s, as thousands of German immigrants crossed the Atlantic, a population of Europeans developed around Milwaukee's lakeside location. They didn't want to drink the dark, muddy ales of colonial influence and instead they wanted the lagers of their homeland. By the beginning of the 20th century, Milwaukee's Pabst, Blatz, Schlitz, and Miller were among the biggest brewers in America. Now only Miller is still brewed in the city but in their place a new lager revolution is taking place, drawing on the heritage and flipping it forward. Lakefront's Riverwest Stein is a great example of this. Amber-colored like a classic Vienna, there's toffee and toast in the middle, and it gets its floral, slight citrusy aroma from American hops, which leave a big, lingering bitterness. Look back to the late 19th century in Milwaukee and the lagers may well have been a little like this...

Les Trois Mousquetaires Oktoberfest

Brossard, Canada
ABV: 6.0%
Hops: Hallertauer, Perle

Les Trois Mousquetaires packs in loads of deliciousness with toasty cereal, brown bread, and roasted nuts alongside a hint of berries and the spicy, floral fragrance of German hops. Malt dominates the mouthful, though it's never heavy, then the hops use the back of the tongue like a slide, giving it an effortless drinkability and a go-back-for-more quench. Drink it with German sausage, sauerkraut, and pretzels. As proof of the health-giving and restorative powers of Oktoberfest beer, an electric wheelchair, a pair of crutches and 370 pairs of spectacles were found in lost property in 2011. Hooray for beer!

Nils Oscar Kalasöl

Nyköping, Sweden
ABV: 5.2%
Hops: Fuggles, Cascade, Saaz

The name of this beer translates as "fest beer," and it's a Swedish take on an Oktoberfest. Originally brewed as a seasonal, it's been so popular that it's now available year-round as part of the broad range of beers that Nils Oscar produce. Kalasöl is copper-colored with a full creamy foam and the aroma is a mix of malt and hops, which ends up like a slice of toast topped with toffee and a squeeze of citrus. As an unexpectedly successful trio, the mix of hops brings together earthy, spicy British Fuggles with their gruff bitterness; grapefruity and floral American Cascade with their oily hop richness; and delicate, fragrant Czech Saaz which balance the others by bringing fruit and herbs. When you drink Oktoberfest, you need food. Put chicken, sausages, pork knuckle, and pretzels on your shopping list. Order more than you think you need.

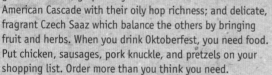

Bamberg De Wiesn

Sao Paulo, Brazil
ABV: 5.7%
Hops: Hallertauer Magnum, Hallertauer Mittelfrüh, Hallertauer Saphir

Wies'n is the local name for Oktoberfest. It means "the meadow" and is named after the land on which it sits—Theresienwiese (which itself is named after the bride for whom the first festival was held). Perhaps a too-serene nickname for the beer party of the year, it's like calling the Rio Carnival a quiet drink with friends. Bamberg's beers, brewed by Alexandre Bazzo, follow the Reinheitsgebot beer order, which decrees that beer can only be made with malt, water, hops, and yeast. As well as this, all of Bamberg's beers are German-inspired and are straight-up interpretations, bringing great German-style beers to Brazil. De Wiesn has biscuit, toast, and caramel in the body with the German hops adding a floral, herbal note. There's a real lightness and a clean, fresh flavor. Matured for a long time in tank, it's a seasonal release coming out ready for September's party.

Avery The Kaiser Imperial Oktoberfest

Boulder, Colorado
ABV: 9.3%
Hops: Magnum, Sterling, Tettnang, Hersbrücker

As part of Avery's Dictator series, The Kaiser Imperial Oktoberfest rules beside The Maharajah (Imperial IPA) and The Czar (Imperial Stout) to create a powerful triumvirate that aims to see how far you can push traditional styles. The Kaiser takes things further than most. Copper-colored, it's dominated by toasty malt, caramel, and bread; it's cake-like with vanilla and almond, plus some boozy baked apples and stone fruit. The hops fight back with spicy, floral, bitter notes, giving balance but not hitting the tongue too hard. It's big, it's dominant, it's powerful, and it sucks you in with outrageous drinkability for its strength—it's an Oktoberfest like you've never had before and yet it still keeps an essential characteristic of the style, which is impressive. You'll want the world's biggest pretzel with this one.

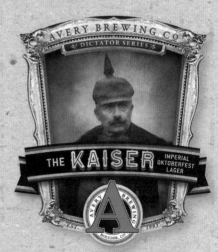

BEFORE MALTSTERS COULD MAKE MALT PALE, BEER WAS ON THE RED-BROWN-BLACK COLOR SPECTRUM, AND IT WASN'T UNTIL THE LATE 19TH CENTURY THAT PALER BEERS WERE BREWED REGULARLY AROUND THE WORLD. SURE, PALER BEERS WERE BREWED LOCALLY BEFORE THAT, BUT THEY DIDN'T GO WORLDWIDE UNTIL THE END OF THE CENTURY. DARK LAGERS EVOKE A TASTE OF BEER FROM YEARS AGO, AND GERMAN DUNKELS AND SCHWARZBIERS, AS WELL AS CZECH DARK LAGERS, ARE THE CLASSICS OF THIS GROUP. "DUNKEL" MEANS DARK AND "SCHWARZ" MEANS BLACK; SCHWARZBIERS CONTAIN MORE ROASTED BARLEY, GIVING THEM A DARKER, MORE MALT-BITTER FLAVOR. BAVARIA IS THE HOME OF DARK LAGER, WHICH USED TO BE THE EVERYDAY DRINK BEFORE HELLES TOOK OVER. IT'S NOT THE MOST POPULAR STYLE OUTSIDE OF CENTRAL EUROPE, WHICH IS A LITTLE UNUSUAL AS IT'S CAPABLE OF BEING BOTH WONDERFULLY DELICATE AND REFRESHING AND INTENSELY COMPLEX AND INTERESTING.

DARK LAGER

Malt leads the way in these beers, but does so with a subtle elegance (in the best examples, anyway). Color can be a red-brown through to opaque black, and body can range from light to full. Bread, chocolate, caramel, and roasted malt flavors provide the background (roasted malt bitterness is low), while hops classically just balance things out, sometimes with a little lift of fragrant aroma. Often lighter in flavor than their darkness suggests, ABV is classically between 4.0 and 6.0%. They are great food beers and work around the world: try with heavy Eastern European meat dishes, light sushi, or Mexican food where the cloak of chocolate cools the fearsome chili heat.

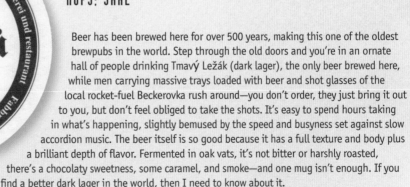

U FLEKŮ

PRAGUE, CZECH REPUBLIC

ABV: 4.6%

HOPS: SAAZ

CLASSIC

Beer has been brewed here for over 500 years, making this one of the oldest brewpubs in the world. Step through the old doors and you're in an ornate hall of people drinking Tmavý Ležák (dark lager), the only beer brewed here, while men carrying massive trays loaded with beer and shot glasses of the local rocket-fuel Beckerovka rush around—you don't order, they just bring it out to you, but don't feel obliged to take the shots. It's easy to spend hours taking in what's happening, slightly bemused by the speed and busyness set against slow accordion music. The beer itself is so good because it has a full texture and body plus a brilliant depth of flavor. Fermented in oak vats, it's not bitter or harshly roasted, there's a chocolaty sweetness, some caramel, and smoke—and one mug isn't enough. If you find a better dark lager in the world, then I need to know about it.

Port Brewing
Hot Rocks

San Marcos, California
ABV: 6.2%
Hops: Hallertauer
Magnum, Tettnang

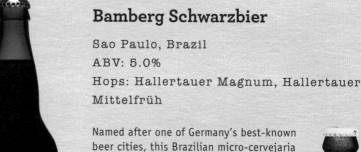

This is a stein (or stone) beer, a rare brewing method practiced for hundreds of years until the beginning of the 20th century. As some brewers were using wooden vessels, which didn't do so well when heated from beneath by fire, stein beer involved adding red-hot rocks into the mash or wort to give a sudden super-boil of heat. A particular type of rock was used, called "gray wacke," which could handle the transition from fire to liquid without breaking apart. Playing with fire isn't exactly a safe process and it fizzled out as the world went stainless until craft brewers started throwing rocks on fires again. A March and April seasonal release, Port Brewing's version is cola-colored, the body is substantial, there's some subtle roast, some toffee from rock-caramelized sugars, a fiery smokiness, an earthy-ashen bitterness, and a floral hop aroma. It rocks!

Bamberg Schwarzbier

Sao Paulo, Brazil
ABV: 5.0%
Hops: Hallertauer Magnum, Hallertauer Mittelfrüh

Named after one of Germany's best-known beer cities, this Brazilian micro-cervejaria makes a wide range of classic German beer styles (and wins many awards for them), among them a Dunkel called Munchen plus this Schwarzbier—fans of dark lager should try both. The Schwarz is almost black, the kind of black that's just slightly red at the edges. The big foam settles to a thin wisp, then there's chocolate, coffee, and crackers, but nothing overpowering, keeping a light touch to the beer. Hop and malt bitterness combine at the same time to be dry, roasty, floral, and quenching. The Munchen is lighter in color, bringing nutty caramel instead of roast. Both are classically made and finished as skillfully as a Brazilian striker facing a German goalkeeper. Drink with feijoada, a Brazilian stew of beef, pork, beans, and veg.

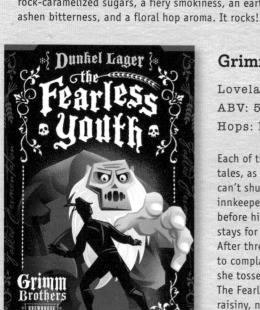

Grimm Brothers The Fearless Youth

Loveland, Colorado
ABV: 5.2%
Hops: Magnum

Each of the Grimm Brothers' beers is German-styled and themed around old German tales, as the name might suggest. The Fearless Youth is a simple-minded boy who can't shudder with fear, even when faced with chilling challenges. One day, an innkeeper tells him to spend three nights at a haunted castle. Many have tried before him but no one's succeeded. The castle will teach him to shudder or, if he stays for the three nights, he will win the king's daughter and the castle's riches. After three shudderless nights of ghoulish challenges, he marries the princess only to complain to his new wife that he still doesn't know how to shudder. One night she tosses a pail of freezing stream water over him and he wakes up shivering. The Fearless Youth pours a ruby-brown. It's wonderfully clean and light-drinking—raisiny, nutty, a little caramel and toast, but reserved not sweet; the malt rules this tale with the hops finishing things like "The End" written after the final sentence.

Ca l'Arenys Guineu Coaner

Valls De Torroella, Spain
ABV: 4.7%
Hops: Galena, Saaz

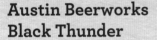

Spanish craft beer has been slow to catch up, but it's on the way and gaining momentum. Guineu make a range of really interesting brews from a heavily hopped 2.5% ABV Pale Ale to a bulky American Stout. Coaner is a ruby-brown dark lager, sitting somewhere between a Schwarz and a Dunkel, and made with a little smoked malt. It gives some chocolate and roast malt first, followed by brown sugar, plums, and raisins, a little sweet smoke, and even a hint of festive spice. More of the same inside with the smoke working like an excursion-tour leader and keeping everything together. Dried fruit, cocoa, toasted nuts, and then some floral hop and dryness, as 37 IBUs of bitterness sees it out. Bring local beer and food together, and go with cured pork or local sausages (botifarra), or with tomato-based stews where Coaner's hint of smoke smothers the tomato sharpness.

Austin Beerworks Black Thunder

Austin, Texas
ABV: 5.3%
Hops: Magnum, Tettnang, Saaz, Hallertauer

"Keep Austin Weird" has become a bumper-sticker slogan for the capital of Texas and a way of promoting the ingenuity of local businesses. While not weird, Austin Beerworks are definitely different and definitely doing something good for local beer. Black Thunder is their take on a German Schwarz. Dark brown to look at, chocolate, roasted nuts, burnt toast, and caramel come first, then a hint of roasted fruit. Clean and light to drink, a snap of carbonation makes it refreshing in the Texan sun before the hops finish deliciously dry, telling you they are there but not screaming in your face. This is a beer for grilled or smoked meat where the dark, roasted flavor in the beer balances the burnt bits from the barbecue. Drink from the can as you grill stuff.

Pretty Things Lovely St Winefride

Cambridge, Massachusetts
ABV: 7.0%
Hops: Hersbrücker

I take notes on the beers I drink in a little black book. Some of them take up five or six lines; most of them stretch to a full page. Only one has ever gone over one page and that's this beer—eventually filling two full pages. Lovely Saint Winefride is a brown lager that pours with a tan foam and a big aroma of chocolate, toasted nuts, vanilla, earthy and floral hops, and a touch of smoke. The body is the thing that makes this such a joy to drink: full and slick, each mouthful is incredibly satisfying with a little sweetness, a little dark malt, a perplexing lightness given the big body, an appetizing savory note, and a lingering, dry bitterness, all with a refreshing breeze of hops. My notebook reads like a gushing love letter, starting with "How do they make this so good?" and finishing with a "Wow!"

DARK LAGER 61

THE BOCK FAMILY

MEET BOCK, DOPPELBOCK, HELLERBOCK, AND MAIBOCK, A GERMAN FAMILY OF STRONG LAGERS. BOCK AND DOPPELBOCK WERE DEVELOPED IN THE 16TH AND 17TH CENTURIES RESPECTIVELY. EINBECK, IN CENTRAL GERMANY—A TOWN KNOWN FOR ITS STRONG TASTY BEER, WHICH WAS EXPORTED AROUND EUROPE—IS THE HOME OF BOCK. DUE TO ITS POPULARITY, A BREWER WAS BROUGHT FROM EINBECK TO MUNICH, IN A SIMILAR FASHION TO A MODERN-DAY, BIG-MONEY SOCCER-TRANSFER, TO PRODUCE BOCK IN BAVARIA AND THE STYLE DEVELOPED FROM THERE.

DOPPELBOCK WAS BORN IN A CONVENT IN MUNICH WHERE BREWING MONKS MADE A STRONGER VERSION OF BOCK AND HAD THE TRAILBLAZING FORESIGHT TO PRECEDE CRAFT BEER'S PENCHANT FOR IMPERIAL AND DOUBLE VERSIONS OF STYLES. EPITOMIZING BEER'S "LIQUID BREAD," DOPPELBOCK WAS SIPPED BY MONKS DURING THE LENTEN FAST. MAIBOCK AND HELLERBOCK ARE AMBER AND GOLD VERSIONS OF THE STYLE, TRADITIONALLY RELEASED IN SPRING, AND ARE MORE VIBRANTLY HOPPY.

The equivalent of sleeping on a grain sack, Bock and Doppelbock have a soothing malt depth that is the defining quality of the beers. There is a liquid-bread and toasty malt sweetness (richer in Doppelbocks), a low hop presence, and the color can range from gold to black, though typically it's on the red-brown spectrum. Body is medium, often with some residual sweetness as it gets stronger. Bitterness rarely reaches the 30s. Bocks, including Mai and Heller, are 6.0–7.5% ABV and Doppelbocks cross over with 6.5–8.0%. Expect these beers to be monologs of malt's magnificence.

AYINGER CELEBRATOR DOPPELBOCK

AYING, GERMANY
ABV: 6.7%

CLASSIC

Every beer lover should have a collection of small plastic goats taken from each of their previous Ayinger Celebrator conquests. Why they hang a goat around the neck of the bottle, I don't know, but it's a nice treat when you drink one. Bock means "billy goat" in German, and many brands feature a goat on the label. One amusing story about why this came to be explains how a duke and a knight were in a weird drinking contest in which the knight fell down drunk and blamed it on a goat. Given that Einbeck was the home of the style, it's most likely that ordering "ein beck" soon evolved to be pronounced "ein bock" and the goat came from there. The beer pours dark brown with a tan crown. Not sweet, there's chocolate, dried fruit, a hint of roast (which comes through with a wisp of smoke), a great complexity, and a softly balanced hop flavor.

Emelisse Lentebock

Kamperland, Netherlands
ABV: 7.5%
Hops: Saaz, Motueka

Think of Bocks like a seasonal spectrum. Traditionally released in the fall, they come out as the first beers made with the new harvest of ingredients. As it gets colder and darker, Doppelbocks warm you against the chill of winter, leading around to the liquid bread needed to get you through Lent. Then, as the days get brighter, so the Bocks get lighter and Maibock or Hellerbock are released. Pale, springtime versions of the style, they are lighter in alcohol and livelier in hop finish. Maibocks freshen things up before Bocks take a break as Helles and Pilsner ride shotgun in the summer sunshine. Emelisse's Lentebock is bright amber, there's apricot and peach, tropical fruit, citrus pith, cut grass, and a little grain. Honeyed and floral, with toffee malt in the middle, a bold spike of hops gives lots of fresh bitterness. It tastes like a fine spring day.

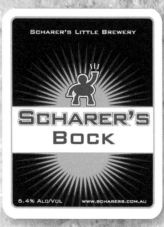

Scharer's Little Brewery Bock

Sydney, Australia
ABV: 6.4%

Geoffrey Scharer is a pioneering Australian craft-beer hero. When he asked for a form to apply for a license to open a brewery, he was told that one didn't exist, though there was a stack of forms for closing a brewery... In 1981 he got Australia's first on-premises brewing license, meaning he could make the German-inspired beers he loved and sell them in the pub he owned, the George IV Inn. His first beer didn't leave the taps until 1987, and then Burragorang Bock became his famous brew. In 2006, David Wright and Luke Davies took over the pub and the brewing, and they continue to make the Bock, now renamed Scharer's Bock. The beer is dark brown, toasty, chocolaty, a little roasty; there's dried fruit and a bitterness that balance everything out behind the light body. Geoffrey Scharer died in early 2012. Aussie brewers owe a lot to him.

Great Lakes The Doppelrock

Cleveland, Ohio
ABV: 6.2%
Hops: Hallertauer

We'd ordered a tasting flight of six beers each. In front of us were now 18 beers. "Wow, this Doppelbock is delicious!" I said, drinking The Doppelrock. I was with my mates, Matt and Mark, drinking in a bar in Milwaukee. They looked up, shocked. "That's the only time you'll ever say that!" Matt said. The thing is, Doppelbock isn't a style like Pilsner or Pale Ale that refrigerators get filled with, mostly because Doppelbocks can be sweet and strong and, personally, it's not a style I drink much of, craving hop over malt most of the time. As we sip each of the samples, with excited oohs and disappointed oofs, Matt and Mark each stop at The Doppelrock and say "Wow, this Doppelbock *is* delicious!" You get bread and dried fruit plus a hint of chocolate; the body is full and satisfyingly mouth-filling (that liquid bread thing). It's dry and not sweet, complex, interesting, and—as we all said—delicious.

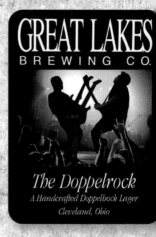

Birrificio Italiano Bibock

Lurago Marinone, Italy
ABV: 6.2%
Hops: Magnum, Hersbrücker

We're in Ma Che Siete Venuti a Fà in Rome. It's also known as the Football Pub for those with a less nimble tongue. The name means something like "what are you doing here?" I order Bibock and immediately fall in love with the freshness of the aroma: it's like dipping my head into a German's hop sack as the fruity, grassy, floral aroma swirls out of the glass. For a Bock, not known for its hop presence, it's got a stunning nose. Bibock pours a caramel-red color; there's a soft, caramel maltiness underneath that hop, then it finishes dry and crisp, and more hop comes out as you drink, giving a spicy, grassy freshness—I could still taste the hops the morning after. Italiano make cracking interpretations of classic beers by following the brewing book and then making their own tweaks with the hops. Ma Che Siete Venuti a Fà? Drinking Bibock.

Coney Island
Human Blockhead

New York, New York
ABV: 10.0%
Hops: Warrior, Tettnang, Liberty, Crystal, Cascade

An Imperial American Bock. Looking at the label of a mustached man hammering a nail into his nose gives you a clue to the minds behind the madness at Coney Island (or their parent brewery, Schmaltz). Blockhead is a big Doppelbock brewed with German and American hops. Malt dominates with caramel, toast, brown sugar, bread, nuts, and dried-fruit sweetness. The hops balance it out and give a floral, spicy note and a botanic kind of bitterness. Imagine the circus's fat lady walking the tightrope and that's the kind of thing you're getting: big and ungraceful, yet you can't take your eyes off it, craving more. Look out for the bourbon-barrel-aged version—she's now tightrope walking while juggling fire.

Cervejaria Way
Amburana Lager

Pinhais, Brazil
ABV: 8.4%

Aging beer in wooden barrels has happened for hundreds of years. Steel took over but now brewers are bringing back wood and using different varieties deliberately to impart flavors and textures into their beer. While oak is the most common, a wide variety of woods can be used. Wooden barrels are filled with beer (these barrels may have previously held a wine or spirit) or wood chips are added to the steel tanks. *Amburana cearensis* is a tree native to South America, and Way use it as chips, which soak up the beer and impart their flavor in return. The Amburana gives the beer a vanilla, woody depth plus a hint of cherry and sharp fruit depth beneath the chocolate, caramel and dried fruit from the malt base. A dry, herbal bitterness mixes with wood tannin at the end. A uniquely brilliant Brazilian flavor.

Baden Baden Bock

Campos do Jordão, Brazil
ABV: 6.5%

Brazil has a large German population and that's clear when looking at the dominant beer styles brewed around the country, with variations on Pilsners, Helles, Dunkels, and Weizens spread throughout Brazil, and, while the American craft influence is there, it hasn't yet grabbed the same strong hold. Blumenau, a city in Southeast Brazil, was founded by Germans in 1850 and still remains a pocket of German life, where each year they celebrate Oktoberfest with around 1 million visitors (it's also home to one of the top craft breweries, Eisenbahen, who make a large range of German-influenced beers). Further north, between São Paulo and Rio de Janerio, is Cervejaria Baden Baden whose bottom-fermenting line-up includes a Pilsner and this Bock. Copper-colored, it's loaded with toasted malt, hints of chocolate raisins and coffee, and then a peppery and grassy hop bite. It's a German Bock with sexy, shimmying Brazilian hips.

GERMAN CURIOSITIES

THIS IS A BUNCH OF UNUSUAL AND RARE TOP-FERMENTING BEERS ORIGINATING FROM OLD WORLD CENTRAL EUROPE, EACH WITH A REGIONAL BASE. THEY CAN BE LOOSELY SUMMED UP AS SOUR OR SMOKY WHEAT BEERS (SOMETIMES BOTH) AND THEY ARE STYLES THAT DATE BACK HUNDREDS OF YEARS AND JUST ABOUT SURVIVED EXTINCTION TO BE BROUGHT TO MODERN DRINKERS BY BREWERS AIMING TO RE-CREATE THE TASTE OF YEARS AGO. THE SHARPNESS IN THESE STYLES GENERALLY COMES FROM LACTOBACILLUS BACTERIA OR LACTIC ACID, THOUGH ORIGINALLY THEY MAY HAVE BEEN SPONTANEOUSLY FERMENTED LIKE BELGIAN LAMBIC.

Look out for: Berliner Weisse, which is a low-ABV, light, and tart beer—this is the most common of the group, with a refreshing sharpness, traditionally mixed with a syrup of raspberry or woodruff to sweeten it; Gose, the regional style of Leipzig in Germany, is a sour, salty, wheat ale, traditionally made in the spontaneous fermentation style and brewed with coriander and salt; Grodziskie, or Grätzer, is an indigenous Polish style which is smoky and sometimes sharp with a biting bitterness; Lichtenhainer, which is somewhere between a Berliner Weisse and Grodziskie, is light, sour, and made using smoked malt. Some beers are essentially extinct, but expect a revival any time now... Broyan is a dark, lightly hopped, sweet-and-sharp-tasting, low-ABV predecessor to Berliner Weisse, dating back to the 16th century; Mumme is a dark, sweet, strong, and bitter beer.

BAYERISCHER BAHNHOF GOSE

LEIPZIG, GERMANY
ABV: 4.5%
HOPS: PERLE

CLASSIC

Gose is a rare regional German style that is getting to travel the craft-beer world through the thirsty imaginations of brewers. The beer is named after the river Gose, which runs through the town of Goslar. At some point in history, the beer was transplanted east to become Leipzig's local beer style. Now brewed with salts, originally the beer was made with the saline and mineral-rich local waters of Goslar. Becoming unfashionable in the 20th century, it's now coming back, with brewmasters adding salt and coriander to their tanks and getting an intentional sharpness from lactic bacteria. Bahnhof's is a classic. Ozone, lemons, minerals, and spice, it's got a unique freshness and appeal with its refreshing, salty-sharp, unusual, and delicious flavor. Bahnhof's brewmaster, Matthias Richter, makes some mad brews including a 10.5% ABV Gose aged in Tequila barrels, beer made with Gewürztraminer, and Porter with Brettanomyces.

Bell's Oarsman

Kalamazoo, Michigan
ABV: 4.0%

The coming-together of a few separate strands of popular beer trends is pushing Berliner Weisse forward as an increasingly popular beer style. Sour beer is seeing a surge of appreciation as drinkers look for different tastes; there's a growing interest in old beer styles; lower-strength beers are getting more attention; more wheat is being used in brewhouses; and a maturing of the tastebuds is seeing drinkers look for subtlety instead of the stamp of a hop's size-10 boot. Berliner Weisse has it all, and Bell's Oarsman is a very approachable version of the style. Pouring a hazy, white gold, it's got a clean and light, lip-smacking, lemony freshness, a little pith, low bitterness, a hint of lactic sharpness, and a flavor that is as refreshing as an iced drink in the summer sun. Unquenchably thirsty on a hot day? Have this.

Freigeist Bierkultur AbraxXxas

Köln, Germany
ABV: 6.0%
Hops: Spalter Select

This is a pumped-up Lichtenhainer made by a German craft brewery that does things differently. Lichtenhainer is a smoked, soured wheat beer, typically drunk young, and is low in ABV and bitterness. It's an almost-dead style now apart from a couple of rare examples, which makes this bigger version like seeing a unicorn dancing at the end of a rainbow. Lichtenhainer is typically fermented with ale yeast and then soured with lactic bacteria afterward. Smoked malt makes up some of the grain bill and peat smoke and ash ar the first things you notice when you take a sniff, as smoke whirls out of the glass. Hazy gold in color, this smoke mixes with a sharp lactic aroma, giving citrus and grapes as if a fruit bowl had fallen on the fire. Puckering to begin with, the smoke lingers at the end. Unusual, taking complexity almost as far as complicated, it's got an unputdownable weirdness.

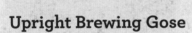

Upright Brewing Gose

Portland, Oregon
ABV: 5.2%
Hops: Hallertauer

Gose reminds me of sipping Champagne while sitting by the sea. There's the air of saltiness, a breezy freshness, brisk bubbles, and a crisp sharpness. Upright's Gose has got that wonderfully appetizing salt presence you expect from the style, which is a kind of background button that drives straight to the hunger switch in the brain. Combine that with the touch of tartness, savory/spicy coriander, and a dry, refreshing finish, and this is a beer that makes you want to eat while you drink. Go with something meaty, as the savoriness in the beer will make the meat taste meatier, or hit some creamy cheeses, where the sharpness adds a fantastic freshness. As well as this Gose, Upright have an excellent range of other beers, including barrel-aged and funked-up brews, some great Belgian interpretations, and modern American brews.

Professor Fritz
Briem Piwo Grodziski

Freising, Germany
ABV: 4.0%
Hops: Perle, Saaz

It's the last bar of the night in Chicago. We're at Local Option and we've walked in the rain for too long to get here. It's dark and we're tired, and all we want is a brash IPA to awaken our slumbering senses. But as soon as I see the draft beer list, my beer-geek radar starts flashing and I jump to the bar before the other two can choose which hop bomb they want. I return with a Grodziski, a Berliner Weisse, and a Gose. Seriously. I don't even really know what a Grodziski is; I just want one. I'm excited; the others are less enthusiastic. The Grodziskie, or Grätzer, is a soured, top-fermented wheat beer made with beech-smoked malt. It looks safe enough, swirling a hazy, pale yellow, but that belies what the tongue gets delivered: citrus and lactic sharpness, clove spice, bonfires, banana sweetness, and also a brutal bitterness.

Farmers' Cabinet
Layover in Berlin

Philadelphia, Pennsylvania
ABV: 3.0%

The first beer of the day is the most important one you can choose. Pick the wrong one and it's like you've got your shoes on the wrong feet, as you stumble from beer to beer trying to regain balance. Choose correctly and you're laughing. This beer literally left me laughing with joy after I picked it as my first beer soon after landing in Copenhagen for a beer festival. I chose it because it's light and sharp, so a perfect livener to get me going, but it surprised me and excited in so many ways. Clean and delicate, it was like a light Sauvignon Blanc with mango, gooseberry, passion fruit, and grape, refreshing but also complex, sharp, and remarkably fresh. I kept going back for more.

The Bruery Hottenroth

Placentia, California
ABV: 3.1%
Hops: Strisselspalt

Traditionally, Berliner Weisse is mixed with a syrup of raspberry or woodruff to sweeten the sharpness of the style. Personally, I like mine straight up, loving its clean, refreshing nature. The Bruery are known for their range of delightfully esoteric, European-influenced beers, which also include a large barrel-program of sour beers. Hottenroth is made with lactobacillus bacteria, which adds a sharp and citric quality, and Brettanomyces yeast, which makes beer dry and funky (horse blanket is the classic quality of brett) without sourness. Pouring a very pale yellow, it's got a lemony, lactic aroma; it's clean with just a little sharpness, some earthiness, a bite of apple, and a dry finish (with only 2 IBUs of bitterness). It'd be hard to find something more refreshing than this. Feeling lavish? Open a bottle with breakfast or mix up some beer mimosas.

Grimm Brothers Snow Drop

Loveland, Colorado
ABV: 5.2%
Hops: Magnum

Snow Drop is a German style of beer called Köttbusser. An ale brewed with honey, oats, and sugar, it was like two fingers in the face of the Reinheitsgebot, the German beer purity law, which originally only allowed barley, water, and hops (later letting in yeast, wheat, rye, and sugar) to be used when brewing. The Reinheitsgebot won in the end, and Köttbusser became extinct. Each Grimm Brothers' beer is linked to an old tale and the story of how Snow Drop became Snow White, though the original has a far less Disney-friendly ending, with the evil stepmother forced to dance herself to death in red-hot iron shoes... The beer, made with molasses, is as gold as the apple in Snow Drop's hand, there are hints of floral honey, estery notes of banana and pear, plus some citrus pith. The body is smooth, the hops are delicate, and there's a clean finish. In your face, Reinheitsgebot—Köttbusser is back.

Schremser Roggen

Schrems, Austria
ABV: 5.2%
Hops: Malling

Roggenbier is a German-style rye ale that dates back to the 16th century, but which began to disappear because rye was regarded as a more important ingredient for bakeries than breweries. The style returned toward the end of the 20th century and you can think of modern versions like a Dunkelweizen, with all the wheat replaced with malted rye. Schremser make one of the few examples of the style still around, and it's a good one. A hazy fall-brown in the glass, you get the spicy, bready, herbal depth of rye and a floral background, which mixes with the clove and banana of the yeast strain; it's smooth and medium-bodied, there's rye bread, toffee, spices, mint, an earthy hop character, and a dry, almost-tart, finish from the rye. The food match is easy for this beer: pastrami on rye with loads of mustard and juicy gherkins, New York-style.

Westbrook Lichtenhainer

Mt. Pleasant, South Carolina
ABV: 4.2%
Hops: Millennium

This one is a treat for the eyes and ears even before the nose and mouth get involved: a whirlpool of fierce bubbles whips around the glass, fizzing, feisty, and storming toward a tight white foam forming on top. Tilt your head and that's when the often overlooked sense of sound comes in: you can hear the bubbles whooshing and popping. I spent about five minutes being entertained by the bubbles before I even took a gulp. Sweet, smoky meat and a squeeze of lemon is what you get—and that's coming from beechwood-smoked malt and lactic Berliner-Weisse-like tartness. There's lots of fruit and citrus, and then smoke lingers like a shirt the morning after a bonfire. It's all so oddly appealing, coming together like a mad masterpiece, and it's best enjoyed with the things drawn on the label: pig and pretzel.

A PAROCHIAL BREWING TOWN, KÖLN (COLOGNE) HAS ALWAYS PROUDLY PROTECTED ITS OWN BEER. IN THE LATE 19TH CENTURY, WITH THE ARRIVAL OF PALE LAGERS THREATENING TO BE MORE POPULAR THAN THE LOCAL BREWS, THE KÖLN BREWERS' GUILD DECIDED TO MAKE A COMPETING BEER OF THEIR OWN. KÖLSCH IS ONE OF THOSE WONDERFUL REGIONAL BEER ANOMALIES THAT CRAFT BREWERS HAVE PICKED UP AND TAKEN ALL AROUND THE WORLD. SURROUNDED BY BOTTOM-FERMENTING LAGERS, KÖLSCH IS A TOP-FERMENTING BREW, LIKE ITS NEIGHBOR ALT. KÖLSCH IS SERVED IN STRAIGHT-SIDED 200ML (7FL OZ) "STANGEN" GLASSES, AND THE BEER HAS A PROTECTED DESIGNATION OF ORIGIN (PDO)— LIKE CHAMPAGNE AND ROQUEFORT—IN THE EUROPEAN UNION. IT'S AN ALE DRESSED UP LIKE A LAGER.

Fermented with an ale yeast, Kölsch is cold-matured slowly like a lager. The brewers of Köln define the beer as light-colored, highly attenuated, and strongly hopped. The warm fermentation gives some fruitiness in the aroma, and soft water gives a soft body and smooth texture, which is cut off by the dry bite of hops in the finish. That dry and hoppy finish is accentuated by filtering the beer. Traditionally, ABV will be around 5.0% with about 25 IBUs. It's a delicate and endlessly drinkable style that is becoming popular around the world as an alternative to lagers.

PÄFFGEN KÖLSCH

KÖLN, GERMANY
ABV: 4.8%

CLASSIC

Whereas you can buy other Köln-brewed Kölschs in bottles (such as Früh, Gäffel, Dom), you need to go to the brewery to drink Päffgen. That's a good thing. While it's sometimes nice to sit at home, relax, and have the beer come to you, it's far better to go to the beer, especially for something like Kölsch, which is so inextricably linked to one place. By going to the beer, you get the full experience of it: you get to see where it's made and share it with others. And when you go to Päffgen, you drink Kölsch. They only make one beer. It comes in small glasses and when you finish one in a couple of gulps, you order another. Bright and clean, there's a hint of malt in the flavor but the hops push forward, giving a dry, herbal fruitiness and balanced, quenching finish. Drink local.

Bi-Du Rodersch

Olgiate Comasco, Italy

ABV: 5.1%

Hops: Magnum, Perle, Styrian Golding, Select

Looking at this beer, pouring a hazy gold with a full white foam on top, makes you thirsty. Rodersch is hoppier than many interpretations of the style but that's what makes it so delicious: floral and grassy, fruity with oranges, peaches, and apricots, and with a little sweet herbaceous note at the end, a smooth body, and a touch creamy from being unfiltered (which is untraditional for a Kölsch). There's also a hint of white bread and biscuit malt before the lingering, dry, fruity finish. Kölsch is a great style for food, being light but still assertive and crisp enough that it isn't wimpishly overpowered. Italian food is especially good, particularly with an Italian Kölsch: try seafood pasta, white risotto, or just a big slice of pizza.

Thornbridge Tzara

Bakewell, England

ABV: 4.8%

Hops: Perle, Tettnang, Mittelfrüh

While some beers are tied to one place, the nature of brewing means that it's possible to replicate a beer style perfectly anywhere in the world by balancing the water composition, getting the right malt, hops, and yeast, and having great brewers. Tzara is a textbook Kölsch and a teleporter for the tongue—a sip in Sheffield carries you straight to Köln. It pours a pale gold with a white wisp of foam. The aroma is subtle and clean, a little lemony, fruity, and floral from the hops with a tiny pop of bubble gum; the sort of aroma that is delicate yet intriguing and makes you chase it around the glass, trying to figure out its come-get-me complexity. The mouthfeel is soft from the water, the yeast is a Kölsch strain, and the hops are all German. It's excellent.

Metropolitan Krankshaft

Chicago, Illinois

ABV: 5.0%

Hops: Santiam

The Metropolitan Brewery is in the Andersonville area of North Side Chicago. Along with Milwaukee, Chicago is an important home for American lager brewing. With a large German population in the middle of the 19th century, many of whom settled in the North Side of Chicago, there was a big market for German-style beers. A great fire, gangsters, Prohibition, and brewery buy-outs combined to drive lager and brewing out of the city for a long time, and only in the 2000s has Chicago seen a resurgence in beer making. Krankshaft isn't a lager but it's bringing German flavors and styles back to the city. This is Metro's bestseller—take a gulp and you'll see why, as the juicy fruit character lifts out of the glass, the body is soft, clean, and smooth, while the cling of bitterness makes you want more.

ALTBIER IS A GERMAN ALE ORIGINATING IN DÜSSELDORF AND IS OFTEN MENTIONED ALONGSIDE KÖLSCH AS THE RENEGADE BROTHERS OF GERMAN BEER. "ALT" MEANS OLD, AND IS NAMED AFTER THE OLD STYLE OF BREWING RATHER THAN BEING A BEER THAT IS AGED. LIKE KÖLSCH, IT WAS PALE LAGERS THAT BECAME THE CATALYST TO KEEP ALT AROUND; WHEN PILSNERS THREATENED TO TAKE OVER, ALT WAS PROTECTED AND PUSHED FORWARD AS DÜSSELDORF'S LOCAL BREW. THE BREWING PROCESS PUTS IT BETWEEN AN ALE AND A LAGER WHERE IT'S COOL-FERMENTED WITH AN ALE YEAST (WHICH TYPICALLY LIKES A WARM FERMENTATION) AND COLD-MATURED LIKE A LAGER. SHARING ANOTHER SIMILARITY WITH KÖLSCH, IT COMES IN 200ML (7 FL OZ) GLASSES CALLED "BECHERS". STICKE IS A STRONGER (UP TO 6.5% ABV), MORE BITTER VERSION OF ALT; DOPPEL STICKE (UP TO 8.5% ABV) IS A STRONGER VERSION OF THE STRONGER VERSION OF ALT.

ALT

Copper-colored, perhaps veering toward brown, Altbier is typically 4.5–5.5% ABV. Bitterness is pronounced and pushed forward by the hardness of the brewing water. Classic Alt is medium-bodied, malty but not sweet, sometimes with a little fruitiness, and German hops are traditional. The extended lagering time gives a clean, mellow depth to the beer, separating it from its non-cold-lagered cousins. Some Alts are dressed up to be the more fashionable Amber Ales (or vice-versa, with Amber lagers being a confusing middle ground). It's all in the hopping and labeling.

UERIGE ALT

DÜSSELDORF, GERMANY
ABV: 4.7%
HOPS: HALLERTAUER, SPALT

CLASSIC

The provincial pride of the local brew is what keeps top-fermenting Kölsch and Alt going—that and they are both wonderful drinks. While overall Alt makes up a tiny percentage of the beer drunk in Germany, in its hometown it accounts for around half of the beer sold. The joy in drinking an Alt is that you get a clean, elegant subtlety that comes only from a long time in tank, producing a lightness that makes a non-lagered equivalent look chubby and clumsy. The few weeks that it's chilling out also allows the yeast to clean up the beer, reabsorbing the fruity esters you'd usually get in ale. Uerige is a beautiful brewpub in Düsseldorf's Old Town, just a Becher-glass-throw from the Rhine. Pouring a russet color with a thick foam, it's medium-bodied, toasty with brown bread and a nutty maltiness before the bitterness bowls through with a spicy earthiness.

Nils Oscar Ctrl Alt Delete

Nyköping, Sweden
ABV: 4.5%
Hops: Spalt

Copper-colored with a lacy, off-white foam, and an aroma of berries and brown bread, this is clean to drink, breezy, with a hint of berry fruit, maybe a little citrus, and an earthy drag of bitterness to finish it off. There's more in there, too—things I can't quite get my tongue around: a subtle complexity, an unexpected generosity with the hops, great depth... I'm looking at the beer while I drink it and trying to think hard about it. What's that flavor I can't pick out, what tricks are the hops playing, what malt are they using to give that depth? But the beer is looking back at me and saying: "Just drink me and stop thinking about it, you idiot!" Ctrl Alt Delete. Restart your brain. Just drink it. It's that kind of switch-your-brain-off brew that doesn't demand attention but is still damn good.

Freigeist Bierkultur Hoppeditz

Köln, Germany
ABV: 7.5%
Hops: Spalter Select, Tettnang, Hersbrücker, Saphir, Northern Brewer

While tradition rules most German brauhäuser, Freigeist Bierkultur is laughing at all of the other guys. It does something different by making a range of untraditional beers, including a soured Porter, re-creations of unusual styles, such as Gose and Lichtenhainer, as well as adding fruit and herbs to beers, something the Reinheitsgebot shakes its head at. Hoppeditz is a Doppel Sticke, a strong German ale similar to a Barley Wine in its big base of malt and liberal hopping. It pours on the amber side of brown and immediately the aroma tells you to expect something different: toffee, dried fruit, dates, berries, and lots of earthy, grassy hops. Big-bodied, it carries the same flavors through with raisins and chocolate, tea and spice, plus a big whack of pepper and woody pine at the end to give a really complex mix of malt and hops. It's Alt's alternative side.

Metropolitan Iron Works

Chicago, Illinois
ABV: 5.8%
Hops: Mt Hood, Vanguard, Horizon

Düsseldorf and Köln are just 40km (25 miles) apart and rivalry exists between them. The towns are split by two things: being on opposite sides of the Rhine River and their beer. Metropolitan's attitude is to try to bring them closer together with a big hug of appreciation for both styles, so they brew an Alt and a Kölsch. Iron Works is a copper-red Alt and the beer is dominated by fruitiness from the American hops, giving berries and a grassy, citrus, and herbal aroma. Bitterness is big and lasting, with a dry roughness at the end being a nice counter to the brown-bread maltiness. The website suggests it goes well with, among other things, speed dating, air hockey, and punk rock. Combine all four and send out the party invitations.

CREAM AND STEAM BEER

TWO INDIGENOUS AMERICAN BEER STYLES, CREAM AND STEAM BEERS ARE
HYBRIDS OF AMERICAN AND EUROPEAN BREWING, BORN TO BATTLE THE PALE
LAGERS SPREADING AROUND THE COUNTRY.

Cream beer shares similarities with Kölsch in that it's top-fermented (or a blend of top- and bottom-fermenting yeast) at a cool temperature and then undergoes a cold conditioning. It dates back to the late 19th century and developed as an ale alternative to the popular lagers. It's now an unusual style and it seems that no one really knows much about it or where the name comes from... Pale blonde to amber in color, ABV from 4.0 to 5.5%, with bitterness in the 20s, typically with old-school American hops (Cluster and Northern Brewer) adding balance not boldness, it threatens to be replaced by more fashionable styles such as Kölsch and Amber, but it's still hanging around.

Steam beer developed as Americans migrated west during the 19th century to the warmth and potential wealth of the Pacific coast. There, lager brewers who didn't yet have artificial refrigeration or easy access to ice made their yeast work in warmer temperatures than usual, gradually evolving a specific yeast strain for this type of fermentation. San Francisco is the home of these beers, which are also known as California Common. The beer is gold to amber in color, with toasty malt in the middle, and hops that range from polite to punchy. Woody, herbal American hops varieties such as Northern Brewer are typical. ABV is 4.5–5.5% and IBUs can range from 25 to 45.

ANCHOR STEAM BEER

SAN FRANCISCO, CALIFORNIA
ABV: 4.9%
HOPS: NORTHERN BREWER

CLASSIC

Anchor Steam owns the trademark to Steam beer, which is why California Common is the alternative name. The beer was once cooled on the brewery roof, so it looked like steam was rising from the building, giving a nickname that has stuck. Another etymological explanation is that the beer was highly carbonated and the barrels let out a burst of steam when they were tapped. Anchor Steam is made with a special strain of yeast and fermented at an ale temperature. It uses Northern Brewer hops, with their woody, minty freshness, and these have come to be the style's defining hop. It pours the sort of sparkling color that the Gold Rush prospectors dreamed of finding; it's got a fine carbonation, a depth of toasty, caramel malt, virtually no esters, and a dry, quenching hop finish. It's been brewed in San Francisco since 1896, though has probably been good only since the 1970s.

Gadds' Common Conspiracy

Ramsgate, England
ABV: 4.8%
Hops: Northern Brewer, Cascade

This one was originally a joint effort between Ramsgate Brewery's Eddie Gadd and two brewing buddies, Phil Lowry and Steve Skinner (hence the ESP production on the badge). While drinking Anchor Steam one day, they started discussing the story and history of the style, and the idea for Common Conspiracy was born—it's now a yearly-released brewery special. There's a bulky body of pale malt, which gives a backbone to the lively, citrusy American hops and botanic, herbal hit. There's some grapefruit, soft herbs, candy, and a floral fragrance before the long, dry finish sets in. The brewery is named Ramsgate Brewery, although everyone calls it Gadds' after the affable Eddie, the head brewer and owner. Not much beer leaves the East Kent coast, which makes it a good excuse to visit the seaside and drink some good beer.

Bad Attitude Bootlegger

Stabio, Switzerland
ABV: 6.94%
Hops: Amarillo, Perle, East Kent Goldings

If I owned a brewery, I'd put my beer in stubby bottles like the ones that Bad Attitude use. They remind me of the slabs of cheap French lager my dad would bring home from the booze cruise across the Channel, and holding them brings back an unusual childhood nostalgia: it's seeing the adults drinking from them, it's remembering how my small hand couldn't reach all the way around the cold glass, it's that first bitter sip as a boy. Bootlegger is a California Common brewed in Switzerland by Italians. Made with American, German, and English hops, plus coriander and cane sugar, it's fermented with a lager yeast at warm temperatures. It pours a hazy gold, with the hops hitting first with a floral, peachy, and citrus note; the body has a creaminess and the finish is dry and peppery. Drink it from the bottle—it's more fun.

Sixpoint Sweet Action

Brooklyn, New York
ABV: 5.2%
Hops: Horizon, Glacier, Cascade, Centennial

Even the brewery don't really know how to classify this one, placing it somewhere between a Pale Ale, Wheat Ale, and Cream Ale. I like all three styles, so that's fine by me. Amber-colored, there's pine plus zesty orange and grapefruit in the aroma, pointing toward Pale Ale. The malt fills the mouth, there's a smooth creaminess to it, and a hint of honey, showing off the cream and wheat parts before a dry, citrus-pith and peppery bitterness passes it back to pale, which does a one-two with cream. I'm not sure there's a better place to drink this than in Barcade in Brooklyn, which might be the world's hippest beer bar. In this dark, garage-like space, quarter-a-play retro video games light a line around the edge while impossibly cool people furiously button-tap or drink from a joyous line-up of beer taps. Sweet video-game action and kick-ass beer.

THE WEISSBIER FAMILY

WEISSBIER, HEFEWEIZEN, OR WEIZENBIER; IT'S ALL THE SAME AND THEY ARE PART OF THIS FAMILY OF GERMAN-STYLE WHEAT BEERS. "YEAST WHEAT" IS THE PROSAIC TRANSLATION OF HEFEWEIZEN AND THOSE TWO THINGS DEFINE THE BEERS: THEY USE DISTINCTIVE YEAST STRAINS, WHICH GIVE AN ESTERY, FRUITY AROMA. YOU CAN EXPECT BANANA, VANILLA, CLOVE, BUBBLE GUM, AND SOMETIMES A CITRIC EDGE. THE WHEAT WILL MAKE UP AT LEAST 50 PER CENT OF THE GRAIN BILL, ADDING A SMOOTHNESS TO THE BEER AND A TURBIDITY THANKS TO THE PROTEIN IN THE GRAIN. THE YEAST IS KEY TO THIS STYLE, SO HOPPING LEVELS ARE GENERALLY VERY LOW—TYPICALLY THERE TO ADD BALANCE, BUT NOT TO BE NOTICED. CARBONATION IS HIGH AND THE BEERS ARE WELL ATTENUATED, SO ARE DRY TO FINISH; THEY MAY TASTE SWEET AT FIRST, BUT NOTICE HOW THAT DISAPPEARS AT THE END.

There are a variety of wheat beers and the best way to understand them is to look at the color: gold is classic Hefe; amber is known unpronounceably in the style guides as Bernsteinfarbenes (or South German style); dark brown is the Dunkelweizens. In these, the malt flavor develops from subtle and bready to caramel to chocolate. You can also look at size: Leichtes (which means light) is a smaller version of Hefe, found in Germany but not many other places, coming in at around 3.0% ABV, while a Weizenbock is a stronger version (6.0–9.0% ABV). Kristalweisse is a filtered version that arrives without the yeast in it.

WEIHENSTEPHANER HEFE WEISSBIER

FREISING, GERMANY
ABV: 5.4%
HOPS: PERLE, MAGNUM

CLASSIC

The world's oldest brewery makes the world's best Weissbier and it's the definitive example of the style; it's so definitive that many other breweries use the Weihenstephan yeast strain in their wheat beers. In 1021, a monastery was founded on top of Weihenstephan Hill and in 1040 brewing started there. In 1803, the Benedictine Abbey ceased and the Bavarian State Government took over the brewery. The Hefe is Weihenstephan's flagship beer. It's hazy, pale amber with a creamy white foam, and the aroma is what the beer textbook writers were smelling when they wrote Hefeweizen into the style guide: banana, bubble gum, clove, a little lemon, and a hint of floral hop. A sip and you get a hint of sweetness, some toasted nuts and caramel, then it dries right out and the ester aromas fold into the taste. Mouthfilling and satisfying to drink, it needs to be poured into a big vase glass to appreciate the elegance of the beer, which is light yet so full of flavor.

Live Oak
HefeWeizen

Austin, Texas
ABV: 5.2%
Hops: Saaz,
Hallertauer, Saphir,
Tettnang

Started by two homebrewers,
Live Oak brings German-style
beers to Texas by brewing
classic styles in traditional
ways. HefeWeizen is a bang-on,
brilliant example of a German
Weissbier and it's rightly seen as one of the best in the
United States. Hazy gold with a big foam on top, it's got
banana, peppery clove, vanilla, a little cheeky stone
fruit, and some floral hops. There's a lush creaminess to
it, which I love in this style, a richness that's also light,
and a depth that makes you go back again and again.
At the end of this one there's some fruity hop plus a
little citrus as it waves goodbye on the way down. Live
Oak also make Primus, a wicked Weizenbock, which is
bigger, bolder, and stronger than the Hefe.

Matuška
Pšeničné

Broumy, Czech
Republic
ABV: 5.1%
Hops: Saaz,
Premiant

No, I don't know how to
pronounce it either. And
I had no idea what style it
was when I went to order
it in a bar in Prague. All
I knew was that I wanted
to drink the beer from
Matuška, whatever it was.
Spitting out an awful
attempt to say "Pšeničné"
and failing miserably—it
means "wheat" but I still don't
know how to say it—I managed to point and wave before
the bartender asked in perfect English what I wanted.
Matuška (pronounced Mah-toosh-ka) make some of the
most interesting and exciting modern beers in the Czech
Republic. They also make great versions of classic styles,
which is exactly what Pšeničné is. Hazy gold, with a fat
white foam on top, it's got everything you want and a
little more, giving full body and depth of flavor. There's
also an excellent stronger version, which is blissfully
easier to pronounce. It's simply called "Weizenbock."

Bogota Beer Company Chía Weiss

Bogota, Columbia
ABV: 4.6%
Hops: Magnum, Golding

A modern brewery in Columbia's capital city, Bogota Beer Company is one of only a
small number of craft breweries in the country. Chía is an excellent brew, pale gold in
color with a light haze; the esters are there but are not like someone's pushing a
mashed banana up your nose. Clean, crisply carbonated, a little creamy, and it has a
fresh citrus edge which makes it ever-so drinkable. With a bunch of pubs around the
city, BBC are making a wide range of good beer available to thirsty Columbians. To
authenticate your drinking experience, try this with one of the region's dishes: ajiaco,
a soup of chicken and corn, thickened with potatoes, and served with cream, capers,
and avocado. Chía will match its rich creaminess and give a citrusy poke that mirrors
the capers.

Moo Brew Hefeweizen

Tasmania, Australia
ABV: 5.1%
Hops: East Kent Goldings

You'll notice a recurring pattern throughout this book: I like beers that look good. Not just in the glass, but before they even get that close to being drunk. Some bottles of beer are works of art and Moo Brew make a few of them, though knowing that the brewery started in the Museum of Old and New Art in Hobart, Tasmania (in a cylindrical, glass-fronted block overlooking the sea like a superhero's lair), you expect them to look good. Typically Aussie in their down-to-earthness, the brewery say, "The distinctive Moo Brew Bottle has John Kelly's art on the front, bullshit on the back, and beer in the middle." The beer in the middle is a hazy blonde color, the aroma is a subtle lift of banana, vanilla, and clove, more gentle than the thrusting German versions. The body is smooth and clean, and then finishes sharp, making it refreshing and a smart mix of old German and cool new Australian.

Birrificio Italiano VùDù Weizen

Lurago Marinone, Italy
ABV: 5.5%
Hops: Hallertauer Magnum

I reckon that Italiano make the best modern interpretations of European classics of any brewery in the world. Pilsners, Bocks, and wheat beers—they do them all with such skill that they even make the classics look dull. Their B.I. Weizen is full of depth and deliciousness, smooth and creamy, and yet refreshing and light. VùDù is a Dunkelweizen brewed once or twice a year. Milk chocolate in color with a rocky foam, it's a visual delight. Lots of banana and chocolate in the aroma, dried fruit, apple, and cinnamon, and a creamy depth plus a frisky carbonation. The hops come through with slight citrus and herbal bitterness and give more than you'd usually expect from the style, which leaves it satisfying to drink as well as making you thirstier. Magic. Or brew voodoo, perhaps.

Schneider Aventinus Weizen Eisbock

Kelheim, Germany
ABV: 12.0%
Hops: Hallertauer Magnum

This is a Weizenbock that has been partially frozen. As alcohol freezes at a lower temperature than water, the ice which develops first is just water. This is then removed, concentrating the alcohol and sugar, and making the beer stronger. The original story (though now probably creatively mythologized) is that one icy night, when beer was being prepared for shipping, a lazy brewery worker left some barrels outside and the beer partially froze. Fearing a firing, he removed the ice and found that the beer tasted excellent. This form of brewing is technically a partial distillation and is illegal in some countries, including America. Schneider's Eisbock pours mahogany with a cream-colored foam. There are raisins, apples, plums, dark fruit, marzipan, roast bananas, vanilla, festive spice, and chocolate. Smooth, warming, sweet, complex, and rich.

Schneider Weisse Tap 5 Meine Hopfenweisse

Kelheim, Germany
ABV: 8.2%
Hops: Hallertauer Tradition,
Hallertauer Saphir

"Hoppy fireworks" is how Schneider describe this beer. For a brewery that's been making the same beer since it opened in 1872, especially in a traditional country like Germany, this Hopfenweisse exploded into the beer world. It started with a two-way collaboration with Brooklyn Brewery in which both made a Weizenbock and then dry-hopped it—Schneider using Hallertauer Saphir, and Brooklyn going with Amarillo and Palisade. The beers were so good that Schneider introduced theirs as a permanent addition. Tap 5 is an incredible brew, combining the banana, estery aroma of yeast with the orange, apricot, and grassy freshness of the hops—it's an olfactory masterpiece. Smooth-bodied and rich with malt, there's also a lot of hop flavor, giving an earthy bitterness, a dry botanic finish, and a clinging hop presence, like a Weizen IPA. It's traditional Germany meets trailblazing America.

Fujizakura Heights Kougen Weizen

Yamanashi-ken, Japan
ABV: 5.5%
Hops: Perle

Fujizakura don't make a wide range of beers, but the ones they do make are excellent. Weizens seem to be a favorite, with a smoked version, a chocolate Weizen, and a Weizenbock. Their straight-up Weizen is the one to get thirsty for. Hazy yellow with a creamy white foam, there's banana, bubble gum, apple, vanilla, and clove, all gently humming rather than yelling like a mad gameshow contestant. Smooth, balanced, more creamy than most, and authentically German, with a lift of carbonation to keep it light. It's definitely one for sashimi, where the subtle spice and creaminess in the beer matches the creamy texture of the fish, and fire-blankets the wave of wasabi. Weizen's fruity aromas and slick depth have made it one of the most popular beer styles in Japan.

Piece Dark-n-Curvy

Chicago, Illinois
ABV: 6.0%

Piece is a brewpub and pizzeria, and both sides of the business are seriously good. It was karaoke night when I went and while we ate fantastic, thin-crust pizza (made in a city famous for deep dish), too many people climbed on stage to belt out bad versions of classic songs. Thankfully, when it comes to the beer, brewer Jonathan Cutler totally nails the classics, especially the wheat beers, which are dazzling with medals and awards. Dark-n-Curvy is a delicious Dunkelweizen, chocolate brown in color, with that great aroma of banana and bubble gum, plus a little chocolate from the dark grain. It fills the mouth with body and yet finishes with a spicy dryness along with some brown sugar and vanilla. Also try Top Heavy, a superb Hefeweizen, smooth, massively drinkable, clean, and full of flavor. Great with pizza, fun with karaoke.

AMERICAN WHEAT

THIS IS A MODERN AMERICAN STYLE THAT FALLS SOMEWHERE BETWEEN HEFEWEIZEN, WIT, KÖLSCH, AND AMERICAN PALE ALE. GENERALLY VERY PALE IN COLOR AND MADE WITH A HIGH PROPORTION OF WHEAT IN THE MASH (30–60 PER CENT), THESE ARE HANDSOMELY HAZY BEERS BREWED WITH AMERICAN ALE YEAST AND NOT THE TYPICAL BAVARIAN OR BELGIAN STRAINS. THIS MEANS THAT THE BIG BANANA ESTERS OR CLOVE-LIKE, SPICY CHARACTER SHOULDN'T BE DOMINANT, THOUGH A LITTLE OF IT MIGHT FIND ITS WAY IN AND CAN WORK WONDERFULLY. HOPS STEP FORWARD HERE AND AMERICAN VARIETIES, WHETHER GENTLE OR GENEROUS, ARE OFTEN USED. THE USE OF LATE- AND DRY-HOPS TO GIVE A DOUBLE-WHAMMY FRUITINESS FROM HOP AND YEAST MAKES A GREAT COMBINATION IN THESE SMOOTH, EASY-DRINKING, AND FRAGRANT BEERS.

ABV for this style is around 4.0–6.0% with bitterness starting low and reaching 40 IBUs in the most bitter examples. The style is nearly always unfiltered, though sometimes not, and the suspended yeast gives a fullness of body and a satisfying depth of flavor. As beers brewed with wheat spread around the world, this will likely become a more popular style, taking the European classics and combining them with an American influence.

Three Floyds Gumballhead

Munster, Indiana
ABV: 5.5%
Hops: Cascade, Amarillo

I first tried this beer at the brewery. I was there for Dark Lord Day, a once-a-year event that releases Three Floyds' blockbuster Imperial Stout, Dark Lord. With 6,000 people crammed into a space not big enough for 6,000 people, and many queuing in line to pick up four bottles of the rare beer, my defining memory of the day was the first mouthful of Gumballhead. I was lost in the middle of a beer mosh pit, but the tropical, peachy, lemony, and mango fruitiness of the beer made me stop caring whether I was here or on a beach paradise somewhere. The body is a little creamy and super smooth, the bitterness is balanced, and the beer comes alive through the fruity and juicy hops. A perfect, style-defining beer—even if the second pint pushed my bladder to its upper fill line while I still had a long line of people in front of me.

Bell's Brewery Oberon

Kalamazoo, Michigan
ABV: 5.8%
Hops: Saaz, Hersbrücker

Oberon pours a cloudy, golden orange color. Pick it up, hold it to the light, and your fingers look like distant shadows through the glass. There's something sexy about an unfiltered beer, a sexiness that a brightly filtered beer rarely has, seeming too clean or polished. Subtle fruitiness, from both ester and hop, lifts out of the glass and makes you want to dive right in. The beauty of this beer is how clean and smooth it is to drink. It's a little lemony, a touch earthy, and finishes with a peppery kind of bitterness, exactly what you'd expect from the European hops. It's effortlessly drinkable and massively thirst-quenching. It's a style that's good with chili heat as the cool, full, unfiltered body is able to extinguish the flames of Scoville. It's also excellent with lighter food—think salads, creamy cheese, and grilled fish.

Jandrain-Jandrenouille VI Wheat

Jandrain-Jandrenouille, Belgium
ABV: 6.5%

This is what happens when Belgian hop merchants working with the Pacific Northwest's finest crops decide to start a brewery in their homeland. Inspired by American and Belgian beers, J-J does a better job than all the others of combining the two influences and ending up with elegant, balanced, and fantastic brews. VI Wheat is a wheat beer made with American hops (the specific varieties are a brewery secret). Hazy yellow with a cloud-like foam on top, it has a beautiful, wafting aroma of tangerine, peach, and pineapple. Orange, sweet basil, and blossom linger in the background like a soft summer breeze, while the bubbles pop on your tongue and tickle your tastebuds. Bitterness is quite low, a hint of clove dips its toe in and kicks toward its homeland, but then runs off again, chased away by the cheeky American hops. It's an astonishing beer. Drink it fresh on draft, if you can.

3 Cordilleras Blanca

Medellin, Columbia
ABV: 4.6%

At the forefront of Columbian craft brewing, 3 Cordilleras is putting better beers in front of new drinkers. It takes two seconds of looking at their social media pages to see that they're doing a great job; with regular tours and band nights held in the brewery, it's become a party spot for hot young Columbians to hang out, all smiling widely for the camera while holding bright glasses of beer. Blanca is a pale wheat beer fermented with an American ale yeast and hopped with British and German varieties. You get floral and earthy notes, an intriguing fruitiness from the yeast, a good body, and a playful kind of bitterness, which is light yet hangs around. If you happen to be in Columbia, then also look out for Mestiza, 3 Cordilleras's American Pale Ale—citrusy, juicy, fun, and *muy bueno*.

A Belgian-style white beer is known as Witbier (or Bière Blanche in France). Its current popularity owes two high-fives of thanks, each in a different direction: one to Pierre Celis, the man behind Hoegaarden, and the other to Blue Moon, a craft brand made by MolsonCoors.

WIT BEER

This is a sharp, cloudy, spicy style, which was popular for hundreds of years in Northern Europe, particularly in the Flemish area, which was surrounded by the crops needed for the beer—barley, wheat, and oats—and close to the spices of the Netherlands. The last white beer brewery, Tomsin in Hoegaarden, closed in 1955, and the beer style was gone. Pierre Celis, a local postman who had worked at Tomsin when he was younger, decided to bring back white beer and in 1966 he opened a brewery and named his beer after his hometown. Others started to copy his style of beer, and Hoegaarden grew to be the most famous white beer in the world. Hazy yellow, with a nose that points at coriander and citrus peel, and a body that is sharp and smooth, balanced and refreshing, it's a great beer. Hoegaarden was successful in America, where Celis later started another brewery in Texas. Both of his breweries have been bought out by the big guys. Pierre Celis died in April 2011—looking around the world, a lot of Wit beer is brewed and all of it links back to Celis.

The popularity of Wit is also due to Blue Moon, which has gone from nowhere to everywhere in no time at all. But no need to be worried about the rapid growth of a macro-made craft brand; instead, we should celebrate its success because of the number of craft Wit beers now being brewed. Serving as an approachable crossover style for those not yet ready for the all-in commitment of ordering a Double IPA, Wit beer is converting many drinkers to the craft beer side. Made with orange and coriander, Blue Moon encourages a slice of orange to be added to the glass. This pulls out all the orange flavor in the beer, but it also means drinking with a piece of fruit in your glass... I prefer naked with no gimmicky fruit, where the beer is unchallenging, subtle, smooth, orangey, and clean.

Belgian Wits are made with wheat and sometimes unmalted wheat and oats; they are also spiced, typically with coriander, curaçao, and orange peel. They are hazy and pale in appearance, thanks to the grain bill, while the yeast strain adds a lot of character, giving citrus, clove, and spice flavors that are accentuated by using those ingredients in the brewing process—the combination of spices and spicy yeast differentiate Wits from German-style Weizens. ABV will typically go from 4.5 to 5.5% and IBUs are low, rarely reaching into or beyond the twenties. Expect a smooth creaminess in the body, often with a little spike of citrus or acidity, and a depth of spice. White beer has spread around the world, so now sit back and watch as exciting new things happen to it, including turning it sour, spicing it more exotically, or making it bigger.

Hitachino Nest White Ale

Ibaraki, Japan
ABV: 5.5%
Hops: Perle, Styrian Goldings, Sorachi Ace

This is a seriously good Wit, one of those beers that is capable of making you re-evaluate what you thought you knew about a beer style. Made with the classic combo of coriander and orange peel, this also includes nutmeg and orange juice, the latter adding a fantastic fruitiness and smooth depth, while the nutmeg gives a festive kind of background that is great with the floral, earthy double-act of orange and coriander. Plenty of spice bursts out of the glass and then dives back to tickle your tonsils on the way down, making it taste lively and exciting, but it's the fullness of body that makes this a joy to drink—it fills the mouth, but is light and elegant.

Einstök Icelandic White Ale

Akureyri, Iceland
ABV: 5.2%
Hops: Hallertauer Tradition

If you want to know what good water can do to a beer, then drink this. Einstök is brewed in the fishing port of Akureyri, in north Iceland, just 97km (60 miles) south of the Arctic Circle. Surrounded by mountains, glacial water flows over ancient lava fields and into a modern mash tun where Einstök make a Porter, Pale Ale, and seasonal Doppelbock, but it's the White that I love—and it's the water that makes it so good. There's a crisp minerality, a fresh softness, a clean, dancing lightness, and that all comes from the great water. Mix that base with coriander, orange peel, and delicately spicy yeast, and you get a smooth, refreshing, very orangey beer with a spritzy kind of citrus sharpness. You don't generally notice water quality in a beer unless it's very bad or, with Einstök White, very good.

BrewRevolution Venus' Wit

Tamanique, El Salvador
ABV: 5.3%
Hops: Willamette, Mt Hood, Sterling, Mittelfrüh

Say hola to BrewRevolution, El Salvador's first craft brewery and their beer savior! Inspired by American craft brewing, BrewRevolution make a tight range of interesting beers, each with a local ingredient added, such as honey, coffee, fruit, or flowers. Mercurio IPA (made with unrefined whole cane sugar) and Venus' Wit (made with pineapple and maracuya, a local kind of passion fruit) are the two core beers that sit next to a range of other brews. Venus' Wit is pale gold and cloudy, the fruit comes out to play first with the sweetness of pineapple and the sharp, floral flavor of passion fruit—it's a wonderful combination in a Wit. Spicy and dry to finish, it's an exotic spin on the style. Have Venus' Wit with Salvadorian pupusa de queso, a corn tortilla filled with soft cheese—the beer's fruity sharpness is wonderful with the cheese's fruity richness.

Bäcker Exterminador De Trigo

Belo Horizonte, Brazil
ABV: 5.0%
Hops: Amarillo

I think you'd have to be an idiot not to buy a bottle of beer that has a picture of a man riding a crocodile on it, but then I would say that as I'm a sucker for stand-out labels and I've always wanted to sit on a crocodile. Exterminador is part of the Three Wolves series from Cervejaria Bäcker and is a Wit brewed with lemongrass. Unfiltered and made with citrusy American hops, which emphasize the sweet, woody lemongrass, this sits somewhere between a Wit and an American Wheat. The hops are upfront, floral, and pithy and leave behind a snap of bitterness with a tangy, earthy freshness from the lemongrass, while the yeast hides quietly inside, as if scared that the crocodile might bite if it makes a noise.

Good George White Ale

Hamilton, New Zealand
ABV: 4.5%
Hops: Pacific Jade, Motueka, Wakatu

In what used to be the Church of St George is now a divine brewery restaurant. A hybrid of a style, the White Ale is inspired jointly by Belgian Wits and American Wheats, which brewer Kelly Ryan calls a "New Zealand White". It uses American ale yeast in place of the classic spicy Wit yeast, coriander is replaced by indigenous locally grown botanicals and zest comes from NZ navel oranges. A beautiful hazy yellow with firm white foam, the beer is an exercise in controlled subtlety where the sweet orange teases, the botanicals tickle like pepper on the tongue, and hops are juicy NZ varieties giving distant and fragrant fruit. You'll definitely want more than one, so grab the food menu while you drink—this is great with seafood or the smoked chicken pizza. Good George also makes cider, including a dry-hopped version, which playfully skips in the middle ground between apples and ales.

Funkwerks White

Fort Collins, Colorado
ABV: 6.0%
Hops: Saphir

Funkwerks do Belgian-style beer. There are hoppy Blondes, sharp wheat beers, and a stack of barrels aging away in the small, neat brewhouse. The flagship beer at Funkwerks is their superlative Saison. A simply glorious beer, it's elegant, delightfully light, delicately spicy in the background with a soft mouthfeel countered by a brisk carbonation that feels like each bubble is kissing your tongue as it pops—when a brewery gets a Saison right, you know they're good. White is a summer seasonal that's somewhere between Saison and Wit. Brewed with orange and lemon zest, coriander, and grated ginger, it's fermented with the same yeast as Saison with the Wit spicing and zest giving a poke of fruit, fragrance, and earth, emphasizing a refreshing background sharpness. They have a fun little taproom attached to the brewery where they sell local farmhouse cheese to go with your farmhouse-style beer—it's a perfect combo.

BELGIAN BLONDE AND PALE ALE

TWO STYLES HAPPILY PAIRED UP, THANKS TO THEIR BIRTHPLACE AND SIMILAR LIGHT COLOR AND BRIGHT HOPPINESS. THESE BEERS DEVELOPED BY DRAWING INSPIRATION FROM BRITISH PALE ALES AND GERMAN LAGERS. BELGIAN BREWERS TYPICALLY ADDED THEIR OWN INFLUENCE WITH THEIR DISTINCTIVE USE OF HOPS (A BOLD, RAVISHING KIND OF BITTERNESS) AND AN AROMATIC YEAST STRAIN (WHICH GIVES EARTHY SPICES AND FRUITY ESTERS). THE CLASSIC FORMS OF THESE BEERS DATE TO AFTER THE TWO WORLD WARS, WHILE A NEW WAVE HAS ARRIVED IN RECENT YEARS, GIVING BLONDES AND PALES WITH MORE HOP AROMA, FLAVOR, BITTERNESS, AND WOW FACTOR.

Straw to deep gold in color, they hit the booze somewhere between 4.5 and 7.0% ABV. (Pale Ales are typically on the lower side of that range.) Bitterness will be pronounced in both, with the classical use of European hops giving a dry, earthy, and peppery bitterness (up to 30 IBUs). Alongside the traditional examples, the new wave of these beers is showing a bolder use of hops with bigger bitterness (up to 45 IBUs) and utilizing late- and dry-hops to give a winning air-punch of aroma from fragrant, citrus, and tropical varieties. The yeast pokes pepper and fruity esters into it and carbonation will be lively and add a refreshing quality on top of the well-attenuated dryness. While some examples can sadly share a dull ubiquity closer to a mass-made lager, get a good one and it's a beautiful, subtle, teasing style of beer.

ORVAL

FLORENVILLE, BELGIUM
ABV: 6.2%
HOPS: STRISSELSPALT, HALLERTAUER HERSBRÜCKER, HALLERTAUER TRADITION

CLASSIC

This is a Trappist beer made by Abbaye Notre Dame d'Orval. Its name is derived from "Valley of Gold." The legend tells of a countess who dropped a gold ring in a lake in the valley and made a promise to build a monastery if the ring was ever returned, at which point a trout heroically rose from the water with the ring in its mouth. It's the oldest monastery of the Trappist breweries, but modern brewing started as a means of funding post-war renovation. Orval is dry-hopped, and Brettanomyces is added to the bottles: drink the beer fresh, and you get the hops; drink it aged, and you get the yeast. I like it best at around a year from bottling when you get the spicy, earthy aroma from the hops blending with a leathery, lemony, funky note from the brett. Bitterness is bold, accentuated by the dryness of the beer and the sharp carbonation. So wonderfully complex and always interesting, the beauty of Orval is that it always tastes a bit different thanks to how it evolves in the bottle. I think it's one of the best beers in the world.

Brasserie de la Senne Taras Boulba

Brussels, Belgium
ABV: 4.5%
Hops: Saaz

This whole chapter could be given over to just beers made by Brasserie de la Senne. Zinnebir is a 5.5% ABV Blonde; Band of Brothers is a dry, hoppy Blonde made for Moeder Lambic, one of the best beer bars in Brussels; and Brussels Calling is a super-fruity bitter Blonde worth traveling to Belgium for. The thing with Brasserie de la Senne is that they make amazing beers by taking classic styles and decorating them with more hops. Taras Boulba is a pale gold "Extra Hoppy Ale" and it's the beer I always want in my refrigerator. The body has a little fullness without much malt flavor—it's almost not there, hiding, and that launches forward the hops: pithy, grapefruity, floral, spicy, lemon and lime, peach, all just from Saaz. There's spice in the body, pepper, ground coriander, and then a big bitterness, which is at first quenching and then thirst-inducing. Every time I have this beer, I get the feeling of falling in love all over again.

Dieu du Ciel! Dernière Volonté

Montreal, Canada
ABV: 7.0%
Hops: Sterling

Dieu du Ciel's cosy, corner brewpub pulls you in by showing off the shiny tanks as you walk past; walk inside and the long list of beers is what makes you stay. The brewpub makes three or four small batches of beer a week, with lots of variety and experimentation. There's also a production facility nearby with the most successful brewpub creations graduating up to the bigger tanks. Dernière Volonté, meaning "last will," is a hoppy Belgian-style Blonde. Pouring a hazy yellow-orange with a feisty foam, the bold hops give big floral and citrus which hang in that head of foam, hiding a peppery, grassy, stone-fruit depth. The body is satisfyingly big, with a blossom-honey background, while staying light; bitterness grips and is lifted by the aroma and then the yeast adds a spicy roundness. Dieu du Ciel! means "Oh my God!", which is what you'll exclaim when drinking their beers.

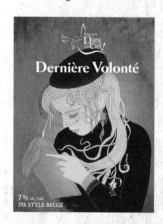

Feral Golden Ace

Baskerville, Australia
ABV: 5.6%
Hops: Sorachi Ace

You could probably give this one its own new style category. Somewhere between a Blonde and a Wit, it's got the depth of Belgian influence and spice, and then you get the distinctly fruity aroma coming from the Japanese-developed Sorachi Ace hops. These are unlike any other hop variety in their flavor profile: lemon, lime, melon, bubble gum, mint, lemongrass, coconut, and pineapple (they can also give off a blue-cheese whiff). In Golden Ace it adds a fruity, tropical twist, which gives a wonderfully unusual aroma that works really nicely with the Blonde base. The yeast is subtle and like great background music in that it makes the whole atmosphere better without you noticing it. With the Thai-like flavor, this is one for fragrant curries, coconut-based dishes, or freshly grilled fish with a squeeze of citrus.

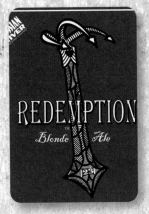

Russian River Redemption

Santa Rosa, California
ABV: 5.15%
Hops: Styrian Goldings, Saaz

Russian River has led the reinvention and revolution of Belgian beers in America simply by doing an incredible job with their interpretations of the classic styles. Redemption pours a beautiful hazy blonde with a fluffy white foam, and the first thing you get from the glass is a hint of orange blossom and pith and some light fruity esters. The body is wonderfully light with a carbonation that feels like the bubbles are ballroom dancing on your tongue, elegant and poised. Subtle, yet complex if you look for it, it's perfectly clean and finishes dry; you could, and would, drink this all day long. As a single (coming before Dubbel and Tripel), this is kind of like a table beer, though that might not do it justice—unless you drink it at the world's most glorious table.

Birrificio del Forte Gassa d'Amante

Pietrasanta, Italy
ABV: 4.5%
Hops: Hallertauer Northern Brewer, Perle, Styrian Goldings

With a name meaning "bowline," which is one of the most important nautical knots, the del Forte beers all share a traveling theme and a sense of adventure: the adventure of starting a brewery, the adventure of making great craft beers, and the adventure of drinking them. The brewery call Gassa d'Amante a companion beer for long voyages, so tie a knot around its neck, sling it over your shoulder along with an emergency travel-kit of bottle opener, beer glass, and a photo of a loved one, and be on your way. It's pale gold, with a gorgeous hop depth of peaches and apricots, plus an ester fruit flavor of bananas and apples. The taste is dry and clean, with the yeast giving pink pepper and spice followed by a refreshing depth of bitterness. If you've got room in your travel bag, then also pack the ingredients for creamy seafood pasta—it's a great combination.

Furthermore Fatty Boombalatty

Spring Green, Wisconsin
ABV: 7.2%
Hops: Perle, Saaz

Imagine a Belgian Wit and a Blonde hook up and decide to make things a little fruitier by inviting along an American Pale Ale wannabe... You can call that a Fatty Boombalatty. It pours an amber color with the yeast making the first advance, giving you banana, bubble gum, and a wink of vanilla. The body is slick and smooth, a little sweet kiss comes in the middle along with a rounded mouthfeel, before the hops bite at the end with earthy spice, peaches, and lemons and citrus enhanced by the orangey coriander used in the brew. Not your straight-up missionary Belgian ale, this one brings three different styles together, Americanized by a supersized use of Saaz going late into the brew, with everything complementing everything else, and makes them fit into one great-tasting, Belgian-inspired beer with a modern influence.

BELGIAN DUBBEL AND DARK STRONG ALE

TRADITIONALLY A BEER BREWED BY BELGIAN MONKS, DUBBEL IS A DARK ALE OF MEDIUM-TO-HIGH STRENGTH. IT'S MOST FAMOUS FOR ITS MONASTIC LINK BUT, LIKE SO MANY OTHER BELGIAN STYLES, IT STUBBORNLY DEFIES LABELS AND ROLLS SEAMLESSLY INTO STRONG DARK BELGIAN ALES. WESTMALLE GET THE CREDIT FOR DEVELOPING THE STYLES WE NOW KNOW AS DUBBEL AND TRIPEL—DUBBEL CAME IN 1926 WHEN THE MONKS MADE A "DUBBEL BRUIN," WHILE TRIPEL CAME IN THE 1930S. OF THE TRAPPIST BREWS, WE CAN ASSUME THAT THE BEERS MADE HUNDREDS OF YEARS AGO ARE DISTANT RELATIVES OF DUBBEL (UNLIKE GOLDEN TRIPELS, WHICH JOINED THE BROTHERHOOD FAR MORE RECENTLY).

These beers are dark in color, ranging from ruby-brown to dark chocolate. They can be made with pale malts and turned dark through the use of caramelized candi sugar (this is the Belgian way of brewing them), although brewers also use dark malts. Typical ABV will be 6.0–7.5% for Dubbels and 7.0–10.0% for the bridging dark ales between Dubbel and Quad. Bitterness is background rather than foreground, adding balance with around 25 IBUs; hops add a herbal or earthy edge. Flavor comes from malt, sugar, and yeast, giving dried fruit, cherry, caramel, chocolate, and fruity esters (mostly banana, which comes from high fermentation temperatures). There might be some residual sweetness left in the beer, though many have a well-attenuated dryness to finish.

ST. BERNARDUS 8

CLASSIC

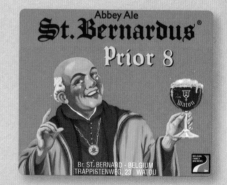

WATOU, BELGIUM
ABU: 8.0%
HOPS: GOLDINGS, MAGNUM

This is not a Trappist brewery, but it's pretty close. In 1946, the abbot in charge of the Abbey Sint Sixtus decided to have beer as less of a focus, so he shifted production of the Westvleteren beers to St. Bernardus. When Westvleteren took back the brewing in 1992 (because a new ruling said Trappist beers had to be produced within the actual monastery), St. Bernardus carried on brewing and released their own range of beers. The 8 is crimson-brown in color; it's got the dried fruit you expect, some cocoa and caramel, some festive spices, and a little nudge of fragrant hops, which are grown beside the brewhouse. Drinkers talk about a similarity between St. Bernardus and St. Sixtus, which is to be expected, as the monks took yeast and recipes across from Westvleteren to Watou. The beer is brewed next to an old cheese factory, so use this information for an inspirational food pairing: the 8 is great with nutty and creamy cheeses.

Hitachino Nest XH

Naka, Japan
ABV: 8.0%
Hops: Chinook, Styrian Goldings

Before 1994, new Japanese breweries couldn't get a license unless they were going to produce 528,300 US gallons (2 million liters) of beer a year. When the law changed, it allowed a yearly output of just 15,850 US gallons (60,000 liters), making craft brewing a realistic option. Since 1994, over 200 small breweries have opened in Japan, creating one of the most varied and interesting beer scenes in the world, with a lot of German and American influence, plus many uniquely Japanese elements. The Hitachino Nest beers from the Kiuchi Brewery are some of the most available and celebrated Japanese beers. At their brewery they also make sake and a distilled version of sake called shochu. XH is a dark Belgian brew matured for three months in shochu barrels. Full-bodied and rich, there are berries, sour cherries, cocoa, stone fruit, festive spices, and floral hop, with the barrel giving a unique flavor and sharp-hot-sweet complexity.

Goose Island Pere Jacques

Chicago, Illinois
ABV: 8.0%
Hops: Saaz

In 2011, Goose Island was bought by brewing giant AB InBev. Those initially worried that this would see G.I. Lite or a reduction in deliciousness have had their fears eased. Production has increased overall and the brewery in Chicago has started to make more barrel-aged beers, as well as a range of Belgian-style beers called the "Vintage Ales," which includes a wine-barrel-aged farmhouse ale, a dark Saison, an Orval-esque Blonde, plus tart fruit beers. Pere Jacques is a dark, Belgian-style ale; there are plums, nuts, candy, banana bread, and brown sugar with a light spiciness. While they're all Belgian-inspired, they aren't direct copies straight out of the recipe book. These are exciting interpretations of classic beers, done with a delicate touch that has, arguably, created new beer styles.

Sierra Nevada Ovila Dubbel

Chico, California
ABV: 7.5%
Hops: Challenger, Styrian Goldings

This is a great story: in 1190, the Santa Maria de Ovila abbey was built near Trillo, in Spain. In 1931, as the abbey was crumbling, William Randolph Hearst, the outrageously rich newspaper magnate, bought the abbey, had it dismantled, and then shipped to San Francisco, where he planned on building himself a castle. That didn't happen and instead the stones were left in wooden crates in the Golden Gate Park until 1994, at which point they were handed over to the Abbey of New Clairvaux in North California, where they began reconstructing the ruins. The Ovila series from Sierra Nevada is a collaboration between the brewery and abbey, with money from the beer helping to fund the abbey restoration work. Great idea and a great beer: deep copper-brown with a custard-like foam; the aroma is softly, sweetly malty with dried fruit, a little tea, nuts, chocolate, and spice. The mouthfeel is creamy and yet lively with carbonation; it's incredibly well balanced and a reverential take on a classic.

Charlevoix Dominus Vobiscum Double

Baie-Saint-Paul, Canada
ABV: 8.0%
Hops: Brewers Gold, Strisselspalt

American breweries may have taken a little while to turn to Belgian beers, but Canadian brewers have been making their own excellent examples and interpretations for many years. Microbrasserie Charlevoix is one of the best. The Double is made with a classic dark Belgian base and also includes ground coriander, curaçao, and camomile. It is burgundy-brown in the glass, with an aroma that is an enticing mix of dried fruit, plums, dark chocolate, licorice, and an earthy citrus background from the spices. With a luscious mouthfeel, the low bitterness makes it rounded and smooth, leaving an aftertaste that mixes all the fruity, malt-forward notes with a hint of peppery, aniseed spiciness from yeast and hops. Dubbels and dark Belgian ales are great with cheeses: with this one go for a strong, blue-vein cheese, where the sweet aniseed notes cut through the richness of pungent mold.

New Belgium Abbey

Fort Collins, Colorado
ABV: 7.0%
Hops: Willamette, Target, Liberty

Before New Belgium was a real bricks-and-mortar-and-mash-tun brewery, there was a Dubbel (called Abbey) and an Amber (called Fat Tire). Homebrewer and cofounder of New Belgium, Jeff Lebesch, had these two beers and built a brewery around them, growing it into one of the most successful in America. Given the name, you can figure out the influence and, indeed, New Belgium were one of the first to focus on classic Belgian beers in the United States. Abbey is a great rendition of a Dubbel. Copper brown, there's banana, bubble gum, and pear, plus earthy spices and a hint of dried fruit. Creamy in the middle, there's caramel, tobacco, dried fruit, and herbal hops before it finishes clean, dry, and peppery—the kind of ending that calls for an encore sip to get another round of sweetness. If you see the Grand Cru Abbey Ale, then it's a bigger, richer, rounder version of the Dubbel.

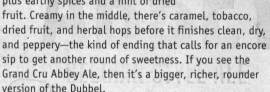

Maltus Faber Extra Brune

Genova, Italy
ABV: 10.0%
Hops: Northern Brewer, East Kent Goldings

Pouring a hazy dark brown with a full foam on top, Extra Brune is like the monk who one day decided to throw off his robes and go on vacation. He joined the gym, watched some movies, went on dates, and generally enjoyed the freedoms of secular life before swaggering back, refreshed and inspired. "Have you been working out?" they comment. "Nice hairstyle," another says. "What's that wonderful fragrance?" one asks. You get all the dried fruit, the cocoa, the tea leaves, the brown bread, earthy spice, and brown sugar, plus an appetizing savory note. The body is full and slick, smooth, soft, and richly malty, with estery yeast giving an overripe fruit bowl of banana, pear, and apple. This is a Dubbel but bigger; refreshed and inspired by new tastes.

BELGIAN STYLE AND FASHIONABLE MONKS

Belgian beer styles are among the most famous in the world, yet style isn't something many Belgian brewers think about, eschewing the need to squeeze beers into catagories. Instead, styles have evolved over many years, becoming so popular that they are copied around the world.

The area of most awareness is among the Trappist and Abbey brews. Trappist beer is rare and only a small number of breweries in the world make it officially; Abbey beers aren't Trappist but are made in the monastic tradition. As the monks are Cistercian, Trappist monasteries follow the rule of Saint Benedict and are self-sufficient. The monks make products that provide enough money to cover their own living expenses and use any surplus to help others.

Trappist isn't a style—it's an appellation used to indicate where the product was made and by whom. The type of beer the monks make doesn't matter (they could thrash out a Trappist IPA if they wanted). What does matter is that it's made according to Trappist criteria, which say that:

1 . The beer must be brewed within the walls of a Trappist monastery, either by the monks themselves or under their supervision.
2. The brewery must be of secondary importance within the monastery, and it should be run according to business practices proper to a monastic way of life.
3. The brewery is not intended to be a profit-making venture. The income covers the living expenses of the monks and the maintenance of the buildings and grounds. Whatever remains is donated to charity for social work and to help persons in need.
4. Trappist breweries are constantly monitored to ensure the irreproachable quality of their beers.

Monasteries have been making beer for a thousand years, stopping and starting periodically due to wars and monastic changes. But the beers we now associate with the brothers date back to the 1930s and 1940s. As these monastic beers gained appeal, secular brewers wanted to make the same types of beer. To keep Trappist and non-Trappist separate, a ruling was made in 1962 that only beers made according to the above criteria could be called Trappist. The others could use the term "Abbey."

Classic Trappist beers generally fall into a few categories: Single (Enkel), which can be light or dark, rarely leaves the brewery and is for the monks to drink; Dubbel is a dark, medium-strength beer with a dried-fruit depth; and Tripel is a strong Blonde with a pervasive hop presence. A newer addition is Quadrupel, the strongest, darkest, most complex beer made in the Trappist tradition. Some other examples don't fit: Orval is a highly hopped and wild-yeast-dosed beer; some beers sit between Dubbel and Quad; La Trappe, the most forward-thinking monastic brewery, make a Wit, Bock, and an oak-aged Quad.

Single, Dubbel, and Tripel get their names from illiterate times, when brews were labeled with crosses to denote their strength: X was the weakest, XXX was the strongest. Originally they would've all been taken from the same brew: the sweet first runnings of wort were strong (XXX) while the third runnings (X) were weak. Over time, the beers were brewed separately, although the names stuck.

To complicate things, or perhaps illuminate the nature of Belgian beer and the brewers lack of a need to define styles, Westmalle and La Trappe are the only Trappist breweries that use Dubbel and Tripel (and Quad for La Trappe) in beer names.

The beers of the monastic tradition are popular around the world, whether made by monks or inspired by them. When it comes to style, Trappist and Abbey brewers have produced some of the most fashionable beers simply by doing what their forebears have done for decades.

BELGIAN TRIPEL AND STRONG GOLDEN ALE

TRIPEL IS A STRONG, GOLDEN, BELGIAN-STYLE ALE. IT WAS ONCE KNOWN AS XXX AND WOULD'VE BEEN A DARK BEER BUT THE COLOR CHANGED IN THE 1930S WHEN WESTMALLE FURTHER DEVELOPED THE BREWING SIDE OF THE MONASTERY. THEY STARTED SELLING BEER AND WITH THIS CAME A NEW GOLDEN BEER, WHICH THEY CALLED TRIPEL. LIKE DUBBELS, TRIPELS HAVE AN EXTENDED FAMILY, STRETCHING OUT TO INCLUDE STRONG GOLDEN ALES, THE CLASSIC EXAMPLE OF THIS BEING DUVEL.

Yellow to deep gold in color, there's often a strong body to the style, though malt flavor is kept low, not interfering with the yeast or hops. The hops give a dominant bitterness (40 IBUs), though are still restrained and not overpowering, alongside the dry finish. Aroma might be herbal, grassy or lightly fruity (stone fruit, citrus pith, or with esters—typically banana and pear—from high fermentation temperatures). European hops are classic. Carbonation, thanks to the bottle-conditioning, will be sharp (kegged versions can never get that same lively carbonation, which is why most Belgian Tripels are bottled only). ABV will be 7.5–9.5%. Tripels and Golden Ales are close, but not the same thing. Stan Hieronymus, in *Brew like a Monk*, explains that the essential difference between Tripel and Golden Ale is the yeast: Tripels are spicy whereas Golden Ales are fruity. New World hops can dress these up to be more like IPAs, but should never overpower the subtle elegance of the style: you want a beautiful dance between malt and hops in which the hops take both the leading steps and the bow at the end, but the malt controls the timing and pace.

Westmalle Tripel

Westmalle, Belgium
ABV: 9.5%
Hops: Saaz, Tettnang, Styrian Goldings

This beer writes the style guide for Tripel. Born in 1934, Westmalle turned their strongest beer pale in color and others followed. The monastery where the beer is made is known as Our Lady of the Sacred Heart. Formed in 1794, it started selling beer in 1856 (though only in small volumes), choosing to sell more commercially in the 1920s, which led to developing the brewery in the 1930s. Now, their output makes them one of the largest Trappist breweries. As the textbook Tripel example, Westmalle is bright gold in color with a heavenly white foam. Peach, orange, banana, pepper, almond, white chocolate, and apple all catch in that foam, which leaves a lace down the glass. Hops are bold, yet elegant. The body has a slick, rich mouthfeel from the malt and alcohol (with a spirit hint but no harsh booziness) and is deeply filled with hop flavor—peppery, fruity, and floral. It's an endlessly interesting beer to drink.

Brasserie de la Senne Jambe de Bois

Brussels, Belgium
ABV: 8.0%
Hops: Hallertauer, Spalt

A strong Blonde, Jambe de Bois (meaning "wooden leg") is another phenomenal beer brewed by Brasserie de la Senne. It pours an appealing opaque orange. The malt gives a smoothness, plus a hint of cakey sweetness with vanilla and almond notes. An assertive use of hops gives bitterness, pineapple, grapefruit, stone fruit, orange, and peppery herbs with an additional, elusive fruitiness that's best described simply as "fruity." While there's a lot of hops, that never overpowers the malt and they stay in harmony throughout. Feisty yet tender, it's one of those beers that you drink fast because you love it and fast because it's got a magical quality, a "je ne sais quoi," something that you can't quite work out. I reckon it'd be brilliant with Thai food where that tropical fruitiness plus the sturdy body would wrap around savory, sweet, hot, and sour dishes.

Duvel Tripel Hop

Breendonk, Belgium
ABV: 9.5%
Hops: Saaz, Styrian Goldings, plus a changing hop each year

Everyone's had Duvel, right? It's the quintessential strong Golden Ale. Luminous gold, massive white foam, apples, apricot, and spice, a quenching dryness to finish, super clean, and light for the 8.5% ABV, it's a beautiful beer that's always interesting. Once a year they release a dry-hopped version of Duvel: "Houblonnage Extra Intense" is what the label says. In 2011, it was made with Amarillo and in 2012, it was Citra. It's a stronger version of the Duvel base beer plus more hops, which go into the kettle and conditioning tank. The Citra version was peaches, grape, apricot, gooseberry, floral and citrus pith in the amazing aroma; the body was slick and hop-oily, juicy, super-fruity, plus a wickedly clean bitterness. After this, you'll never look at Duvel in the same way again, mostly because you'll be craving the Tripel Hop. A classic reinvented.

Falke Tripel Monasterium

Ribeirão das Neves, Brazil
ABV: 9.0%
Hops: Galena, Hallertauer Tradition

Inspired by Belgian monks, Monasterium claims to be the first Tripel to be brewed in Brazil. The celebratory sound of a cork bursting from the bottle is what you get when you open this beer, making you immediately excited to drink it. It's made with ground coriander and curaçao, Pilsner malt, wheat, and oats, plus some dark malt—and that malt grist gives it a rounded body, perhaps rounder than traditional Tripels or strong Belgian ales, with a smooth depth of caramel and cereal grain. It's made light and sharp with the Champagne carbonation, and the hops give stone fruit with a dry bitterness and a hint of warming spirit. Yeast and spice add a peppery, orange quality plus some apple and pear. Contrast the fancy bottle with some traditional street food and try with acarajé, a fried ball of black beans, dried shrimp, and onion.

Anchorage The Tide and Its Takers

Anchorage, Alaska
ABV: 9.0%
Hops: Sorachi Ace, Styrian Goldings

Brace yourself: this is a Tripel that's brewed with Sorachi Ace hops alongside classic Styrian Goldings. It's fermented once in tank with Belgian yeast, then it goes into oak barrels, which used to hold Chardonnay, where it gets a second fermentation from Brettanomyces, and then it gets a third fermentation in the bottle to give a burst of carbonation. Hazy yellow in the glass, the aroma immediately jumps out, giving funky and earthy brett, a little lemon from the Sorachi Ace hop, a bubble-gum sweetness, and some barrel flavors. It tastes like a Tripel, but then there's this whole other complexity around it: wine, oak texture, vanilla, mint, lemon, melon, and perfumey hops; peppery, earthy, spicy, and dry from the yeast; and a blossom-honey sweetness. You might never manage to work out the chase-me complexity on this one but you'll love every sip as you try to understand it.

Allagash Curieux

Portland, Maine
ABV: 11.0%
Hops: Tettnang, Hallertauer

Inspired by Belgian beers, Rob Tod founded Allagash in 1995 and now the brewery make six Belgian-style beers all year round. Curieux is a bourbon-barrel-aged version of their terrific Tripel. The base beer is golden, smooth, dry, and spicy; there's nectarine, pineapple, and banana in the aroma; it's got the quintessential complexity of Tripel while remaining light, giving a lift of herbal and floral hops. Put that into a bourbon barrel for eight weeks, where you pick up coconut, vanilla, cola, and toffee notes, and you get a beer that's rounder and sweeter than the original with an oaky-bitter finish from tannin, plus a great depth of flavor that works well with the fruity yeast. The barrel doesn't overpower it, keeping the base beer in balance. This is a treat alongside dessert: carrot cake, vanilla cheesecake, or apple crumble all work with the bourbon's caramel depth and the base beer's dry bitterness.

Red Hill Temptation

Red Hill, Australia
ABV: 8.0%
Hops: Golding, Hallertauer

Not many breweries have their own hop yard onsite, but Red Hill does. They grow Hallertauer, Tettnang, Willamette, and Golding, the last being appropriate as the brewery was started by Karen and David Golding. The hops are grown, harvested, dried, and used in all the house beers. Temptation uses Golding to get the 30 IBUs of bitterness and then Hallertauer to give a floral and fragrant aroma of herbs, grapes, and a faint hint of tropical fruit—it's Hallertauer the southern hemisphere way. Big banana esters say hello at the beginning and a subtle yeast spiciness waves goodbye at the end. In between there's a hint of toffee without being sweet, and the carbonation lifts it, making it clean and light, belying its 8.0% ABV. A classy Aussie Tripel with the special addition of home-grown hops.

BELGIAN QUADRUPEL

A MONASTIC OR ABBEY BEER THAT'S BIGGER THAN DUBBELS AND BIGGER AND DARKER THAN TRIPELS, MAKES QUADRUPEL THE NEXT LOGICAL STEP. YET IT'S A STYLE THAT DOESN'T HAVE THE SAME HISTORY AS THE OTHERS AND IS A RECENT ENTRY INTO BREWHOUSES, WHERE THE NAME IS CONTENTIOUS. LOOK AT THE BREWERS ASSOCIATION AND THE BJCP STYLE GUIDELINES AND "QUADRUPEL" ISN'T THERE—YOU GET DARK STRONG ALE INSTEAD; THERE ISN'T AN ENTRY FOR IT IN *THE OXFORD COMPANION TO BEER*; MICHAEL JACKSON DOESN'T USE THAT WORD IN HIS *GREAT BEERS OF BELGIUM*... QUADRUPEL WAS NAMED IN THE 1990S BY DE KONINGSHOEVEN BREWERY AND THE TERM HAS STUCK AND SPREAD. YOU WILL ALSO SEE THEM CALLED "ABT," WHICH MIGHT BE A MORE APPEASING NAME, GIVING A BREWERY'S STRONGEST BEER A STANDING EQUAL TO THE HEAD OF A MONASTERY, THE ABBOT.

Expect ABV to be 9.0–14.0% and beers that are a dark ruby-brown in color with a full foam. Flavor is dominated by depth of malt and yeast, which combine to give dried fruit, tea, chocolate, spices, caramel, berries, and bread. The use of a dark candi sugar is common to add color and flavor. Hops are traditionally German, English, or Belgian—some brews can be well hopped (expect 20–50 IBUs), though, typically, they give a peppery earthiness at the end, emphasized by the brisk carbonation. Some can be well attenuated, while others have a lick of sweetness to them. Complex and interesting, they are sipping beers to take your time over. Some of the world's most revered beers are in this saintly style.

ROCHEFORT 10

CLASSIC

ROCHEFORT, BELGIUM
ABV: 11.3%
HOPS: STYRIAN GOLDINGS, HALLERTAUER

Abbey de Notre-Dame de Saint-Rémy is home to Brasserie de Rochefort, where beer was first brewed around 1595. They make 6, 8, and 10, all dark, lusciously plummy, and rich, getting stronger and more complex as the number increases. Brewed with pale malt and then turned dark with candi sugar, Rochefort 10 also includes some ground coriander, though the dominant profile of the beer is its smooth, complex body, which gives dried fruit, toasted nuts, banana, figs, malt loaf, dark chocolate, and caramel, though it never threatens to be sweet. The hops are earthy and typically peppery, adding further complexity to this world-renowned brew. Thanks to the high ABV and bottle-conditioning, these beers age well for a number of years, after which you can expect more tea-like maltiness, more dried fruit, and maybe even a hint of nutty, sherry depth.

Sharp's Quadrupel Ale

Rock, England
ABV: 10.0%
Hops: Centennial, Hallertauer, Aurora, Simcoe

Alongside the regular range of cask beers, Stuart Howe, the bluff, plain-talking, rugby-playing head brewer at Sharp's, makes a range of Connoisseurs Choice brews, a selection of specials that are released each year, taking old and new inspirations. One look at the hop line-up will tell you that this one's not like other Quads. Made with four different hops (including the Simcoe as a dry hop) and four strains of yeast, the body and malt are classic with berries, raisins, licorice, nutty Oloroso sherry, and a roasty, dark chocolate depth, but the hops, which bring pine, citrus pith, flowers, and grapefruit, are like a team of brightly shirted American tourists powering through Brussels hollering and yee-hawing. It's a great take on the style, giving it a new hop accent above the classic base.

Struise St Amateus 12

Oostvleteren, Belgium
ABV: 10.5%
Hops: Challenger, Styrian Goldings

Westvleteren 12 is the most famous Quadrupel in the world. It's a blockbuster brew, regarded as one of the world's best beers. In Oostvleteren, the next town over from Sint Sixtus, is De Struise Brouwers and they make St Amateus 12, ostensibly their riff on Westvleteren 12. A tongue-in-cheek, wry Belgian smile at their neighbors, St Amateus is a dark ruby beer with a thick foam. Get it fresh and the hops dominate; let it age and they mellow into the beer and allow the yeast and malt to come forward. Dried fruit, spice, cherry brandy, perfumey hops, coconut, cocoa, some banana and pear esters; it's got a medium body with bread, berry pips, treacle, and more bitterness than most Quads. There's depth of flavor, complexity, and just a hint of brewing bravado: anything you can do, I can try to do better.

Dieu du Ciel! Rigor Mortis

Montreal, Canada
ABV: 10.5%

Made and released once a year, get Rigor Mortis when you can. With a full, creamy foam above the dark body, this one looks fantastic and that's just the start. There's banana and rum in the aroma, cherries, dried fruit, and a sweet bready depth. It's strong, but it drinks like a far lighter beer with a smooth and wonderful creaminess; there's raisins, prunes, chocolate, caramel, anise, vanilla, and then spicy, earthy hops at the end. Every mouthful is different and more interesting than the last, which is a good quality in a beer like this and it makes you dip your nose deeper and deeper into the glass each time you go back for more. The brewery say that the beer gets better after six months, so try and make it last if you can—or just buy extra.

Lost Abbey Judgment Day

San Marcos, California
ABV: 10.5%
Hops: Challenger, East Kent Goldings, German Magnum

Lost Abbey and Port Brewing are two halves of the same brewery, a short drive out of San Diego. Lost Abbey make a range of superb Belgian-inspired beers, including barrel-aged and sour brews, while Port Brewing is the fist-pumping, American all-star, cranking out hop-forward beers. Port Brewing came first, and then Lost Abbey developed from sideline to frontline. They have a fantastic tasting room where you can try beers from both sides and here's a beer-geek fact: when Stone Brewing moved out of their San Marcos location, Port Brewing and Lost Abbey moved in. Judgment Day is a Quad brewed with raisins. It pours a deep ruby-brown color and you get cocoa, toasted nuts, dried fruit, caramel, berries, plus an earthy hop background. Dark and intense, it's one for sipping while contemplating your day of judgment (or just watching TV).

Boulevard Brewing Bourbon Barrel Quad

Kansas City, Missouri
ABV: 11.8%
Hops: Perle, Hallertauer Tradition

The flavor of a Quad naturally fits with the profile of bourbon (toffee, dried fruit, spice), so it's no surprise that there's an increasing number of Quads going into barrels. That's what this is, plus the addition of some cherries, and it's a rare release from the Kansas City brewery. The Quad, Boulevard's "The Sixth Glass," goes into various barrels, some for up to three years, and then it's blended before bottling to get the best balance of flavor. Toffee, vanilla, oak, sharp cherries, sweet cherries, cola, figs, festive spices, raisins, and brown sugar all come out and you get the best of the beer and the barrel both bursting out of your glass. It's layered with a smooth, warming depth and it's the sort of beer to share with friends, preferably over a dessert of crème brûlée or cherry pie.

Cervejaria Wäls Quadruppel

Belo Horizonte, Brazil
ABV: 11.0%
Hops: Galena, Styrian Goldings, Saaz

Cachaça is a Brazilian spirit distilled from fermented sugarcane juice. It can come white, which is unaged, or gold, which is matured in wooden barrels, and it's similar to rum. It's Brazil's most popular spirit and makes up the base of Brazil's most famous cocktail, Caipirinha—a refreshing mix of cachaça, sugar, and lime served over lots of ice. Cervejaria Wäls' Quadruppel is aged with French oak soaked in cachaça, adding a warming spirit background, some banana, and an exotic, tropical-fruit twist to the vanilla, caramel, roasted figs, molasses, and chocolate in the beer. It's smooth, creamy, and full-bodied with the wood adding texture before 35 IBUs of hops give a firm bitterness. A great local take on the style, the spirit works wonderfully well with the rich beer and makes it perfect with brigadeiro, a Brazilian chocolate truffle.

BELGO AMERICAN

BELGO AMERICAN BEERS AND BELGIAN IPAS LOOK LIKE THEY SHOULD SIT SIDE BY SIDE ON BEER'S FAMILY TREE, BUT THEY DON'T. THEY ARE STYLES THAT BRING TOGETHER BELGIAN AND AMERICAN FLAVORS, BUT THE DIFFERENCE LIES IN WHERE THEY START OUT: BELGO AMERICAN BEGINS AS A BELGIAN BEER AND IS THEN PIMPED WITH AMERICAN OR NEW WORLD HOPS (GIVING THEIR CITRUS, FLORAL, OR TROPICAL FLAVORS), WHILE BELGIAN IPA STARTS OUT AS AN AMERICAN IPA AND IS THEN FUNKED UP BY BEING FERMENTED WITH A BELGIAN YEAST STRAIN (GIVING A PEPPERY, ESTERY, SPICY DEPTH). LIKE A COMPLEX VENN DIAGRAM, THERE ARE STYLES THAT MOVE BETWEEN THE TWO, AND IT ISN'T BLACK AND WHITE, BUT BOTH ARE ZEITGEIST BEER STYLES THAT BRING TOGETHER THE OLD WORLD OF BELGIAN WITH THE FRUIT-FORWARD FLAVOR OF AMERICAN CRAFT BEER.

These beers generally defy a single categorization, which makes them especially exciting. They might start as a Saison, Blonde, or strong ale; ABV might range from 5.0 to 10.0%; bitterness from 20 to 80 IBUs; and they may include spices, wild yeast, or barrel-aging. The link is the use of fragrant, fruity American and New World hops to give a juicy aroma and flavor profile, which blends gently with the malt and yeast depth. This still remains true to its Belgian home with its subtle complexity—ultimately, they taste like Belgian beers with an American accent.

JANDRAIN-JANDRENOUILLE IV SAISON

JANDRAIN-JANDRENOUILLE, BELGIUM
ABV: 6.5%

CLASSIC

This was the first beer I drank after proposing to my girlfriend, Lauren. On a private beach on a little Greek island, just as the sun was setting, I asked the question, she said "yes," and later, back in our hotel, I had a bottle of this chilling in the fridge. Why this beer? Because it's one of my favorites. I first had it in Belgium and it was love at first sniff. Fruity American hops give peaches, apricots, a wonderful floral freshness, citrus, and pineapple. The body is light, the carbonation makes it tingle (like a heart in love), and the spice is as delicate as fairy dust. It's not an explosive kind of beer, just so fresh and light, and with a hop presence that lifts everything up like a smile on a pretty face. A pretty face that just said yes to the most important question I'd ever asked.

Extraomnes Zest

Marnate, Italy
ABV: 5.3%
Hops: East Kent Goldings, Citra

The Italian craft beer scene is making up its own rules as it develops, though inspiration is coming from Belgium and America, plus a little local flair and a nod toward their wine-making countrymen. Together this is creating exciting new flavor profiles; which are uniquely Italian. Extraomnes Zest is a great example of that; a Belgian Blonde dry-hopped with Citra, combining that dry, clean, and light body with hop fruitiness. Mango, passion fruit, apricot, grapefruit, and peach all come from Citra. The body is clean, with a hint of dried herbs and pepper, before the huge bitterness bounds in; it hits unexpectedly and then grows, clawing at your tongue, threatening to overpower. Aggressive yet playful, it has that classic botanic type of Belgian hop bitterness, which the dry hops lift and lighten with a perfumey, fruity freshness.

Houblon Chouffe

Achouffe, Belgium
ABV: 9.0%
Hops: Magnum, Hallertauer, Amarillo

This "Dobbelen IPA Tripel," made by Brasserie d'Achouffe, was one of the first Belgian beers (released in 2006) to have a supersized hop influence and it's still one of the best. Pouring a hazy gold with a bright white foam, there's a teasing, tantalizing hop aroma, giving citrus pith, fresh grass, apricots, nectarines, hop sack, and floral herbs, all rounded out by some banana and spicy esters. The body is full yet light, the malt is smooth on the tongue, giving a hint of sweetness and hiding the 9.0% ABV, and making you drink in gulps. The hops give more in the mouth with stone fruit, pith, and a herbal bitterness mixing with the peppery spice of the yeast. This is great with paprika-roast chicken, especially if it's stuffed with herbs and garlic.

Anchorage Love Buzz Saison

Anchorage, Alaska
ABV: 8.0%
Hops: Simcoe, Amarillo, Citra

It doesn't get more craftbeertastic than this. Belgian ale re-imagined: tick. American hops: tick, tick, tick. Unusual ingredients: tick each for rose hips, peppercorns, and fresh orange peel. Barrel-aged: tick for French oak Pinot Noir. Wild yeast: tick for Brettanomyces. And a bonus tick awarded for a great label. It pours a hazy orange with a blush of pink through it. Take a sniff and you get pepper: freshly cracked (savory and floral), peppery hops, and peppery yeast. The hops and orange peel combine to give a fruity, floral background to the Brettanomyces, which gives a little lemon and leather. The wine provides a tangy sharpness through the spicy body and there's a lasting bitterness that is like a three-way hug between hops, spices, and oak. For such disparate ideas to be thrown together in a barrel, you might expect a riot; instead, everything helps to complement or emphasize something else. Ten ticks and a big smiley face.

FARMHOUSE ALES

TRADITIONALLY MADE IN FARMHOUSES, BUT LONG SINCE MOVED INTO BREWHOUSES, THESE BEERS WERE ORIGINALLY BREWED IN THE WINTER ONLY, BECAUSE THE LACK OF ARTIFICIAL REFRIGERATION MEANT THAT SUMMER TEMPERATURES WERE TOO HIGH TO ACHIEVE CONSISTENT OR QUALITY RESULTS. THE BEERS WERE DESIGNED TO SLAKE THE HUGE THIRSTS OF HARD-WORKING FARMERS DURING THE DAY, TO BE A FORM OF SUSTENANCE IN THE FIELDS, AND TO SIT AT THE TABLE AFTER THE DAY'S WORK WAS DONE. NOW BREWED YEAR-ROUND, SAISON IS BECOMING A FLAGSHIP BEER STYLE AND ONE THAT IS OPEN TO CREATIVE INTERPRETATION.

Saisons are from the Hainaut region in Belgium. Dry and spicy (from hops, yeast, and sometimes the addition of spices), aromatic, elusively fruity (citrus, orchard, and stone fruits), and refreshingly bitter, they are quenching yet complex, rustic yet refined. Expect 5.0–8.0% ABV, bitterness up to 40 IBUs, straw to gold in color, and highly attenuated. Bière de Garde, meaning "beer for keeping," is France's only indigenous beer style and developed in the north of the country, along the border with Belgium. The beers are more malt-forward and rounder than Saisons, gentler, softer, sweeter, with a herbal quality and maybe a cellar-like funk. ABV will be around 6.0–8.5%, bitterness up to 30 IBUs, and the beers on the gold to amber color spectrum. Both styles traditionally use European hops. Modern versions use the citrus and tropical notes of American and southern-hemisphere hops, which work well in Saisons.

SAISON DUPONT

HAINAUT, BELGIUM

ABV: 6.5%

HOPS: STYRIAN GOLDINGS, EAST KENT GOLDINGS

CLASSIC

This beer is a classic Saison, but as late as the 1980s it wasn't even the main product at the brewery. That's when it was taken to America and turned into a superstar. The house yeast strain gives it a lot of its character: fruity, peppery, spicy, and very dry—other brewers use the same strain to get similar Saison qualities into their brews. Hazy gold with a big foam, it's a handsome beer. The hops give earthiness, peppery spice, and stone fruit before the refreshing, ravishing, dry finish with a lasting bitterness. If you ever see the dry-hopped version, then try it because it's even better than the original: apples, vanilla, spice, pineapple, and almond; there's more aroma, complexity, and depth to it. Both are great with food: the sharpness is perfect with Thai food, the dryness works well with oily fish, and the spiciness loves peppery meat.

Brasserie Theillier La Bavaisienne Ambrée

Bavay, France
ABV: 7.0%
Hops: Brewers Gold

Situated a few miles from the Belgian border, Brasserie Theillier has been in the same family since 1835 and is France's oldest working brewery, only stopping once between then and now when the Germans marched in and requisitioned the brewing vessels during the First World War. La Bavaisienne is a Bière de Garde. Hops come first, giving an earthy, grassy aroma with a hop-sack spiciness. The texture is full and malty, there's toffee, toasted nuts, cereal, and bread, and there's also some phenolic yeast action, adding a waft of smoke in the background. The bitterness eases in but doesn't leave it dry, keeping a fullness that's satisfying and loin-girding, a cap doff to the days of the style's liquid-bread necessity. A hint of farmhouse mustiness makes it especially good with farmhouse cheeses, cured meat, and fresh bread.

Dark Star Saison

Brighton, England
ABV: 4.5%
Hops: Saaz, Styrian Goldings, Belgian Goldings

Dark Star make some of the best beers in Britain and this is one of my favorites. Every year I wait for it to be released (it's a summer special) and then begins my mission to search all the pubs I know until I find it—at which point I order a pint, sit down, drink it, and then order another one. Taking the Dupont yeast, head brewer Mark Tranter creates a cool mix of Belgian and British flavors with a smooth body, some estery fruit, orange pith, peppery hops, lovely orchard and stone fruits, and a glugging drinkability. Served on cask, it's soft, round, and spicy and has a fullness from the low carbonation; served on keg, it gets livelier and sharper with a fizz that pushes the hops out and makes it lighter and brighter. A fantastic, low-strength interpretation of a Saison.

De Glazen Toren Saison d'Erpe-Mere

Aalst, Belgium
ABV: 6.9%
Hops: Saaz, Magnum, Hallertauer Mittelfrüh

This beer comes wrapped in paper. Like most things wrapped in paper—fish and chips or birthday presents—it's very good. When two would-be friends, Jef Van Den Steen and Dirk De Pauw, met at Erpe-Mere's town hall in 1988, they probably didn't realize the future they had together... After starting to homebrew, they enrolled on a brewing course, graduating as brewmasters in 1994. Following a search for the location and kit, they opened their brewery in 2004 and Saison d'Erpe-Mere was the first beer they produced. Hazy yellow in color and an aroma that is as intoxicating as a pretty perfume: there's lemon, apples, pineapple, coconut, and tropical fruit, plus a grassy earthiness and farmhouse funk. Gentle, soft, and light to drink, it's got a gorgeous, elegant texture and quenching fizz. A wonderful gift of a beer.

Hill Farmstead Arthur

Greensboro, Vermont
ABV: 6.0%
Hops: Varies—includes Saaz,
East Kent Goldings

Hill Farmstead. Say those two words and beer-geek knees get weak. They are a brewery with hype behind them: difficult to get hold of, much searched for, and renowned for farmhouse styles and hoppy beers. Arthur is an incredible Saison. It's one of those beers that you drink, sit back, and just wonder what these guys are doing that no one else can achieve. The joy in Arthur is the light, floating, gliding mouthfeel—I've never had a beer quite like it. It's got a beautiful, delicate fruit aroma of apples, apricot, and peach; there's a hint of spice from the yeast; the malt whispers a passing compliment ("You look good today" or "I love your shirt"), but it's all about how this one feels when you drink it—that impossible lightness is astonishing (they use their own well water; perhaps it's enchanted). Hype them up and hunt the beer down.

Del Ducato New Morning

Soragna, Italy
ABV: 5.8%
Hops: East Kent Goldings, Saaz, Chinook

A beer inspired by spring, that hopeful time of year when the world around us comes back to life, stretching out from its winter slumber. The Saison style fits that idea perfectly: there's just something about it that sings of freshness like a cool ephemeral breeze, like dew on grass, like blossom. It's the briskness in the carbonation, the fleeting poke of livening spice, the fresh floral aroma, and the grassiness of hops. New Morning, named after Bob Dylan's song, is spiced and scented with wild flowers, camomile, ground coriander, green peppercorns, and ginger. It's rounded, subtle, and clean, and the camomile gives a dozy sweetness, the pepper perks it up, and the flowers evoke honeysuckle and blossom; there's a hint of citrus, an appropriately crisp body and finish, and a vibrant, smile-inducing loveliness to it. One to drink outside while the flowers unfurl and the sun warms your skin.

Stillwater Artisanal Ales Cellar Door

Baltimore, Maryland
ABV: 6.6%
Hops: Sterling, Citra

Brian Strumke, the man behind Stillwater, has brewed with other people all around the world, making one-off rarities and specials alongside a small range of regular beers, all with a farmhouse influence. He's at the forefront of the fashionable gypsy-brewing movement, which is creating rock-star reputations for brewers who don't own a mash tun but take up tank-time with others or collaborate on new brews. Cellar Door is an American farmhouse ale made with white sage. A pale hazy gold, with a floral, fruity, herbal aroma that calls you in to the delicate body, there's a prickle of carbonation, and plenty of yeast spice and depth. The sage makes it wonderfully appetizing, leaving me craving pork bahn mi or Asian steamed buns. The juicy hops give an uplifting fruitiness and freshness to create a new take on this old style.

SEASONAL DRINKING

My thirst is evocatively attached to the weather as we gradually roll through the year and pass through the seasons. The beer I choose in January is not the same as the one I call for in July, while the satisfaction had from satiating a specific type of thirst is hard to beat.

The beer calendar's most seasonal product is green-hopped beer. Like the rarest of foods, green-hopped beers appear once a year in each hemisphere and last for just the briefest of moments. Hops are usually harvested and then dried immediately. Speed is important because otherwise the hops start to oxidize and deteriorate in flavor. By drying and tightly packing them together, the hops can happily last a year until the next season's fresh crop is ready. Green hop, fresh hop, or wet hop beers take the flowers straight from bine to kettle, thus bypassing the drying process. Brewers located close to hop farms can be there on the day of harvest, collect their sacks of hops, and speed back to the brewhouse. The beers made from these fresh hops are unique products that are specific to a certain moment. Green hops don't have the intensified flavor of dried ones; instead, they are grassier and more delicate, and give a flavor very different from the usual—think about the difference between fresh tomatoes and slowly roasted ones. That's the kind of difference that applies to green versus dried hops.

After September's green rush comes a darkening of brews as the colors of the pints match the leaves on the trees, turning through gold to red and then brown. Hedgerow fruit and earthiness come into the beers until we pass by the smoke of bonfires and into the roasty flavor of winter, spiked with festive spices, stronger to warm against the cold outside, and a real boost against the dreary dark skies. The beers are a reflection inside the glass of what's happening outside, personifying the seasons, the mentality, the feelings, the flavors.

Gradually, hopefully, wonderfully, spring arrives again with a breath of freshness, of life, of brightness and green, and the beers follow suit. Now they're golden and bright, zingy and vibrant with the hops harvested just a few months before. As spring warms into summer, the beers relax, lose their edge of bitterness, and gain a gulping kind of conviviality designed for sharing with friends while sitting outside. And then we lead back into the harvest, the green hops, the darkening days of fall, and the cycle repeats.

The link between sky, glass, and plate is also relevant. This seasonal evolution of tastes extends to what we eat—spring salads work well with bright Pale Ales; Kölsch is the perfect summer beer to drink while grilling meat on the barbecue; Brown Ales work beautifully with the pumpkins of fall; and Stouts complement the hearty stews of winter.

Sure, we all drink Stouts in summer and Wit in winter, but nothing quenches the thirst quite like a beer that tastes like the world around it.

FLEMISH BRUIN AND FLANDERS RED

THESE BROWN AND RED BEERS, ORIGINATING IN BELGIUM, MAY ALSO BE PREFIXED WITH "OUD." BOTH ARE ALES FERMENTED IN TANKS, THEN AGED TO DEVELOP A SWEET-AND-SOUR, VINOUS CHARACTER THAT IS MORE ACETIC (VINEGAR) THAN THEIR ACIDIC (LEMON) NEIGHBORS OF LAMBICS AND GUEUZE. THE SHARPNESS IN THESE BEERS COMES FROM WILD YEAST AND BACTERIA, AS WELL AS THE EFFECTS OF AN EXTENDED AGING TIME—BROWNS ARE AGED IN TANK WHEREAS REDS ARE AGED IN OAK BARRELS. BATCHES COULD BE MATURED FOR UP TO TWO YEARS, AND, KEY TO THE STYLES, YOUNG AND OLD BEERS ARE BLENDED BEFORE PACKAGING TO GET A PERFECT BALANCE OF SOUR AND SWEET. THESE ARE DISTINCTLY FRUITY STYLES, AND BOTH ARE ALSO USED AS BASES FOR MAKING FRUIT BEERS, MOST OFTEN WITH CHERRIES.

Color for both is on the red-brown-burgundy scale. ABV is 4.5–8.0%, with low hop aroma and bitterness (under 25 IBUs) giving way to wood tannin and sourness. Flavor comes from malt, yeast, bacteria, and the aging time, and you can expect fruity, complex beers: reds have fruity esters, vinous depth, cherries, plums, raisins, wood, and an acetic richness; browns typically have more malt characters, no oak, and less sourness than reds, although the styles can converge and blur as they move in mash tuns around the world. Balance is key with these beers: it's about the right blend of sweet, young beer with sour, aged beer.

RODENBACH FOEDERBIER

ROESELARE, BELGIUM
ABV: 6.0%
HOPS: BELGIAN HOPS FROM POPERINGE

CLASSIC

Rodenbach is the classic Flanders Red. The beer is brewed and conditioned for four weeks in tank and then transferred into one of Rodenbach's 300 huge oak vats called foeders (some of which date back to the 1830s) to mature for up to two years in the vast cellars. These vats range in size from 3,700 US gallons (14,000 liters) to a whopping 17,200 US gallons (65,000 liters). The microorganisms inherent in the wood create the sourness, which goes acetic instead of acidic. In the standard Rodenbach, there are three parts fresh beer blended to one part aged, and it's also sweetened. You get a little smooth sharpness but mostly wood, cherries, vanilla, and something freshly floral. Foederbier is available near the brewery only, and is the unfiltered, unsweetened beer pulled straight from the barrels. Sharper, richer, and more woody and intense, it's best tasted on Roeselare's central plaza, with a croque monsieur and a bowl of frites.

New Belgium La Folie

Fort Collins, Colorado
ABV: 6.0%
Hops: Target

If you like getting your mind blown, then go to New Belgium's brewery and see the sour program they've got going on. It's incredible. La Folie is their most famous Wild ale. It's called a "sour brown," but is matured like a red, a link to brewmaster Peter Bouckaert, who used to work at Rodenbach before moving to Fort Collins. La Folie is aged in big, tall oak barrels like the foeders from Belgium. In 2012, they shifted their brewery around to accommodate more foeders (increasing to 28 tanks), including some very big ones at 5,800 US gallons (21,900 liters). La Folie is a blend of one- to three-year-old beer. Cherry, plum, apple, and oak come first, the body is rich with texture, rounded with caramel and chewy malts, and an acetic edge, giving a kick of sharpness, more cherries, more wood, more apples, and spice.

Panil Barriquée Sour

Parma, Italy
ABV: 8.0%
Hops: Perle, East Kent Goldings

An oak-aged sour red, this is fermented in tank first, then it moves to cognac barrels for the next burst of fermentation, and then gets a final fizzing flourish with a third fermentation in the bottle. Deep copper-red, fruit comes first with a platter of cranberries, plums, cherries, and the raisin notes of aged beer and cognac combining. Then comes a light balsamic acetic edge, plus oak depth and a definite tang of refreshing sourness. It's really textured to drink, with beer, barrel, and bacteria all doing different things, but bringing them together like three tenors belting out a ballad. Softly acetic, it adds depth instead of a harsh throat-kick, and it's all softened with more red fruit, tannic and savory wood dryness, a hint of sweetness, and a depth of cognac. It's the sort of beer that makes you hungry, giving you a little of all the five tastes.

Cascade Sang Noir

Portland, Oregon
ABV: 9.2%

Did you ever have daydreams as a kid that you'd get locked in a store overnight and could just eat everything, run around, and do amazing knee slides down the aisles while no one was watching? I did. The grown-up version of that is getting locked in Cascade Brewery's Barrel House with only a glass and maybe a partner in crime (to help reach the high-up barrels). Cascade make some of the most interesting and excellent soured beers in America using a variety of barrels, fruits, blends, and styles. Sang Noir is a Double Red, aged in bourbon and Pinot Noir barrels, and then blended with cherries. Sounds good? It is. Loads of cherry, an acetic kick, sharp wine notes, vanilla and oak, caramel, and a tartness rounded by the bourbon. It's the kind of beer that makes you hug the bartender for suggesting it to you (and then hide under the table until they lock up so you can sneak into the barrel room).

LAMBIC AND GUEUZE

THESE ARE ACIDIC, DRY, BARREL-AGED BEERS SPECIFIC TO THE PAJOTTENLAND REGION OF BELGIUM, WHICH RINGS AROUND AND TO THE SOUTH AND WEST OF BRUSSELS. THERE, NATURAL AIRBORNE YEASTS ARE READY TO JUMP INTO BEER TANKS, HAVE A WILD FEAST ON SUGAR, AND TURN BARRELS OF BEER SOUR. BEFORE YEAST WAS CULTURED AND CULTIVATED, AND BEFORE BREWERS HAD A SCIENTIFIC UNDERSTANDING OF FERMENTATION, MOST BEER PROBABLY HAD AN ACIDIC DEPTH THROUGH WILD YEAST; LAMBIC AND GUEUZE ARE INTENTIONALLY SOUR.

Brewed with up to 40 per cent unmalted wheat, these beers go through a traditional process of mash tun, and then kettle (the hops added are aged hops, there for preservative qualities not bitterness or aroma). After that the beer is moved into a large, wide pan called a "coolship," which is left open to the air outside (usually through holes in the roof), where it cools and welcomes in the airborne yeast and bacteria, which start a spontaneous fermentation—meaning fermentation occurs without yeast being physically added by a brewer. The beer is then transferred to wooden barrels and left for one to three years. The fermentation process is complex and occurs in phases: alcohol, acidity, and then depth of wild yeast flavor.

Lambic is a straight beer, unblended, and served uncarbonated—it's rare to find Lambic, and you need to drink it near to where it's made. Gueuze is a blend of different vintages of Lambic, mixing one-, two-, and three-year-old barrels to create the right balance. Gueuze is carbonated—the young beer in the blend still contains sugars, which start another fermentation in the bottle and this creates the Champagne fizz that the style is famous for. This carbonation takes another few months to develop in the bottle, so the beer is packaged and left in the brewery until ready. Faro is a gently sweetened version of Lambic, so if you like it less sharp, try this. Fruit is regularly added to Lambic, but watch out for artificially sweetened varieties, which can be saccharine or lack the puckering punch of the style.

As complex as beers come, these are very dry, sharply acidic, textured, refreshing, and sometimes challenging to those unfamiliar with the cheek-puckering tartness. The hops used will have been aged for a few years and give oxidized, cheesy, farm-like flavors; the barrel gives oak and tannin; the bacteria and yeast make it acidic and funky with many layers of depth. Once you develop a taste for these beers, you'll want them more and more. As styles, they threatened to disappear as recently as the 1990s, but they are now among the most-loved and most-craved beers in the world, with breweries trying to replicate the sharpness and complexity of Lambic and Gueuze.

CANTILLON LAMBIC

BRUSSELS, BELGIUM
ABU: 5.0%
HOPS: AGED HOPS (THREE YEARS)

CLASSIC

You have to go to Cantillon Brewery. Whether you love sour beers or can't get your tongue around them, just go there. This working beer museum, complete with 19th-century brewing vessels, is inconspicuous from the Brussels side street. The aroma as you walk around is incredible and intoxicating: rich, fruity, woody, vinous, old, mystifying: the sweet smell of fermentation. Barrels squeezed in everywhere, dark worn wood, mold creeping up the walls, cobwebs around dusty skylights; an air filled with life. The Lambic, which has had about 18 months in barrel, is poured burnished gold and still from a pitcher. It has lemon sharpness in the aroma, along with apple and a farm-like earthiness, and it's so smooth to drink; there's a hint of residual sweetness and then comes a quenching kind of lip-smacking acidity followed by a dry, woody finish, which gives a rough, unpolished intensity. Complex, balanced, unrivaled. Go to Cantillon.

Tilquin Gueuze Draft

Rebecq, Belgium
ABV: 4.8%
Hops: Blend of aged hops

Tilquin doesn't have a physical brewhouse. Instead, it's a "gueuzerie," or blender, meaning they buy wort (which has had enough time for the wild yeast to get into it) from different Lambic breweries nearby and then ferment it in empty barrels that they've bought separately from vineyards. Then, a few years later, Tilquin create their own blends between all of the barrels. The draft version is delicate and refreshing, easy drinking, and approachable, yet still mind-bogglingly complex; it's got a Granny Smith apple sharpness, lots of fruitiness, a clean and soft acidity, a hint of spritz, a sherbet-like sweetness, and a savory, woody depth at the end. In the middle of the mouthful it threatens to pucker, but then it suddenly mellows, dropping like a curveball, and rounds out all the flavors. There's also a bottled version called Oude Gueuze Tilquin à l'Ancienne which is 6.0% ABV; both versions are really fantastic.

Allagash Coolship

Portland, Maine
ABV: Varies

Ask a Lambic brewer if you can make Lambic outside of the Pajottenland region and they'll quickly fire back a "no." There's something special in the air there, for sure, but wild yeast strains are everywhere and it's possible to make spontaneously fermented beer around the world. Taking the Belgian inspiration, Allagash installed a coolship in their brewery in 2008 where they've made a number of spontaneously fermented beers, catching the microflora overnight before going into barrels until they're ready. The first brews hit bottles in 2011 and more are coming. Beers like this are the ultimate link to the surroundings, a romantic notion that the local air holds something definitive of a place, and Allagash are trying to capture that essence. Very rare, these beers give unique tastes of a precise space in the world, and combined with the patience needed to wait years until they're ready and the skills of good blending, I think that's pretty exciting.

WILD BEER AND SOUR ALES

FOLLOWING THE PASSIONATE POPULARITY OF LAMBIC AND GUEUZE, WORLD BREWERS HAVE TRIED TO MAKE THEIR OWN INTENTIONALLY SOURED BEERS. IN GENERAL, WILD BEERS, SOUR ALES, OR NEW WORLD SOURS HAVE A DELIBERATE INOCULATION OF SPECIFIC STRAINS OF WILD YEAST (FROM THE BRETTANOMYCES FAMILY) AND SOURING BACTERIA (SUCH AS LACTOBACILLUS AND PEDIOCOCCUS), ALTHOUGH SOME BREWERIES OUTSIDE OF BELGIUM HAVE SUCCESSFULLY STARTED SPONTANEOUS FERMENTATIONS.

These beers follow the Belgian classics in that they are brewed and then aged in barrels; some are fermented in tank and then moved to wood (wine barrels are very popular), while others fully ferment in barrels. Following the practice with Gueuze, these beers are generally blended before packaging, as individual barrels tend to mature differently, even if they have exactly the same thing inside them.

Rules don't apply to this group of beers. The beer could be the palest yellow or the darkest black, under 3.0% ABV or over 12.0% ABV; aged in steel, barrels, or even bottles. Bitterness will usually be very low because bitterness and sourness tend to clash—although exceptions exist. The best in this group are tart but not acetic or vinegary; balanced, dry, refreshing, and complex. Given the nature of these beers, many Wild ales are single-batch beers, which aren't repeated. We can expect to see waves of Sours in the next few years as all the barrels tucked away reach maturity.

Lovibonds Sour Grapes

Henley-on-Thames, England
ABV: 6.0%
Hops: Hersbrücker

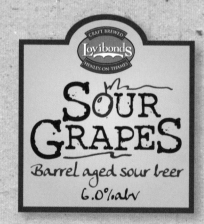

Lovibonds make a pale wheat ale, Henley Gold, which is low in both ABV and hops, and one day a batch caught some bacteria and went sour. Tasting the beer, brewer Jeff Rosenmeier saw its potential (but not before he'd thrown most of it away) and so did others who tried it. When a later batch also soured, Jeff got three French wine barrels and filled them with the beer, adding sour yeast and bacteria. A few years later, in 2012, he's on stage collecting a World Beer Cup gold award for best barrel-aged Sour beer, one of the most coveted categories in the competition. The aroma of the bright-blonde beer is a dream: grapes, citrus, oak, wine, wild yeast, lemons. There's a phenomenal depth of oak, tannin, and tartness plus a smooth creaminess. It's dry and refreshing, light and wonderfully elegant. A very beautiful mistake.

Russian River Temptation

Santa Rosa, California
ABV: 7.5%
Hops: Styrian Goldings (aged), Saaz (aged)

The Russian River beers are regularly listed near to the words "best" or "favorite." It's the mix of brilliance and rarity that does it: the beers all taste great and they are hard to find. Temptation is a Blonde ale aged in Chardonnay barrels and spiked with Brettanmyces, pediococcus, and lactobacillus. It's a pale gold, glistening with bubbles. The aroma gives white wine, wood, citrus, and wild yeast funk. You get the sourness first, a sharp and refreshing shock to the tongue, then you get wine and barrel, and then comes complexity at the end, with a tart yet clean, lingering finish. It's got a fresh, thirst-quenching simplicity to it while also being incredibly complex. Beatification has been spontaneously fermented and is a "Sonambic," as Russian River call it, named after the nearby wine-growing region where the brewery get their barrels.

Captain Lawrence Cuvee de Castleton

Elmsford, New York
ABV: 6.0%

Captain Lawrence make a number of barrel-aged beers. Rosso e Marrone is a Sour ruby ale, matured with red grapes and wild yeast in oak barrels and Golden Delicious is a Belgian Tripel, aged in apple-brandy barrels and dry-hopped with Amarillo to give a boozy, baked-apple-tasting beer with a hint of tartness at the end. Cuvee de Castleton was Captain Lawrence's first Sour and it continues to be a favorite. It's a Belgian Blonde aged in French oak with Muscat grapes and wild yeast, and you get a beer that's sharp and sweet, with lemon, grapes, and vanilla oak in the aroma. It's clean and sharp, there's a real dryness to it that emphasizes the wood, and the sourness makes it elegantly refreshing. The brewery is an hour on the train out of New York City. If you can go, then do—the whole range of beers is great, especially Captain's Reserve Imperial IPA.

Cascade The Vine

Portland, Oregon
ABV: 9.73%

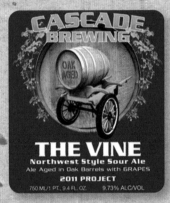

Calling their brews "Northwest style Sours," Cascade give provenance and a new identity to this advancing type of American brewing, which takes inspiration from Belgium and makes it different with the use of new-style base beers, the controlled addition of wild yeast and bacteria, and barrels often sourced locally, including wine and bourbon casks. The Vine is made with pressed white grapes, another popular addition to American Sours, blurring that line between fruit and field. Deep gold in color, there's a sharp, clean, lemon, and grape-skin aroma, farmhouse cider, lots of barrel depth (it gets 12 months in barrel and then another three with the grapes), a rounded, slick, and still-sweet middle balances the sharpness, and then there's more grape and lemon at the end. It's refreshing and astonishingly light given the high ABV.

The Bruery Tart of Darkness

Placentia, California
ABV: 5.6%
Hops: Saaz

The Bruery are one of America's top breweries for their use of barrels and bacteria alongside their fantastic non-sour beers. At the end of 2012 they had an astonishing 3,000 barrels in their cellar, making up around 20 different beers (including bourbon barrels and non-sour beers). Those barrels are maturing slowly and we can be excited about what will eventually leave them. Tart of Darkness is a stout that goes into old bourbon barrels (which previously held Black Tuesday, The Bruery's famous barrel-aged Imperial Stout) with souring bacteria and wild yeast. It's one of those beers that baffles your brain: it looks like it'll taste of chocolate but it smells like lemon, cherry, vanilla, and fruity coffee; there's sourness, then roast, then bourbon, then oak, and it ends tart and dry. A dark, wild rollercoaster of a beer and one of the few Sour Stouts.

Feral Brewing Watermelon Warhead

Swan Valley, Western Australia
ABV: Varies
Hops: Varies

In 2012, Feral Brewing and Nail Brewing decided to pool resources and buy a bigger brewery together, sharing the facilities as both try to make more beer for the thirsty Australian market. With the move, Feral kept their original kit and turned it into Australia's first dedicated Sour brewery. Feral have already released a number of Sours, including the sharply, deliciously refreshing Watermelon Warhead Berliner Weisse (made with locally grown fruit and matured in Chardonnay barrels); the Sour red Dark Funk (also aged in wine barrels), and they've even produced Swanambic, a spontaneously fermented beer from the lively local microflora. Given the time it takes to make some of these beers, it's lucky that Feral already have a bunch of barrels—they are in a wine-making region, so there's access to barrels—souring away, ready to be joined by a whole lot more of them.

LoverBeer BeerBera

Marentino, Italy
ABV: 8.0%

Mixing the grape and the grain, in attitude and recipes, Italian brewers are developing ranges of Wild ales quicker than other brewing countries. With an abundance of barrels and a taste for tart fruitiness, that's no surprise. BeerBera is the midpoint between beer and wine. Brewed like a regular beer, it transfers from the kettle into oak vats where crushed Barbera grapes are added and the beer spontaneously ferments thanks to natural yeast on the grape skins. It pours a purple-brown and you get grapes straight away with dark fruit and sour plums, and then there's a barnyard kind of earthiness alongside the oak. It's vinous to drink; the sharpness of grapes and wild yeast meets the rounded body of malt; there's a poky carbonation; then a sharp hit of berry-like sourness. Interesting, different, and a drink that transcends beer and wine glasses in a great way. An appetite-arousing aperitivo.

BELGIAN INFLUENCE

When I started drinking beer, and taking notice of the differences between each one, it was Belgian beers that I regarded as the best: exciting, unusual, varied, and—this part caught our intrepid eyes—strong. We used to drink in the Belgian Bar, in Ramsgate, in England. It's by the sea, close enough to France so that you can sometimes see the mainland across the English Channel, meaning you can almost see Belgium.

Belgium was tantalizingly close and yet the beers we drank in that bar were so far away from the beers brewed around us, making them wonderfully exotic and different. Getting a taste for Belgian beers was like the ultimate of beer drinking, as we opened bottles painted with pink elephants, puckered up against the sourness of Gueuze, laughed at our precocity to be drinking a beer that was over 10.0% ABV, squared up to devilish Golden Ales, enjoyed fruit beers, spiced beers, beers brewed by monks, blonde beers, brown beers, white beers, red beers. Surely this was beer utopia?

But then our thirst took a sharp turn west as we noticed the punk-rock chords of American craft beer. Forget the subtle complexity of European beer, we wanted our senses to be abused by American hops. We chased those craft beers and the Belgian beers started to look dated on the beer shelves, soon to be replaced with bright new bottles from farther away.

But a change was happening in America, and we hadn't tasted it yet. It was led by New Belgium, Ommegang, Russian River, Allagash, and Lost Abbey, among other breweries, all making faithful interpretations and remixes of Belgian styles. Soon more and more craft brewers started to make their own versions of these styles. Before this, those beer styles were almost untouchable: they were classic, nation-defining beers and brewing them in America was like trying to copy a Da Vinci. But once some had tried and succeeded, others wanted to do the same, and Belgian beers were no longer hallowed. It became okay to brew them, then it became necessary, and then it became exciting to develop them.

Evolving thirsts, inspirations, and styles mean that there's always something "in" right now. IPA, bourbon barrel-aging, Sour beer (inspired by Lambic and Gueuze), and wine barrel-aging have all been there (and stayed popular). Saison was the beer *du jour* for a while as breweries spiked that dry, effervescent spiciness with fruity American hops. Then someone decided to ferment their IPA with a Belgian yeast, getting funky flavors behind the hops. More styles arrived: Tripels showed off brewing skills but also shared the booze and hop-kick of a Double IPA; Quadrupels added another strong beer to the portfolio; Witbier was everywhere; funking yeast stopped freaking brewers out. And other countries around the world starting making Belgian styles—Italian brewers made some of the best—and this knocked back into Belgium. Belgian breweries took American hops and used them in their own beers, giving new flavor profiles to classic styles. And the overall effect was that the classic styles became even more revered: imitations and inspirations led to an increased desire for the originals.

Belgian beer is now influencing so many others around the world, whether it's spontaneous fermentation, monastic tradition, strong golden Duvel, or sharp dry Dupont. Far from falling from fashion, Belgian beer is creating the latest trends. And their brewers are returning the compliment by brewing American-style Pale Ale and IPAs.

FRUIT BEERS

IN BELGIUM, AMONG THE LAMBIC AND GUEUZE BREWERS AND BLENDERS, IT'S POPULAR TO ADD FRUIT TO BARRELS. CHERRY (KRIEK) AND RASPBERRY (FRAMBOISE) ARE THE TWO CLASSICS, BUT YOU'LL FIND MANY OTHERS ARE USED. IN THE BEST BELGIAN VERSIONS, THE LAMBIC HAS ALREADY BEEN MATURED FOR UP TO TWO YEARS BEFORE THE FRUIT IS ADDED; WITH THE FRUIT GOING INTO A BEER THAT IS STILL FILLED WITH HUNGRY YEAST, THE FRUIT'S FERMENTABLE SUGARS KICK ON FURTHER FERMENTATION AND ACTION IN THE BARREL, WHERE THE BEER WILL STAY FOR ANOTHER YEAR OR MORE.

Away from Belgium, fruit is also popular in Sour and non-sour beers. Any fruit can be used and it can get into the beer in many forms: whole and fresh, frozen, puréed, syrup, or extract. The fruit may join the brew at many stages of the process: sometimes added like late hops (end of boil, whirlpool, during fermentation, or in tank after fermentation) or sometimes blended into the beer before packaging. All combinations are capable of producing good beers; just watch out for syrupy, unnatural-tasting fruit from syrup or extract.

Collected here are beers made with fresh fruit. Look out for notes of pips, skin, or stone, plus ester-like flavors that are natural in the fruits. The beer could be tart, fresh, sweet, or delicate and the fruit should be one part of the beer and not the overpowering flavor.

DRIE FONTEINEN SCHAERBEEKSE KRIEK

CLASSIC

BEERSEL, BELGIUM
ABV: 6.0%
HOPS: AGED HOPS

Schaerbeekse are tart, sour cherries that grow in the Lambic-making region around Brussels. At one time they would've been the variety that all Kriek producers used, but now more readily available cherry varieties have replaced this one. Thankfully, Drie Fonteinen still make a Kriek with Schaerbeekse, though it's hard to find. It's deep pink in the glass and you get cherry right away, but it's subtle and delicate alongside a floral, blossomy aroma and some almond and vanilla. Sharply acidic, the cherry bobs along in the background, adding depth and just a hint of fruitiness, as if you've caught the aroma of a cherry tree on a warm breeze—it's not more than that, so don't open this expecting sweet cherry juice. This beer ages really well (so if you manage to find it, get a few), giving berry or plum-like fruit while retaining the sharpness.

Upland Strawberry Lambic

Bloomington, Indiana
ABV: 6.0%
Hops: Hallertauer (aged three years)

Upland make eight fruited Lambics. Eight! Brewed like a Belgian Lambic, the base beer gets a turbid mash of unmalted wheat, aged hops in the kettle, and is put in oak barrels with yeast and bacteria where it's left for as long as necessary to get the right acidity. At this point the fruit goes in, furthering the fermentation process. A few months later the beers are ready to go. The eight (eight!) fruits Upland use are strawberry, raspberry, cherry, kiwi, persimmon, blueberry, blackberry, and peach. The kiwi is particularly interesting, giving a tropical, floral depth to the sharpness, but I like the strawberry for the sharp, berry-seed depth, which adds its own tannic quality—subtle fruit, fresh, and naturally tart. All the beers are dry, sour, lip-puckering, and funkier than most, and definitely on the rustic side of things, which I like a lot.

Baird Brewing
Temple Garden Yuzu Ale

Shizuoka, Japan
ABV: 5.5%
Hops: Motueka, New Zealand Cascade, Santium

Made with yuzu, a Japanese citrus fruit, picked in a temple near to Baird's Brewery, this beer contains rye and wheat in the malt makeup, giving a smooth and spicy depth to the amber brew. The local citrus comes out straightaway—delicate lemon and grapefruit, grapes, floral honey, and some mineral botanic notes. It's dry to drink, there's plenty of citrus, tropical and floral hop flavor, which complements the yuzu and emphasizes its tartness. The fruit goes in as peel and juice, and both elements come through— one is pithy and dry, while the other is bright and sharp. Baird also make a Shizuoka Summer Mikan Ale and The Carpenter's Mikan Ale with locally grown mikan, a sweet and sour, grapefruit-like fruit. At the end of the year, you'll also find Jubilation, a celebratory beer brewed with cinnamon and Japanese figs. The use of local fruits gives the Baird beers a great link to their location.

Upright Fantasia

Portland, Oregon
ABV: 5.75%
Hops: Crystal (aged)

Appropriately named after the musical term for an improvised piece not following any classic style, Fantasia is a limited-release beer made with fresh peaches grown in an orchard close to the brewery. The peaches are chopped up, de-stoned, and then added to oak barrels, which the brewery source from local vineyards. The beer is brewed with barley (not unmalted wheat as in the Lambic style) and aged hops before it meets the peaches in the barrel where it's fermented with Saison yeast plus Brettanomyces and lactobacillus. A few weeks after the yeast has kicked off, the barrels (which were three-quarters filled) are topped up with a different Upright beer and then it gets a year of maturation time. You get the peach plus apricot and lemon, the tartness is refined and refreshing, and there's vanilla and a smooth creaminess before the dry, quenching finish. It's as interesting and beguiling as the label.

Russian River Supplication

Santa Rosa, California
ABV: 7.0%
Hops: Styrian Golding (aged), Saaz (aged)

I have a small suitcase decorated with brewery stickers, which I use when I'm traveling in Europe. I bought that suitcase on the same street as Russian River's brewpub because I got over-excited on my first beer trip to America and I bought way too many bottles to bring home. Now, whenever I see that battered little case, I think of Supplication—the beer I drank after getting my nice new case. Ruby-red in color, Supplication is a Brown Ale aged in Pinot Noir barrels with sour cherries and the typical tarting threesome of Brettanomyces, lactobacillus, and pediococcus. You get the funk first, a lift of lemon, and then come the sharp cherries along with almond and vanilla, followed closely by the barrel and wine—berries, oak, and spices. You could sit and sniff this one all day, but don't because the taste is even better: tart and dry, yet smooth and lush with fruit.

Goose Island Juliet

Chicago, Illinois
ABV: 8.0%
Hops: Pilgrim

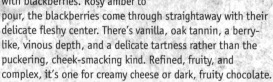

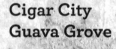

Goose Island have the biggest barrel program in America and walking around the brewery there's evidence of it in every corner: a barrel sitting by the side, a room with unbunged barrels ready to be filled with beer, separate tanks just for the funky yeasts. If you get into the barrel room, you'll be surrounded by a castle of casks and your nose will get the most glorious treat from the evocative, intoxicating aromas of wood, the sweet smell of slow fermentation, red wine, bourbon, vanilla, and red fruit. Juliet is fermented with wild yeast and aged in Cabernet barrels with blackberries. Rosy amber to pour, the blackberries come through straightaway with their delicate fleshy center. There's vanilla, oak tannin, a berry-like, vinous depth, and a delicate tartness rather than the puckering, cheek-smacking kind. Refined, fruity, and complex, it's one for creamy cheese or dark, fruity chocolate.

Cigar City Guava Grove

Tampa, Florida
ABV: 8.0%
Hops: Styrian Bobek, Simcoe

One of the things I like most about beer is when it's a reflection of a specific place. Cigar City shares that same mindset, and their beers showcase the surroundings in great ways, whether that's focusing on their Latino roots, using Spanish cedar to age beers (that's the same wood used to make the cigar boxes that give the area and the brewery their names), or by brewing with the fruit that gave Tampa the nickname of "Big Guava." With a Saison as the base beer, Guava Grove is given a secondary fermentation on pink guava purée and what you get is a beer filled with the fresh-fruit aromas of peach, apricot, lime, guava, and pink grapefruit, plus the clove and pepper spice of the yeast and a camomile floral note. Dry, sharply carbonated, and tart, it's a fruity, refreshing beer, great with fresh seafood from the state's miles of coastline.

Crooked Stave
Wild Wild Brett Indigo

Denver, Colorado
ABV: 7.0%
Hops:
Strisselspalt,
Mittelfrüh,
Cascade

Having studied a
Masters in Brewing
and Distilling, which
focused on wild
yeast, Chad
Yakobson knows
more about Brettanomyces than most and he's happy to
share it: find "The Brettanomyces Project" online to read his
MSc research into brett, which isolated eight strains of the
yeast and investigated their pure culture fermentation to
look for individual characteristics. Now he's using those
strains in his own brewery to produce some wonderful Wild
ales. Part of a 100 per cent brett fermentation series, which
follows the colors of the rainbow, WWBI gets its indigo hue
by being aged with fresh blueberries. It's oak-matured, and
the unique brett strain gives fragrant fruit (think pineapple
and mango), which works magnificently with the light, tart
spiciness of blueberry. There's soft-wood tannin, pepper,
mellow funk, a subtle, teasing background of berry,
and an elegant dry finish. The beers at Crooked Stave
are special and if you want brett-brewed beers,
then this is the place to go.

Whitstable Raspberry Wheat

Whitstable, Kent
ABV: 5.2%
Hops: Perle

There are a few places in the
world where I just love to
drink and the Whitstable
Brewery Bar is one of
them. A relaxed, sparse
shack by day (turning
into a club by night),
it sits on the beach,
making it a great
summer drinking spot.
Whitstable is an English
seaside town in Kent,
which is famous for
oysters, and it's one of my
favorite towns to wander
around before sitting on the
pebble beach outside the Brewery
Bar, staring happily out to sea. They make a Saaz-hopped
Pilsner and an East Kent India Pale Ale, but I love the
Raspberry Wheat on a hot day. It's deep pink, with a
background whisper of lemon juice, and raspberry pips
add a little refreshing tartness at the end—it doesn't taste
like a punnet of raspberries, though; instead, it's clean
and subtle, as if the fruit is feeling shy. Best drunk on the
beach from plastic cups.

Cantillon Fou' Foune

Brussels, Belgium
ABV: 5.0%
Hops: Aged hops (three years)

Cantillon only use whole fruit in their beers and they use a lot of them:
7oz (200g) of fresh fruit per 2 US pints (1 liter) of beer. They have a
Kriek with a teasing, just-there background sweetness of cherry and a
Framboise which bites like raspberry pips in your teeth. Fou' Foune is
made with apricots: skin on, stones in, just cut in half and added to the
barrel. The yeast chomp away all the flesh and leave just the stone at the
end. In return, you get an elegant depth of apricot, a floral and honeyed
creaminess that blends with the Lambic sharpness in an incredible way.
It's not sweet, it's still sharp, there's an earthiness, a pith and stone
character, some funk, and oak. It's too easy to liken this beer to
Champagne, but that's too flattering to the fizz: this is extraordinary.

PALE AND HOPPY SESSION BEER

IN THE UNITED KINGDOM, PALE BEERS, LOW IN ALCOHOL AND HIGH IN HOP FLAVOR AND AROMA, OFTEN FROM AMERICAN AND SOUTHERN HEMISPHERE HOPS, ARE TAKING OVER BAR TOPS. THE LOVE FOR AMERICAN PALE ALES AND THEIR CITRUS AND FRUIT-FORWARD HOPS, COMBINED WITH THE BRITISH DRINKING CULTURE OF GOING TO THE PUB AND SINKING A FEW PINTS, HAS PUSHED THESE BEERS AHEAD AND CREATED A NEW BRITISH BEER STYLE. IN MANY WAYS, IT'S A GREAT TEST OF A BREWER: CAN YOU LOAD FLAVOR INTO A LOW-ABV BEER AND KEEP BODY, BALANCE, AND DRINKABILITY? GO TO ANY BRITISH BEER BAR AND YOU'LL FIND A LINE OF BREWERS DOING A WONDERFUL JOB AT THIS STYLE.

Hitting somewhere between 3.0 and 4.0% ABV, these beers, pale straw to gold in color, are made to be refreshing, light in body, powerfully hopped, dryly bitter, and drunk all day long. Bitterness can be very high set against the lightness of alcohol, reaching 50 plus IBUs, although typically it'll be in the 30s. The malt tries to hide in the background, often giving just a hint of biscuit or light caramel. It's the hops that elevate this from a Golden Mild or Bitter: brightly aromatic, full of fruitiness, and often crisply bitter at the end with a dryness that makes you want to drink more—it's that combination of huge hop flavor and the quenching bitterness that best defines these beers. They are modern British beers at their best and the style has kicked off around the world due to a general desire for flavorsome, low-alcohol brews.

Moor Revival

Somerset, England
ABV: 3.8%
Hops: Columbus, Cascade

Justin Hawke is an American transplant to the moors of Somerset where he brews a superb range of modern British styles, including some fantastic pale and hoppy beers, a session black IPA, and the tremendous JJJ IPA, a 9.0% IPA Barley-Wine beast. Revival is perhaps an oxymoron of a name, as this beer is leading the way for the new style—it was one of the originals and it's still one of the best. It's 3.8% on cask and 4.0% in the bottle, but this gorgeous, hazy orange gold beer drinks the same: the aroma bursts out of the glass with tropical fruit, pineapple, mango, grapefruit pith, and mandarin. It's light in body but strong enough to hold it all together and elevate the hops with the beer, finishing quenchingly, refreshingly dry, making you want a whole lot Moor. Also look for Nor'Hop (American-hopped) or So'Hop (New-Zealand-hopped), both 4.1% ABV, ultra pale, and ultra hoppy.

Uinta Brewing Wyld

Salt Lake City, Utah
ABV: 4.0%
Hops: Simcoe

There are some complicated alcohol laws in Salt Lake City: a beer of 4.1% ABV and upward counts as "heavy" and has different laws from a "standard" beer of 4.0% ABV and under. It's no surprise then that when you look at the strengths of the Uinta beers many of them are exactly 4.0% ABV, although there are wonderful exceptions, such as Hop Notch IPA (7.3% ABV—a beer introduced in 2011 that was so popular the brewery had to buy new tanks just to keep up with the demand for it) and Dubhe Imperial Black IPA (9.2% ABV). Wyld is an extra Pale Ale and it delivers big in the flavor and aroma departments: apricot, peach, blossom, and orange pith; it's got a lovely elegance, a lightness that's neither weak nor underwhelming, a smooth creaminess, and a quenching finish. It's also certified organic, and the beers are made with 100 per cent renewable power.

Matuška Fast Ball

Broumy, Czech Republic
ABV: 3.8%
Hops: Citra, Columbus, Cascade

This is a 9° American Pale Ale and that's the sort of beer that stands out in the Czech Republic—there aren't many Pale Ales and there definitely aren't many 9° beers. But then there aren't many breweries like Matuška. With a great range of Pale Ales and IPAs, Matuška is one of the leading small breweries in the Czech Republic. If you want to drink these beers, go to Prague, which has a few craft-beer bars (Zlý časy should be your first stop), showcasing the growing number of exciting new breweries. Fast Ball is a hazy pale gold, the hops fly forward with citrus, pepper, peach, and floral aromas, which are backed up with smooth, toasty malt. It's light and clean, fragrant and refreshing, loaded with flavor, body, and a sharp bitterness to finish—it's a game-winning fastball flung right in the middle of the strike zone.

Cromarty Happy Chappy

Cromarty, Scotland
ABV: 4.1%
Hops: Columbus, Cascade, Nelson Sauvin, Willamette

One of Scotland's many exciting small breweries, Cromarty have come out firing hops in all directions from their start a few days before Christmas in 2011. Bright and bold-looking, they make a modern selection of styles from Brewed Awakening (4.7% ABV), a coffee-infused Stout, to Red Rocker (5.0% ABV), an American-hopped Rye, to Rogue Wave (5.7% ABV), an extra Pale Ale. Then there's Hit the Lip (3.8% ABV) and Happy Chappy, both pale and hoppy, light in color and body, and heavy in fragrant hops—they are great examples of this new British beer style. Happy Chappy pours a golden color and the body is gentle and smooth, allowing for maximum hop exposure, which gives grapefruit, berries, and floral, and a grassy dryness at the end.

Hawkshead Windermere Pale

Cumbria, England
ABV: 3.5%
Hops: Citra, Goldings, Bramling Cross, Fuggles

"Beer from the heart of the lakes," is Hawkshead's tagline as they are set in one of England's most beautiful areas: the Lake District. Trying to make the most of their location, in 2011 Hawkshead opened a Beer Hall on the side of the brewery. A bright, airy, and modern drinking spot with a great food menu, it's the best place to try all the Hawkshead beers. When you go, start with the Windermere Pale, named after the famous lake nearby. This brew is super pale and super hoppy—mango, grapes, and grapefruit—and has a fresh, English-hop grassiness reminiscent of the expanse of green surrounding the brewery. It's got a delicate body and then a ripping hop flavor, and that's what makes it such an enjoyable beer—it's the sort of beer that makes you pray for rain (which you can almost guarantee you'll get) so that you can stay for another.

Ca l'Arenys Guineu Riner

Valls De Torroella, Spain
ABV: 2.5%
Hops: Amarillo

A low-alcohol American Pale Ale brewed in Spain, Guinea Riner is a brilliant achievement, which brings together big hops (the brewery says a whopping 93 IBUs) and a light body. It's a pale, hazy yellow in the glass with a bright aroma of citrus pith, grassy herbs, lemon, pine, and apricot. It has an intoxicating, perfumey kind of aroma and that leads into the beer, which is delicate and light, yet still has a rounded, full mouthfeel that's big enough to handle all of those hops, the ones that are jumping up your nose and then sliding down your throat with a big, bracing kind of bitterness and a lasting dryness. With such a low ABV and high IBU you might worry that the body will be thin and overpowered, but it isn't. Kicks ass with tapas, especially some calamari or fried anchovies.

Buxton Moor Top

Buxton, England
ABV: 3.6%
Hops: Chinook, Columbus

This is an ode to the gloriously grapefruity Chinook hop. Moor Top is another brilliant example of how beer can be modest in ABV but really punchy with hop flavor and aroma. The thing with these beers is that they combine the old British idea of "sessionability," meaning you drink a few pints after work or slowly sup during the day, and combines that with the super-citrus flavor of American IPAs. You see, we Brits want to drink pints and we want to drink IPAs, and this is the winning result of that combo. Moor Top is a very pale Blonde and it smells like you've lodged a Chinook hop in one of your nostrils: grapefruit, citrus pith, tangerine, and pine resin. It's lip-smacking, dry, and quenching; there's more pithy citrus through the flavor and a clinging bitterness. Buxton make great beer—order it when you see it.

GOLDEN AND BLONDE ALE

THE ARRIVAL OF BRITISH GOLDEN ALES IN THE 1980S HAS PUSHED THIS STYLE FORWARD AND AROUND THE WORLD. IT CAME AS A GENTLE COMPETITOR OR ALTERNATIVE TO THE UBIQUITOUS PALE LAGERS, A FACT REFLECTED IN THE BEERS' SIMPLE, BRIGHT, FRESH FLAVORS. THOSE FIRST PALE PINTS WERE A SEASONAL GLASS OF SUNSHINE REFRESHMENT, BUT PROVED SO POPULAR THAT THEY QUICKLY TURNED INTO YEAR-ROUND BREWS.

Blonde or gold in color, they are a step beneath Pale Ale in both alcohol and hops. The malt body is smooth and clean, giving a biscuit flavor, perhaps some honey or cereal sweetness, and then hops add a delicate depth to the beer (not a brash, barnstorming bitterness), and it remains balanced against the malt, being a beer brewed to be easy to drink and unchallenging. ABV will generally be between 4.0 and 5.5%, with IBUs coming in the 20s or 30s. Any hop profile is acceptable as long as it isn't overpowering: British hops made the classic versions, giving earthy, floral, hedgerow fruit; American and southern hemisphere hops add their citrus and tropical-fruit qualities. Not explosive beers, Golden and Blonde Ales are the giggle to Pale Ale's big laugh; sometimes that cheeky chuckle can give a whole lot more than a room-clearing howl.

Fyne Avalanche

Argyll, Scotland
ABV: 4.5%
Hops: Cascade, Challenger, Liberty

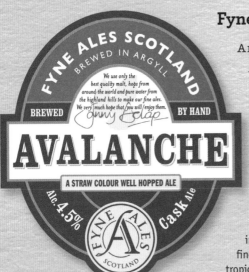

On a list of beers that I want in my refrigerator during the summer, this one always features. Scotland is a country of many really good, interesting breweries, most taking their inspiration from American craft beer and combining it with classic British styles. Avalanche is a modern Golden Ale. It takes a very British base of pale malts, adds some English hops for an earthy, subtle bitterness, and then goes in with the Cascades for a snappy, lemon and citrus finish with grapefruit and floral aromas rounding it all out. Clean, refreshing, light, quenching, and always interesting, Avalanche is a summer picnic kind of beer. Another Fyne beer to find is Jarl, a 3.8% ABV Citra single-hop session ale with a stunning citrus and tropical-fruit aroma, which is rightly regarded as one of Britain's best beers.

Septem Sunday's Honey Golden Ale

Evia, Greece
ABV: 6.5%
Hops: Styrian Golding, Tettnanger

I love Greece. I go there most years, hopping between islands, enjoying the bright sun, golden sand, warm blue sea, and local food. When it comes to drinking, a number of microbreweries are producing a range of different and exciting beers. Septem is the Latin word for "seven," representing the number of days of creation, and each Septem beer is named after a day of the week. Monday's Pilsner is snappy with fruity hops making it aromatic and inviting, and Friday's Pale Ale has a slick, clean hop freshness which is wonderful. On Sunday we get this Honey Golden Ale made with two types of Greek honey. Pale gold in color with delicate floral blossom, peach, and apricot in the aroma, it's a delicious and smooth beer with a gentle, balanced bitterness, rich body and just a touch of sweetness.

Cucapá Clásica

Mexicali, Mexico
ABV: 4.5%
Hops: Amarillo, Cascade, Centennial

Just across the border from California is Cervecaria Cucapá, one of Mexico's top craft breweries who make a range of boldly branded, full-on beer styles, including an American IPA, Double Rye, Imperial Red, and a tequila-barrel-aged Barley Wine. Clásica is a straightforward, easy-drinking Golden Ale. Bright gold in color with clean, biscuity malt, there's citrus and floral hops, which give a little freshness to the aroma, and a 23 IBUs cut of quenching bitterness at the end. It's everything you want and need this beer to be: it's not trying too hard to impress with too many hops, it's not hammering booze down your neck—it's just a great, well-made Golden Ale for drinking in the sun and perfect with quesadillas. Beer by beer, Cucapá are battling the lousy reputation Mexican drinking has of clear bottles with lime stuffed in the neck or the lick-shot-suck of slamming tequila.

Oppigårds Golden Ale

Hedemora, Sweden
ABV: 5.2%
Hops: East Kent Goldings, Pacific Gem, Cascade

This Golden Ale was the first beer brewed when Oppigårds Bryggeri opened in 2004 and it's now the biggest-selling Swedish ale in the Systembolaget. That's a big deal. The alcohol laws in Sweden mean that beers over 3.5% ABV can only be sold in the state-owned Systembolaget stores. Far from being restricted, these stores probably have the best beer selections in the world, with new brews added to the shelves each month. This Golden Ale is a mix of old and new: earthy, marmalade-like Goldings, floral, grapefruity Cascade, and blackcurranty Pacific Gem combine. The malt is chewy and toasty with a hint of caramel, while the 30 IBUs of bitterness ensure it finishes with a bite that makes it quenching with some exotic-fruit pith in the middle. Sweden isn't known for its summer sun, so use this as a placebo dose of Vitamin D.

Stone & Wood Pacific Ale

Byron Bay, Australia
ABV: 4.4%
Hops: Galaxy

Look out across Byron Bay's beautiful sweep of sand and you'll stare, doe-eyed and lovingly, at the endless waves of the Coral Sea. Here, on Australia's East Coast, where people go to surf and party, Stone & Wood was set up in 2008. Just minutes from the sea, it doesn't take a genius to see why they chose this spot. Pacific Ale is an all-Aussie brew that uses malt, wheat, and hops grown in Australia. Galaxy is a great hop: tropical fruit, passion fruit, and peach all explode out of this little green grenade. In Pacific Ale they bring a delicate freshness to those fruits, with zest, grapes, and a grassiness (harking back to Galaxy's parentage as a German hop) above the smooth, clean base of malt, which has a hint of honey before the dry, clean bitterness. It's a beautiful beer, beautifully balanced and made in a beautiful place.

Kern River Isabella Blonde

Kernville, California
ABV: 4.5%
Hops: Cascade

On the edge of the Sequoia National Forest, not far from either Death Valley or Yosemite, is the Wild West town of Kernville. The stars of Los Angeles and the lights of Las Vegas are distant distractions in this small town, which attracts people looking for the athletic pursuits of mountain and river sports. After a day climbing over rocks and hurtling over rapids, you're going to need a beer and Isabella Blonde is the place to start. Named after the lake close to the brewpub, this is a Golden Ale with a subtle malt background and an earthy, grassy, and orchard-fruit depth. Easy-gulping, wonderfully refreshing, brilliantly balanced: it's a beer to calm the adrenaline before you raise it again by ordering a Kern River Citra, their tastebud-thrilling double IPA.

Rooster's Yankee

Knaresborough, England
ABV: 4.3%
Hops: Cascade

When Sean Franklin brewed Yankee in 1993, he was one of the first brewers in Britain to use the new hop variety called Cascade. Working in wine before becoming a beer-maker, Sean was always at the forefront of brewing, especially with his use of hops to get balanced and unique flavor profiles. In 2011, he decided to pass the brewery on and it's now run by the Fozards, with brothers Ol and Tom keeping up Sean's great work, while also moving things forward with new beers. Yankee is a keeper, a classic. Bright gold, it's a brilliant blend of Britain and America: the clean, soft Yorkshire water meets the pale English malt, while the Cascade hops give a wonderful grapefruit, floral, and grassy freshness. Look out for the regular brewery specials and also Buckeye and Wild Mule, that are well-hopped modern British styles, perfectly executed.

AMERICAN PALE ALE

THE FIRST TRUE AMERICAN CRAFT-BEER STYLE, THIS TOOK INSPIRATION FROM THE PALE BEERS BREWED IN EUROPE AND THEN MADE THEM AMERICAN BY USING THE HUGELY FRUITY HOPS GROWN ON THE WEST COAST OF THE UNITED STATES. THOSE EARLY BEERS—SIERRA NEVADA IS THE CLASSIC AND STILL ONE OF THE BEST—IGNITED AND EXCITED BEER DRINKERS, AND KICK-STARTED CRAFT BREWING.

Cascade hops are the original American C-hop used in the style and have all the necessary attributes: floral, juicy citrus, pine and pith. Bitterness could be gentle or aggressive with 25–50 IBUs. A large dose of late hops and dry hops gives the beer a big aroma and flavor, which is like sitting in a grove of citrus trees. These beers, blonde to amber in color, often have a hint of sweetness and a rounded body, although some will finish very dry. Yeast is typically a neutral American ale yeast, which gives a few fruity esters and a clean depth. ABV could be a broad 4.5–6.5%. The shift from Pale Ale into IPA is a blurred line and a 6.0% brew could be on either side of it; ultimately, the difference lies in the use of hops, and IPAs will have a bigger hop presence. Going in the opposite direction, Pale Ale shifts down into Amber or Golden Ale as the hops are lightened. American Pale Ale has started breweries, converted drinkers, opened bars, and, ultimately, changed beer forever.

Half Acre Daisy Cutter

Chicago, Illinois
ABV: 5.2%
Hops: Centennial, Amarillo, Columbus, Simcoe

If Sierra Nevada is the classic example of an American pale ale—which it indisputably is—then Daisy Cutter is one of the best modern examples. Beer styles renew themselves regularly by combining old inspirations with new ingredients and new ideas. The aroma is grapefruit, mandarin, floral, and mango, but it's so much more than just those four things. This golden pint is clean and smooth to drink, while the flavor is so well defined with a clean malt simplicity. It's easy to over-hop beer and be left with brash noise instead of tuneful clarity, but Daisy Cutter has this unbeatable fresh, juicy flavor with a bitterness big enough that it clings to the tongue, but not so big that it kills the taste buds. This means you want to drink more, teased by that beguiling bitterness and pleased by that fantastic aroma. There's also Double Daisy Cutter, a bigger version of the beer, which is just as good.

Magic Rock High Wire

Huddersfield, England
ABV: 5.5%
Hops: Centennial, Columbus, Citra, Cascade, Chinook

Magic Rock went from nought to brilliant in no time, Their first brew came out in 2011 and since then they've been on the lips of every British beer geek, thanks to their great range of American-inspired brews. High Wire is their West Coast IPA. Order a pint of this, take a big gulp, and it's like a teleporter straight to the sunshine of San Diego (which sure beats the gray Yorkshire skies). Mandarin, grapefruit pith, passion fruit, roasted pineapple and orange; the body has a hint of toffee sweetness to balance the hops, then it finishes dry, peppery, and bitter, demanding you drink some more to get that calming hint of sweetness back on your tongue. Cannonball is their American IPA, which is magic stuff, or try Curious, an exceptional 3.9% ABV pale and hoppy session beer that wows the delighted taste buds as they experience the hop showcase.

Three Floyds Alpha King and Zombie Dust

Munster, Indiana
ABV: 6.66% and 6.4%
Hops: Alpha King: Centennial, Cascade, Warrior. Zombie Dust: Citra

Alpha King and Zombie Dust are too good to leave out, so both are in. Three Floyds are hop heroes in the brewing world and while their wide range of beers takes you around all of the styles you can think of, it's the Pale Ales (and the brilliant Gumballhead) that I want to go back to. Centennial, Cascade, and Warrior hops hit Alpha King with 66 IBUs. Orange pith, mandarin juice, pineapple, pine, and dried herbs drive the olfactory senses wild. Zombie Dust achieves the same hollering, cheering, high-fiving sensation using only the tropical-fruit festival that's Citra hops for more mango, grape, and floral flavors. Everything fits perfectly together in these beers with unrivaled balance working toward giving the most amazing hop experience with freshness, vibrancy, and deliciousness. Three Floyds are hop heroes.

Dancing Camel American Pale Ale

Tel Aviv, Israel
ABV: 5.2%
Hops: Citra, Cascade

Israel is one of those unexpected craft-beer hotspots with a growing range of breweries and interesting beers, taking local inspiration but also a lot of ideas from America. Dancing Camel was one of Israel's first craft breweries, opened by American David Cohen in 2006. The American Pale Ale is on the amber color scale and made with Israeli date honey. It's dominated in aroma by American hops with grapefruit, pineapple, and orange pith; it's got a toasty, caramel kind of malt depth, with a hint of honey before the simple, quenching finish. LeChaim is the toast—it's Hebrew for "to life." We can all raise a cold one to that.

Hill Farmstead Edward

Greensboro, Vermont
ABV: 5.2%
Hops: Centennial, Chinook, Columbus,
Simcoe, Warrior

Shaun Hill is the man behind Hill Farmstead, which is a brewery in a farmhouse on land that's been in his family for over 220 years. The Ancestral Series of beers is named after and inspired by members of the Hill family. Edward is Shaun's grandfather and he lived on the land where the brewery is now situated. It's an all-American Pale Ale: American malt, American hops, house yeast strain, and well water pulled from beneath the farmstead. I definitely think the water is special there; it gives the beers this unbelievable, incredible, teasing elegance, which is so light on the tongue. Combine that with hops—grapefruity, peach, orange pith, freshly floral, and grassy—which taste fresher and cleaner than you've ever had before, and it makes for a phenomenal-tasting beer: it's a beer with story, made in a special place.

Lambrate Ligera

Milan, Italy
ABV: 4.7%
Hops: Chinook, Amarillo, Cascade,
Willamette

A visit to Milan isn't complete without a few beers in the Birrificio Lambrate brewpub. Dark-wood clad, beer memorabilia all around, chalk board scratched with what's on, bronze taps all pouring pints topped with a thick crown of foam—it's got the feeling of an old English pub meeting an old underground speakeasy. The whole range of Lambrate beers is excellent, so plan to stay a while: dark beer lovers should get a Ghisa, a bellissimo smoked brew with coffee and dark fruits mixing with a whirl of smoke. Hop fans should get a Ligera, but don't expect a boom of lupulin—this one is fragrant, delicate, and flavor-driven, and not a bitter bomb. Peach, mandarin, and citrus pith fill the beer; the body is clean before a lasting dry and balanced bitterness. Ligera is lush and lovely—try it with the delicious risotto cooked in wort from the brewpub.

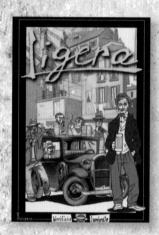

Camba Bavaria Pale Ale

Truchtlaching, Germany
ABV: 5.2%
Hops: Cascade, Golding, Willamette

This one came as a huge surprise to my preconceptions. An American Pale Ale brewed in Germany? Whatever. It'll taste like lager, right? They won't know what to do with the hops, right? I opened and poured it while I was busy doing other stuff, but then I caught this fragrant wave of citrus and tropical fruit filling the air... I love having my expectations smashed to pieces and this Pale Ale is sensational. If this were brewed by any well-known American brewery, then it'd be one of the most famous Pale Ales around, I reckon. The brewery is linked to Braukon, a brewery manufacturer that builds kits for craft breweries around the world. That worldwide inspiration has come back to their own tanks. The Pale Ale is super fruity and juicy with tangerine, blossom honey, and mango; the body is full and so smooth to drink before the bitterness, which is clean and balanced. A game-changer.

Firestone Walker Pale 31

Paso Robles, California
ABV: 4.9%
Hops: Fuggle, Cascade, Centennial,
Chinook

From 1996, when Adam Firestone and David Walker
started the brewery, it seems as if Firestone Walker
have won every beer award going,
including "Mid Size Brewery of the
Year" at the biennial World Beer Cup four
times—that award is given to whichever
brewery's beers do best in that
year's competition. What makes that
such a great achievement is that the
beers are blind tasted, so flavor
alone is what wins it. Taste Pale 31
and you'll want to put a gold medal
around your glass. With a bursting,
brilliant aroma of mango, melon, and
mandarin, so vibrantly (almost
impossibly) fresh and juicy, the beer
is light and clean; there's so much
hop flavor and just a little
bitterness—it's one of the best
because it makes you smile when you
drink it and excited about what beer
can be. Pale Ale perfection.

Great Lakes Crazy Canuck Pale Ale

Ontario, Canada
ABV: 5.2%
Hops: Centennial,
Chinook, Citra

Toronto's oldest craft
brewery, Great Lakes has
been making beer since
1987 using an open fire
under handsome copper
tanks. You can't beat the
look of copper in the
brewhouse—shiny
stainless steel is nice but
there's just something
special about copper.
Crazy Canuck is a
West-Coast-inspired American Pale Ale. Pouring the color
of a well-scrubbed, copper brewing kettle, it's got the
exact aroma you want: grapefruit, floral, pine—it's like
chewing on C-hops. Light and dry to drink, it allows the
resiny hops to come forward before kicking on the way
down with their pithy, clinging bitterness. Canada does
California and it makes me want to eat a big plate of fried
chicken, where the hop fruitiness cuts the chicken's
crunch and the spiced richness.

Tuatara APA

Waikanae, New Zealand
ABV: 5.8%
Hops: Chinook, Simcoe, Zythos

You know, when you write about 10 beers of the same style, which all share similarities in
ingredients, processes, and intention, the words on the page can get a bit repetitive. We know
American hops give grapefruit and orange, pine and flowers, so it all becomes a bit similar. The
thing is, that's just how they taste. And there are thousands of them around the world doing
similar things. Yet some beers just stand out from the others in their styles. It's a lift or
freshness in the aroma, the way it feels when you drink it, the way the hops and malt play, and it
comes down to the small details. Tuatara's APA stands out for the amber color, the bursting citrus
aroma of American hops, the ravishing 50 IBUs which wrap the tongue in bitterness, while a
caramel and berry sweetness fills the background and balances everything out. Tuatara also make
the excellent Aotearoa Pale Ale, which is a New-Zealand-hopped version of the same beer.

WHILE AMERICAN PALE ALE STARTED IT ALL AND MOVED THE WHOLE WORLD FORWARD, IT'S IPA THAT IS THE UNDOUBTED AND UNRIVALED RULER OF THIS WORLD. THE STORY OF AMERICAN IPA TAKES THE IDEA OF CENTURIES-OLD INDIA PALE ALE, A HIGHLY HOPPED BEER THAT TRAVELED BY SEA FROM ENGLAND TO INDIA, AND FAST-FORWARDS IT TO SUIT THE AMAZING HOPS GROWN IN AMERICA'S NORTHWEST. NOW, IPA HAS NOTHING TO DO WITH INDIA OR LONG SEA JOURNEYS—IT'S A STYLE BUILT AS A CENTER STAGE FOR HOPS. THIS IS ONE OF THE MOST EXCITING AND PROMINENT BEER STYLES AROUND. IT SHOWS JUST HOW DIFFERENT A BEER CAN BE FROM THOSE LIGHT LAGERS THAT LINE REFRIGERATORS EVERYWHERE: THE JUICY, FRAGRANT FRUIT PROFILES, THE BANG OF BITTERNESS, THE RICH BODIES OF MALT, AND THE TINGLE OF ALCOHOL ALL COMBINE TO PRODUCE BEERS FULL OF FLAVOR.

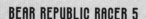

AMERICAN IPA

An American IPA can be many things: from very pale to a deep amber color; delicately floral to brutally bitter; sharply dry to sweet and round. What these beers have in common is the nose-grabbing aroma of American hops, which give citrus, resinous pine, dried herbs, stone fruit, and a floral freshness. Bitterness is usually high, sometimes tongue-splittingly so (50–80 plus IBUs), but this is balanced by malt body and sweetness. Alcohol will typically range from 6.0 to 8.0% ABV. Within American IPAs there's a rough split: West Coast IPAs tend to be more "in-your-face" citrusy, dry, and bitter, whereas East Coast IPAs are a little fuller-bodied and less aggressively hopped. American IPA is craft beer's flagship beer style—craft beer's hero.

BEAR REPUBLIC RACER 5

HEALDSBURG, CALIFORNIA
ABV: 7.0%
HOPS: CHINOOK, CASCADE, COLUMBUS, CENTENNIAL

What is the classic, quintessential, definitive American IPA? Asking 50 different people will probably get 50 different responses, so why Racer 5? IPAs can often be too sweet or too bitter, but Racer 5 slams it straight down the middle with its mix of rounded, toasty malt, big hop aroma and flavor, and a bitterness that makes you want more straightaway. The hops are all American, they give loads of orange blossom, tangerine, mango, and tropical fruit, plus a piney and dryly herbal quality, which is closer to gin than ale. The balancing act is performed by a swathe of sweetness that makes the fruity hops taste fruitier and rounds out the bitterness. It's hard to choose a favorite beer, but this one is near the top of my list, especially with a cheeseburger and fries in the Healdsburg brewpub where the Racer is poured from serving tanks.

The Kernel IPA

London, England
ABV: 6.5-7.5% (batches vary)
Hops: See the bottle label

In early 2010, The Kernel started brewing under a railway arch near London's Tower Bridge. By March 2012 they had already moved to a bigger site to keep up with demand. Evin O'Riordain and his team brew a huge variety of beers, including Stouts, Porters, and interesting takes on classic European styles, but it's the hop-heavy Pale Ales, IPAs and Black IPAs that grab the attention. Each batch is different and named after the hop varieties used, so try as many as you can to see what qualities different hops can give to beer. Flame-colored, with caramel and bread from malt, The Kernel IPAs can be defined by a full, textured body, which helps carry the hops and throws them at you while you drink—expect lots of bitterness and amazing aromas, but always balanced.

Epic Brewing Armageddon IPA

Auckland, New Zealand
ABV: 6.66%
Hops: Cascade, Centennial, Columbus, Simcoe

Despite there being a hop shortage in New Zealand at the time of first brewing, Luke Nicholas, the man behind Epic Brewing, decided not to hold back on the hops, instead choosing to put in as many as possible. I love that attitude. I love the beer, too: the hops give an apocalyptically big bang of grapefruit, juicy tropical fruit, and then pine, while the bitterness is long and rasping above the just-sweet-enough malt body, all combining to make a beer that's addictively drinkable. Love hops? Also look for Epic's Hop Zombie or Mayhem. IPA can be a feisty food choice and many point it at hot and spicy food, but I think that's like putting a fire out with vodka, as hops and Scoville start punching each other in the face. Belly pork is excellent, a hamburger is hard to beat as the beer rips through the richness, and carrot cake makes a surprisingly good match.

Klášterní Pivovar Strahov Svatý Norbert IPA

Prague, Czech Republic
ABV: 6.3%
Hops: Amarillo, Cascade

Walking up the steep cobbled street to Prague Castle is thirsty work. Thankfully, Strahov Monastery, complete with brewery, is one of the first things you see when the hill levels out. Inside, the copper tanks sit in the corner, shiny enough to check your hair in as you pass. The Stout and Wheat beer are delicious, but it's the IPA that's good enough to make you consider a life in the brotherhood. While beer has been made here on and off for centuries, not many of them would've tasted like this: a color close to the copper vessel in which it was made, you get grapefruit, mango, apricot, peach, and honeysuckle, and it's bitter-sweet in all the right ways. This is world-class IPA made in a monastery in a country better known for pale lagers. I didn't make it to the castle in the end; I just stayed drinking the IPA.

Birra del Borgo ReAle Extra

Borgorose, Italy
ABV: 6.2%
Hops: Amarillo, Warrior

American IPAs are beers that need to be drunk as fresh as possible. The hops start to fade, the bitterness draws back, and the brilliant aroma dulls quickly. This means that if you want to drink the best IPAs, then you need to go somewhere close to where they're made. The best place to drink ReAle Extra is Open Baladin in Rome, a bar jointly run by Leonardo di Vincenzi of del Borgo and Teo Musso of Birra Baladin. After a day of wonder-filled sightseeing, you walk into a bar and see the awe-inspiring wall of bottles—a beer lover's Coliseum—and then you see the list of beers on tap, which is like the eyes-wide walk around the Sistine Chapel, seeing all of these famous names. ReAle Extra is ripe with peaches, tangerine, orange blossom, and loads of floral fragrance with a botanic and perfumey bitterness around an almond-cake sweetness (it smells like the most heavenly Italian bakery). A magnificent work of art.

Feral Hop Hog

Swan Valley, Australia
ABV: 5.8%
Hops: Cascade, Galaxy, Centennial

Because this is a hoppy Australian beer I can't resist adding a few 'roo references: a group of kangaroos is called a mob; kangaroos are marsupials; they can't move backward; they are herbivores; in the sea, kangaroos can move their legs independently, but on land they can only hop together. Let's skippy onto the beer: the aroma is as aromatic as IPAs come with lush lemon, plump peaches, and juicy pineapple with the expected grapefruit and orange rolling in with their pithy, juicy mix of tangy sharp fruit—it's got more hops than a mob of kangaroos(!). The body is soft and clean, while the citrusy hops give a lip-smacking dryness at the end. Grab a few bucks (FYI: male kangaroos are called bucks, so that's another kangaroo reference) from your pocket and pouch (pouch, marsupials... it's too easy) a six-pack when you see this.

Pizza Port The Jetty IPA

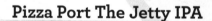

San Diego, California
ABV: 7.6%
Hops: Simcoe, Chinook, Cascade, Amarillo

My flight home from San Diego was at 8 p.m. That gave me an afternoon to grab a final few beers, so I jumped on a bus and rode it out to Ocean Beach. A street lined with hippie shops, fast-food outlets, and tattoo parlors led straight to the sea. I had to get to the ocean—I couldn't go all the way to the West Coast and not sit by the sea and watch the surf. A few blocks back from the beach is Pizza Port, a brewpub (part of a small group of Pizza Ports) that makes damn good pizza and champion beers. The Jetty is their house IPA and it's got that addictive "gotta-go-back-for-more" quality of the best IPAs, which balance the sweet kiss of malt with the bitter hit of hops. Loads of citrus and tropical fruit and a dry, sharp finish. Have it with a pizza.

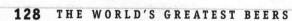

La Cumbre Elevated IPA

Albuquerque, New Mexico
ABV: 7.2%
Hops: Chinook, Magnum, CO2 extract, Cascade, Centennial, Crystal, Zythos, Columbus, Simcoe

We're in good company with the beers in this chapter, many of them shining with medals, and Elevated IPA has won some of the biggest world competitions, getting gold at the Great American Beer Festival in 2011 and bronze at the World Beer Cup in 2012 (the American IPA category is like the Best Film Oscar, so that's a big deal). In 2012, Elevated IPA hit cans because, as Jeff Erway, President of La Cumbre Brewing says, "canning is simply a better package than glass." This one hits 100 IBUs of hop pleasure, given to it by the long list of American hops. The malt body pulls this one together, giving some toffee and toast, and pushing forward the citrus, pine, florals, and orchard fruits. The clarity of hop flavor is what makes this special: everything is so sharp and clean.

Fat Heads Head Hunter IPA

Middleburg Heights, Ohio
ABV: 7.0%
Hops: Columbus, Simcoe, Centennial

Fat Heads started as a craft-beer saloon in Pittsburg, serving great beers alongside great food. In 2009, a second Fat Heads site opened, this time in Ohio, and this one added a brewery. Then, in 2012, after barely rivaled success, Fat Heads opened a production brewery to the cheers of beer fans everywhere. Head Hunter is as golden as all the medals that it's won (and there have been a lot of medals and awards for this beer). The aroma fills your head with fragrant citrus, pine, and tropical fruit, somehow smelling fresher and lovelier than most of the other IPAs. A subtle sweetness and an oily texture come before the 87 IBUs lupulin lash on your tongue. A powerhouse finish of hops is kept from being overpowering by the wonderful freshness in the aroma and a subtle sweetness. Go head-hunting and collect the bottle caps as conquests.

Craftworks Jirisan Moon Bear IPA

Seoul, South Korea
ABV: 6.8%
Hops: Centennial, Cascade, Chinook

IPA really is a worldwide beer style. From Oregon to Osaka, Sydney to Santiago, Buenos Aires to Bristol, Amsterdam to Auckland, it's made in the majority of craft breweries. It's come from the popularity of the American versions, which started a new generation of brewers and drinkers interested in big flavors and that distinctive smack of citrus fruit that grabs the attention. I've never been to South Korea, but now I really want to... Craftworks Taphouse & Bistro is a craft-beer bar in Seoul. Their beers are made at Kapa Brewery in Gapyeong. Jirisan is an American IPA that hits 95 IBUs from its triple attack of C-hops. It's one of those beers that you have to travel to in order to taste it (and when there you can order a flight with their Kölsch, Oatmeal Stout, Hefeweizen, and others). If anyone else is interested, I'll meet you there for a pint sometime.

IPA RULES THE CRAFT BEER WORLD

If one beer style defines craft beer, it's IPA. And it all started with hops and a story. Go back to the 18th and 19th centuries, when beer traveled from England to India by sea, maturing during the six months that it took to make the journey. The mythology behind India Pale Ales, as they became known (though only years after they were first loaded onto boats), talked of them as beers made with lots of hops and more alcohol than usual, perhaps to survive the sea journey without souring or perhaps just to suit the thirsts of drinkers in the warm weather.

That idea—higher alcohol and lots of hops— created IPAs as we know them now. No longer related (or only through the stories), India Pale Ale and IPA are different things, and my view is that IPA has become its own noun and not just an initialization of India Pale Ale—an IPA is a beer around 6.0–8.0% ABV made with lots of hops, simple as that. The difference between IPA and India Pale Ale? One is a beer from the history books, while the other is a beer for now.

The transition from old to new is relevant because IPAs have always been evolving and changing. At one point in time they would've been strong amber beers loaded with British hops, but then in the 20th century they fell from favor and changed into beers under 4.0% ABV, never reaching the popularity of best bitters on British bar tops. It was the pioneering American craft brewers' interest in the story of those early seafaring beers that brought them back to our attention.

American IPAs work because they show off the hops. More than anything else, IPAs are there to be incredibly flavorsome beers with amazing aromas and big bitterness. Put a massive, hop-forward IPA next to a glass of macro lager and the difference is stark. And it's a difference that is converting more drinkers to craft beer as they see that beer can be so much more than they realized.

Beer styles evolve, and that's what's happened with the India Pale Ales of the 1800s and IPAs of

the 2000s. Now they are evolving further, and taking the IPA idea (alcohol of 6.0–8.0% and vibrantly hoppy) and warping it. Black IPAs might be an oxymoron; they might also be hoppy Black Ales or Porters, but they take the hop profile of an IPA and combine it with a black body of beer. Belgian IPAs mix the fruity, spicy, estery Belgian yeasts with juicy American hops. Pacific IPAs leave the American hops behind and use varieties from Australia and New Zealand. Imperial IPAs turn up the volume on booze and bitterness. English-style IPAs hark back to the old style of India Pale Ale, minus the sea journey, and use British ingredients for a very different flavor profile from American versions. Knocking on, there's Red, Brown, and White IPAs and the typical hop profile of American IPA has evolved almost every beer style in the world, giving more alcohol, bolder bitterness, and that citrus smash to the gustatory unit—IPA rules the world and it's changed many times during its kingship.

Go to London, and you drink a pint of cask bitter. If you go to Brussels, you drink a still, sharp Lambic. Go to Munich, and it's a mug of golden Helles. Go to anywhere in America, and it's an IPA: the style has become nation-defining in the beer world. But while IPAs are synonymous with the States, they are brewed everywhere with brewers trying to achieve that wonderful, perfumey, exotic, and exciting flavor from the hops. What's your favorite style of beer? I'll take a fresh American IPA.

AMERICAN IMPERIAL IPA

WHAT I LOVE ABOUT IPAS AND IMPERIAL OR DOUBLE IPAS IS THAT TO DRINK THEM IS TO FIGHT HUMAN INSTINCT. THE BRAIN SEES BITTERNESS AS A BAD THING: TO OUR ANCESTORS BITTER FOOD COULD HAVE BEEN LACED WITH POISONOUS TOXINS, SO THE BODY SENDS A WARNING AND QUICKLY PRESSES THE "DISLIKE" BUTTON—IT'S WHY CHILDREN DON'T LIKE BITTER VEGETABLES OR WHY THAT FIRST PRIMITIVE SIP OF BEER WE TASTE AS A CHILD IS SO DISGUSTING. THIS HARDWIRING MEANS THAT BITTER IPAS ARE A SHOCK TO THE BRAIN, BUT COMBINE THAT PAIN WITH THE SWEETNESS OF MALT AND THE RELAXING PLEASURE OF THE ALCOHOL AND THERE'S AN ADDICTIVE, FUN, AND DANGEROUS EDGE TO DOUBLE IPAS.

The "let's-make-it-bigger" bravado of American craft-brewing has brought us the Imperial or Double IPA: ABV from 7.5 to 10.0% plus, bitterness from 50 to 100 plus IBUs, color from gold to dark amber. But the thing that makes these beers jump out of the glass is their explosive use of hops: hugely aromatic, outrageously citrusy, pithy, and potent, with a tidal wave of bitterness at the end. The body is often full and can be sweet, though some lighter examples finish very dry. The best DIPAs are balanced in the extremities of malt and hop: smooth bodies, layered with alcohol and malt, a scythe of hop flavor through it with bitterness, and the fresh uplift of aroma. Not an easy style to get right, meaning the best really stand out as the best, while the worst fill your sinus cavity with a dank hop harshness that bursts its bitter guts down your booze-burnt throat.

Stone Ruination IPA

Escondido, California
ABV: 7.7%
Hops: Columbus, Centennial

There's a video on YouTube of a fireworks display that didn't go to plan. Instead of being a 10-minute extravaganza of lights, whooshes, whistles, and bangs, someone made a remarkable error and all of the fireworks went off simultaneously: 10 minutes of fireworks exploded in 10 seconds. Ruination IPA tastes like all the fireworks going off at the same time. I still remember the giddy-headed, giggling pleasure I had when I first drank this beer: in that moment I became a lupulin-chasing hop-head. You get an outrageous aroma of orange and grapefruit pith, pine and perfumey floral, while the malt middle is smooth before more than 100 rasping units of bitterness punch in; yet, somehow, it stays incredibly, addictively drinkable—as the bottle says, it's a liquid poem to the glory of the hop. Drink it as fresh as possible, preferably at the brewery, to experience the full-on hop explosion.

Liberty Brewing C!tra

New Plymouth, New
Zealand
ABV: 9.0%
Hops: Citra

This is everything you want from a
Double IPA: outrageously aromatic,
slick with malt, madly bitter, covertly
loaded with booze, and yet still
somehow balanced. The aroma on
this one is ridiculous: potent
passion fruit, raspberry, grapefruit,
and mangosteen all fire out, and
it's hard to know how so much
fruity hop flavor got into your
glass. Some malt sweetness softens
everything, while the hops leave a
big pithy kind of bitterness
beneath. It's a mega mouthful of
massive flavors, assaulting the
senses in a very pleasurable way with
punches, kicks, and caresses. The Liberty beers are brewed
on a small scale (79 US gallons/300 liters at a time) in the
garage attached to Joseph and Christina Wood's house. But
making beer is only half the business: the other side is
selling homebrewing ingredients, though presumably there
aren't many hops left after they're finished brewing this one.

Avery
The Maharajah IPA

Boulder, Colorado
ABV: 10.24%
Hops: Simcoe, Columbus,
Centennial, Chinook

I was in the Avery taproom with this guy
named Reno whom I'd met a few hours
earlier. It was our first beer of the day,
ordered soon after I'd landed in Denver,
Colorado, and driven to Boulder. I eased
myself in with a Joe's American Pilsner
while Reno went for a pint of The
Maharajah. He finished it in about a
minute, ordered another, and slammed
that down in the same time. "Woah, was I
thirsty!" he said, before ordering another
beer. I immediately respected my new
friend Reno. A year later, I drank The
Maharajah in New York with my mate
Matt. It was midnight and we'd already
had a few beers so we just had a small sample of it on a beer
flight. It was so damn good that both of us ordered a pint.
I love this beer for the taste—massive, juicy, tropical citrus,
and bitter herbs—and for those memories.

Alchemist Heady Topper

Waterbury, Vermont
ABV: 8.0%
Hops: Styrian Goldings, Saaz, Perle

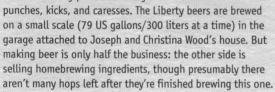

After running The Alchemist Pub and Brewery for a few years, the owners John and
Jennifer Kimmich decided to step up the brewing side of things, so they increased
production and bought a canning line. So dedicated were they in their pursuit of
heady hop perfection that they started by only brewing this one beer, but one is
all you need when it's this good (though an increase in capacity in 2012 means
more range is coming). Heady Topper is an orange-gold color, and out of that
gorgeous liquid come peach, apricot, grape, and orange blossom—astonishingly,
all from glorious European hops and no C-hops in sight. It's mesmerizingly light,
yet there's still a fullness to it, there's a tropical loveliness, and somehow the
120 IBUs give balance and freshness—this is DIPA at its best. It's hard to get hold
of, so buy it when you see it.

Brouwerij De Molen Amarillo

Bodegraven, Netherlands
ABV: 9.2%
Hops: Sladek, Saaz, Amarillo

The De Molen brewery is in an icon of the Dutch landscape: a windmill (De Molen means "The Mill"). The mill was built in 1697, but the brewery is much newer and is on the frontline of European craft beer, where they've been for many years. Every September, De Molen's Menno Olivier arranges the Borefts Beer Festival, which brings together some of the world's best brewers in one place. If you can't make it to the festival, De Molen has a tasting room on site that also does great food. Amber in color, Amarillo is a sensational Double IPA, showing off all the wonderful apricot, peach, and tangerine of the hop the beer is named after. The aroma whirls out of your glass and there's a smooth sweetness before a very European, earthy kind of bitterness from the Sladek and Saaz hops, but this one is really all about the aromatic awesomeness of Amarillo.

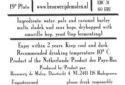

To Øl Final Frontier DIPA

Copenhagen, Denmark
ABV: 9.0%
Hops: Simcoe, Centennial, Columbus

Before there was To Øl, there was Tobias Emil Jensen, Tore Gynther, and their teacher Mikkel Borg Bjergsø. Upset at the lack of good beer in Denmark, they decided to start brewing their own, using the kitchen at the school where they were studying and teaching. Mikkel went on to start Mikkeller in 2006 and then, in 2010, Tobias and Tore started To Øl. Now both teacher and apprentices are pushing Denmark forward as one of the most interesting and progressive brewing nations in the world. Final Frontier is an enormous DIPA. Fiery amber to look at, it smells like you've stuffed your face into a fermenting bowl of fruit: orange, peach, grapefruit, and mango. Resinous, slick on the tongue, malt is there but hiding scared behind the hops, and the bitter finish is intense, giving a sappy, resinous, and peppery kick. Denmark is making some of the world's best beers—go to Copenhagen and see for yourself.

Russian River Pliny the Elder

Santa Rosa, California
ABV: 8.0%
Hops: CTZ, Simcoe, Cascade, Centennial, Amarillo, CO2 extract

I think there's an unwritten rule for beer book writers: you have to include Pliny the Elder. It's one of those beers that fires up the thirsts of beer drinkers: those who have had it know just how good it is and those who haven't tried it yet dream about the day they can say the wonderful words: "a pint of Pliny, please." I'd landed in San Francisco a few hours earlier. I was lost, it was dark and raining, and I'd been awake for 24 hours, but I finally found the Toronado beer bar and said those words. Standing alone in this heaving, rocking bar, I won't forget that first mouthful of Pliny. Yes, it's got the incredible hop aroma you expect, but this is the best because of the base: clean, smooth, and dry, there's no bulging malt sweetness, while the lasting bitterness and hop flavor hang around like grapefruit pith in your gums. It's better than everyone says it is.

ENGLISH PALE ALE AND IPA

LONDON AND BURTON-ON-TRENT ARE THE HOMES OF THIS STYLE, AND THE ORIGINAL PALE ALES AND IPAS ARE PART OF BEER'S ROYAL FAMILY. MADE IN ENGLAND USING ALL-ENGLISH INGREDIENTS, WORLD-TRAVELING, AND HISTORY-MAKING, IT'S A STYLE OF BEER THAT'S BEEN BREWED FOR HUNDREDS OF YEARS, EVOLVING EVERY DECADE OR SO TO RENEW ITSELF FOR NEW DRINKERS. THE FIRST PALE ALES WOULD'VE BEEN DARK AMBER IN COLOR—THEIR "PALENESS" MEASURED IN COMPARISON WITH THE DARK PORTERS OF THE TIME—AND WEREN'T SO MUCH A "STYLE" AS JUST PALE BEER. AND IT'S ALL EVOLVED FROM THERE, THOUGH IT WAS NEVER REALLY THE POPULAR STYLE WE NOW CONSIDER IT, WITH BITTER, MILD, AND PORTER ALL PROVING MORE POPULAR.

An English barley base, providing a depth of chewy, tangy malt, holds this beer together. English hops give their characteristically earthy, hedgerow, and floral qualities and a pronounced rough, herbal bitterness. Water is typically hard, giving a dryness which emphasizes hop flavor. ABVs range from 3.5 to 7.5% with pale passing to IPA around 5.5% (although some IPAs will be under 4.0%, harking back to the mid-20th century when this was the way of the style). IBUs will be 30–70 plus. Not as popular as the American style, these have a more malt-dominated flavor and don't share the same citrus fragrance as the style's American offspring. Where American IPAs demand to be drunk fresh, English IPAs can age nicely for a year or two, though fresh is best if you want the maximum hop hit from the British varieties.

Fuller's Bengal Lancer

London, England
ABV: 5.3% (draft version 5.0%)
Hops: Goldings

Released as a special in 2010, Bengal Lancer was so popular that it became a regular addition to the Fuller's range. Despite a wild hop-rush happening in London, where drinkers and brewers were looking to get as many American and southern hemisphere hops into their drinks as possible, the British-hopped Bengal Lancer has been met with a lot of love from beer fans. Named after the famous troops of the British Empire who fought in India, Bengal Lancer is caramel-colored, giving a glorious Goldings aroma of hop sack, warm woodland, earthy spice, and candied orange, while the body has a great richness, as if it's been bolstered by the army of hops. The finish smacks with spicy, earthy hops and a little sweet marmalade, and it tastes very British in a modern way—it's a new interpretation of a classic beer style.

Firestone Walker Double Barrel Ale

Paso Robles, California
ABV: 5.0%
Hops: Magnum, Styrian Goldings, East Kent Goldings

The Burton Union fermentation system was pioneered in Burton-on-Trent from the mid-19th century. The system involves a bank of wooden casks with swan necks leading up to a trough; as the fermentation takes place in the barrels, the yeast (plus some beer) is pushed up the swan necks into the trough where they then separate and the beer flows back into the Union system while the yeast is removed—it was designed to remove excess yeast without wasting any beer. The Firestone Union modernizes that process and uses it to impart delicate wood character from medium-toast American oak, spending six days in barrels before moving into stainless steel. This process gives DBA a soft, oak background to the floral, peach, apricot, and berry-fruit character, which mixes marvelously with the toasty malt.

Hitachino Nest Japanese Classic Ale

Ibaraki, Japan
ABV: 7.5%
Hops: Chinook, Challenger

Of all the beer styles in the world, India Pale Ales have one of the most interesting stories, the sort of story that can ignite imaginations and flames beneath mash tuns. Being a style surrounded by myth, legend, and hundreds of years of history, it's vociferously argued about. The thing with India Pale Ale is that, like all other styles, it's continually evolving. Japanese Classic Ale is the Hitachino Nest evolution. It takes American and English hops, giving floral, lemony, spiciness, and stuffs them into an amber brew bursting with toffee malt richness. Then it's matured in cedar casks (a modern move reminiscent of the wood that India Pale Ale would have originally traveled in) that are more commonly used for sake, which give a woody sweetness, some orange peel, and a dry texture. A classic ale done the Japanese way.

Cervejaria Colorado Indica

Ribeirão Preto, Brazil
ABV: 7.0%
Hops: Galena, Cascade

Lovers of India Pale Ale need to read Pete Brown's fascinating book, *Hops & Glory*, which tells the story of the style as Pete recreates the old sea journey from England to India with a cask of beer by his side. The ship he took went via Brazil and, had he had time, he could've stopped for a few pints of Brazilian IPA. Indica is a dark copper color and the American hops give an English-type depth of earthy, peppery, hedgerow spice (like the smell of an English woodland on a hot day), roast apples, and a deep grassiness. It's quite sweet to the taste, but then the hops rough it up with their potent bitterness. The Colorado beers are made with water from Guarani Aquifer, an enormous underground source of fresh water lying beneath Argentina, Brazil, Paraguay, and Uruguay, so this is a real mix of local ingredients and far-away inspiration.

Gadds No. 3

Ramsgate, England
ABV: 5.0%
Hops: Fuggles,
East Kent
Goldings

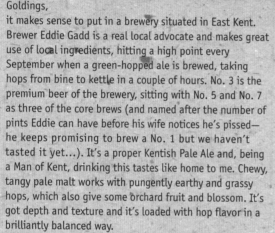

With most of
these beers
going for
East Kent
Goldings,
it makes sense to put in a brewery situated in East Kent.
Brewer Eddie Gadd is a real local advocate and makes great
use of local ingredients, hitting a high point every
September when a green-hopped ale is brewed, taking
hops from bine to kettle in a couple of hours. No. 3 is the
premium beer of the brewery, sitting with No. 5 and No. 7
as three of the core brews (and named after the number of
pints Eddie can have before his wife notices he's pissed—
he keeps promising to brew a No. 1 but we haven't
tasted it yet...). It's a proper Kentish Pale Ale and, being
a Man of Kent, drinking this tastes like home to me. Chewy,
tangy pale malt works with pungently earthy and grassy
hops, which also give some orchard fruit and blossom. It's
got depth and texture and it's loaded with hop flavor in a
brilliantly balanced way.

Carlow Brewing
O'Hara's Irish Pale Ale

County Carlow, Ireland
ABV: 5.2%
Hops: Cascade, Amarillo

Ireland has been slower on the uptake of
craft beer than other countries. Big brands
have a huge hold over the country and they
loom like an impenetrable wall, but that
hasn't stopped some and there's a
consumer group called Beoir
(www.beoir.org) set up to help spread
the good word about small Irish
independent breweries. Carlow are one
of the original Irish craft brewers and
one of the most widely available. This
beer is another modern interpretation
of an IPA: an Irish Pale Ale. A style
jointly influenced by Britain and
America, it has the malt profile of its
nearby neighbors and the hop flavor
of further away. There's a sweet pithy
aroma of grapefruit, the malt is toasty
and chewy, and bitterness fills the
mouth and then hangs around in an
English, earthy hop kind of way
before a little poke of citrus finishes
it off.

Three Floyds Blackheart

Munster, Indiana
ABV: 8.0%
Hops: East Kent Goldings, Admiral

Blackheart brings back this old style by brewing a beer with all-English
ingredients and adding some toasted oak to replicate the barrel the beer
would've once sailed in. Copper-colored, you get those spicy, punchy,
fragrantly earthy and floral hops coming out of the glass and, because
Three Floyds use more hops than most, you also get bonus extra aromas
like pine forests and orchards on sunny days. There's a little sweetness
and a lot of bitterness (70 IBUs), emphasized by the tannic dryness from
the oak, which fills out the already-full mouthfeel. Whereas the original
India Pale Ales were drunk aged after maturing at sea, Blackheart is a
beer to drink fresh because that way you get the full-on impact of British
hops, something not enough beers give us.

PACIFIC PALE AND IPA

AMERICAN IPA GOES ON A WORLD TOUR, TAKING PALE ALE AND IMPERIAL IPA WITH IT, STOPPING IN NEW ZEALAND AND AUSTRALIA, AND PICKING UP THE DISTINCTIVE ACCENT. THE BEERS ARE JUST THE SAME AS AMERICAN PALE ALE AND IPA, BUT MADE WITH HOPS GROWN DOWN UNDER. THESE HOPS HAVE A HUGE FRUIT PROFILE, BUT IT'S NOT THE CITRUS OF AMERICA; INSTEAD, IT'S TROPICAL FRUIT, LYCHEES, TANNIC GRAPES, GOOSEBERRIES, LIME, A VANILLA CREAMINESS, AND PASSION-FRUIT ZING—SIMILAR TO THE WHITE WINES MADE IN THE REGION. THERE'S AN ELEGANCE TO THE HOPS, A LESS-BRASH FLAVOR, AND THEY ARE LIGHTER AND FRUITIER THAN THOSE GROWN IN AMERICA: IT'S AS IF A HEAVY-FOOTED AMERICAN TOURIST RETURNED FROM A TRIP DOWN UNDER IN A MORE RELAXED, EASY-GOING, LIGHT-HEARTED MOOD.

Many of the hops grown in New Zealand are named after the areas they grow in: Nelson, Motueka, Riwaka. Many southern hemisphere hops are bred from classic European varieties, made bigger, and then given the unique influence of the local land. This gives incredibly aromatic beers that are like intensified Noble hops, hugely fruity while keeping a grassy, clean, delicately herbal depth beneath. Cascade hops are also grown successfully in New Zealand, holding onto the grapefruit and floral flavor of those grown in America, but also adding tropical fruit. While their popularity rockets, there is still only a small volume of hops grown down under, so, no matter how wonderful they are, there will be a lot of demand for them.

Yeastie Boys Digital IPA

Wellington, New Zealand
ABV: 7.0%
Hops: Pacific Jade, Nelson Sauvin, Motueka, New Zealand Cascade

The recipe for this beer is online. Not just a hopeful list of ingredients; it's got it down to the nearest kernel of caramalt, the exact water composition, the full hopping regime, and even the color you should get. It's an open source kind of beer, one for sharing with others in more ways than just grabbing two glasses. The cool thing about this recipe for me as a hop-freak is seeing what goes in and when: Pacific Jade gets the brew to 77 IBUs, there's some flavoring hop and dry hop, but the biggest addition comes at flame-out with a mountain of Motueka going in. That gives the huge aroma of passion fruit, mango, honeydew melon, and juicy sweet citrus. A golden (7.3 SRM, to be precise) glassful, it's got a lot of bitterness and hop flavor lingering beneath that burst of aroma.

Toccalmatto
Zona Cesarini

Fidenza, Italy
ABV: 6.6%
Hops: Pacific Gem, Sorachi
Ace, Citra, Palisade, East
Kent Goldings, Motueka

Zona Cesarini is a sporting term,
starting on the soccer pitch and
carried into casual conversation, that
means the final moments of the
game—its etymology is from Renato
Cesarini, an Argentine who played in
Italy and had a habit of scoring last-
minute goals. Like a 93rd-minute
winner, this beer has never failed to
wow me and every time I get it in my
glass it impresses and excites me more
and more. Packed with fruit, there's an intense, perfumey,
grape flavor, kind of like a dessert wine aged with lychees;
there's also tangerine, grapefruit, peach, blossom honey,
and apricot—it's ridiculously fruity in a way that screams
"drink me now!" The body is amber-colored and rich,
but not sweet, and the bitterness is powerful yet not
overpowering, with a tannic grip as it goes down, finishing
dry, dry, dry until you drink some more. A game-winning
screamer.

Alpine Beer Company
Nelson IPA

Alpine, California
ABV: 7.0%
Hops: Nelson Sauvin,
Southern Cross

"Dude, have you tried any Alpine
beers?" this guy asks me in a San Diego
beer bar. "'Cos, I don't know what they
do over there, man, but it's something
special, you know. The hop flavor is
just... it's just... better." He points me
five blocks away where they have Nelson
IPA on tap. Made with a little rye, it's
Nelson Sauvin-hopped, showing off the
crazy breadth of flavor possible with
New Zealand's most-famous hop variety.
It pours a blushing orange that's almost
impossibly bright and inviting, and one
sniff tells you that they do do something
special with hops at Alpine. Smooth, impeccably clean,
so juicy (jammy, even) with passion fruit, lychee,
perfumey grape, and tropical fruits, it's a total joy to
drink. As Pacific IPAs go, this is hard to beat.

Thornbridge Kipling

Bakewell, England
ABV: 5.2%
Hops: Nelson Sauvin

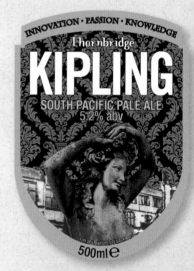

Just as Britain was knocking its neck back and opening wide to pour in American
IPAs, Kipling came along and made everyone look in the opposite direction.
Thornbridge were one of the first breweries in the United Kingdom to use Nelson
Sauvin hops and this brought an entirely new flavor profile to the bar top. Pale straw
in color, it's wonderfully light yet has a great structure to the body. The hops give
passion fruit, lime, gooseberry, and a creaminess that adds a wonderful depth. The
bitterness is balanced and it's all just so easy to drink, working wonderfully in bottle
and on cask. It's the sort of beer that calls out for a Thai curry where the creamy
coconut, chili, and lime love the softly citrusy brew, giving an exotic taste to a beer
made in a sleepy market town in the Peak District.

Santorini Brewing Company Yellow Donkey

Santorini, Greece
ABV: 5.2%
Hops: Aurora, Styrian Golding, US Cascade, Motueka

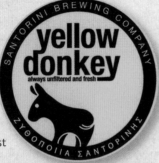

When you go to Greece on vacation, you drink cold lager. This is fine. Good, even: the cold beers are refreshing in the Mediterranean sunshine. But there's definitely more than just Mythos on Santorini, a rugged diamond of an island famous for its sunsets. The Santorini Brewing Company was started in 2011 by a Greek, a Serbian, a Brit, and an American. The Brit, Steve Daniel, is a wine buyer who specializes in Greek grapes, but loves beer so much that he also started a brewery in London—Rocky Head. Yellow Donkey is a Pale Ale that's slightly hazy thanks to being unfiltered. The body is full and smooth, and the Motueka hops give all of the juicy, fresh tropical-fruit aroma. They also make Crazy Donkey, an IPA with a similar hop profile, only bigger and fruitier. Enjoy with the stunning Santorini sunsets.

8 Wired Hopwired IPA

Blenheim, New Zealand
ABV: 7.3%
Hops: Southern Cross, Motueka, Nelson Sauvin

This is an explosive, remarkable IPA. Made in New Zealand with all New Zealand hops, it's like a flare directed at American hop fanatics that says, "Oi, look at what we've got!" Gone is the orange and pine of the American Northwest and in comes the pineapple, mango, passion fruit, lime, gooseberry, and grape of New Zealand; potent, perfumed, aromatic, and also laced with a slick, hop-oil texture flowing through the beer. Once a year you'll find a fresh-hopped version when the harvest takes place in March—this has a grassier, more floral side to it, veering toward kiwi fruit and lychee. No. 8 wire is something Kiwis use to fix just about anything that needs fixing and the name has entered into the local lexicon to show the ingenuity of a New Zealander: a No. 8 wire can sort anything out. As can an 8 Wired IPA.

Murray's Angry Man Pale Ale

Port Stephens, Australia
ABV: 5.0%
Hops: Motueka, Pacifica

Made on Bob's Farm, which the brewery share with Port Stephens Winery, Murray's brew a wide range of colorful, esoteric, and fantastic beers. Angry Man Pale Ale borrows sackfuls of hops from its New Zealand neighbor to give a distinctly antipodean flavor and a beer that shares similarities with the grape-guzzlers next door. Clean malt, with a hint of blossom-honey sweetness, which is exactly what you want in the Aussie sunshine, there's loads of delicate fruit (grape, citrus, and pineapple) and a sharp, dry bitterness. For those who want to step up their drinking, Murray's also make the 10.0% ABV Spartacus Imperial IPA brewed with all-New-Zealand hops. At the brewery there's a restaurant, where they suggest a beer and a wine for each dish on the menu; there's a beer and cheese menu; or you can grab a slab from the Cellar.

BELGIAN IPAS TAKE AMERICAN (AND PACIFIC) IPAS AND CHANGE THE PROFILE BY FERMENTING WITH A BELGIAN YEAST STRAIN, GIVING THE SPICY, ESTERY, AND FRUITY FLAVORS WE ASSOCIATE WITH BELGIAN ALES, WHETHER IT'S BLONDE, FARMHOUSE, OR TRAPPIST. CHANCES ARE THIS BEER STYLE DEVELOPED WHEN A BREWER DECIDED TO CHANGE THE YEAST STRAIN ON HIS FLAGSHIP IPA TO SEE WHAT A BELGIAN ONE WOULD DO TO IT. THE INTERPLAY OF YEAST AND HOPS HAS IMPRESSED MANY AND THE STYLE HAS DEVELOPED AND GROWN EVER MORE POPULAR, TURNING INTO A BIG BEER GROUP HUG WITH BREWERS AROUND THE WORLD TRYING IT OUT. PERHAPS MORE IMPORTANTLY, THIS STYLE HERALDED A WILLINGNESS TO EXPERIMENT MORE FREELY WITH YEAST STRAINS AND THAT HAS KICKED ON INTO MANY OTHER BEER STYLES.

BELGIAN IPA

Belgian IPA, Pale Ale, and White IPA all come together here. Pale Ales and IPAs give that juicy hop flavor with the added depth from the yeast which sometimes brings clove and phenols (which tastes like bathroom cleaner to me: phenolic clove and citrus? No thanks). Other times, it's a peppery, spicy, estery (banana, pear, and apple) addition, which can be wonderful, rounding out flavors and poking more fruit depth into the brew. White IPA comes somewhere between Wit and American Wheat, and adds lots more hops. American hops are popular but southern hemisphere hops are even better, I think, as the tropical fruit works really well with the yeast esters. As an experimental style it's still developing around the world and some brews are better than others; the best are fantastic, the worst taste like perfume or detergent.

Green Flash Le Freak

San Diego, California
ABV: 9.2%
Hops: Amarillo

Green Flash is a fun brewery to visit. The taproom puts you right inside the big brewhouse so that you can see and hear the beers getting made as you sit and sip. The rainbow-color brightness of Green Flash also makes you feel like you've just walked into a candy store, as your eyes jump between the orange of Palate Wrecker, the yellow of Imperial IPA, and the green of Barleywine. The lipstick-pink of Le Freak gives you a wonderful meeting of Belgian Tripel and American IPA. Loads of bright hops burst out with grapefruit, floral, orange, mango, and pine, and then comes the yeast, peppery and herbal, mixing with hard-hitting and bracingly bitter hops at the end. Similar to Le Freak, there's also the blue of Rayon Vert, a Belgian-American Pale Ale with Brettanomyces in the bottle to give a peppery, funky depth.

Anchorage Bitter Monk

Anchorage, Alaska

ABV: 9.0%

Hops: Apollo, Citra, Simcoe

If you've read through from page one, you'll be familiar with Anchorage by now. However, if you've just landed on this page by chance, hold on tight: Bitter Monk is a Belgian-style Double IPA. It's American-hopped, fermented with Belgian yeast in tank, and then aged in French-oak Chardonnay barrels with Citra hops and Brettanomyces. It's a head-spinning, tongue-twisting kind of brew, giving loads of tropical fruit, a background of grape and vanilla, a spike of lemony and farm-like brett, plus a Belgian yeast which drags at the back of the tongue. Imagine a farm. On one side is a pine forest, on the other are citrus and mango groves. Someone has just smashed open a barrel of wine and thrown flowers and pepper all over it while screaming, "Hell yeah!" just because they can. That's what Bitter Monk tastes like to me.

Westbrook Farmhouse IPA

Mount Pleasant, South Carolina

ABV: 7.3%

Hops: Columbus, Centennial, Amarillo, Cascade, Galaxy

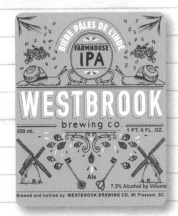

This takes Westbrook's flagship IPA and throws three yeast strains at it plus some extra hops. First it gets a farmhouse yeast, making it peppery, spicy, and distantly phenolic. Then two different types of Brettanomyces tear through it, munching at any remaining sweetness and turning the beer dry, while also giving it funky farmhouse flavors of horses, hay, and lemon balm. On top of all that are the hops: mango and pineapple from the Australian Galaxy and juicy citrus and fragrant floral from the American varieties. The amber body is full before it rips into that dry finish; the carbonation sends a fierce updraft into the foam; there's a solid smack of bitterness; and yet, with all of that, it keeps an incredible balance between hops and yeast with the brett adding an unusual funkiness which works so well with the punchy hops.

Troubadour Magma

Ursel, Belgium

ABV: 9.0%

Hops: Simcoe and others

Made by the Musketeers Brewery, which was started by four friends, the range of beers are called Troubadour, named after those men of medieval times who moved from village to village, bringing music and joy with them. Troubadour Magma is a Tripel IPA: a Belgian Tripel, plus more malt and hopped like an American IPA. Of the new fashion of Belgian beers, those that bring influence from home and away, this is one of the best. Flame-colored, the aroma grabs you right away: roasted pineapple, tropical fruit, mango, and tangerine. The body is full and rich, there's some vanilla and almond-cake sweetness in there, a little rounded pale malt depth, and then the 50 IBUs of bitterness cuts it off and it finishes dry with a second wave of juicy hops coming out. Troubadour also make a brilliant Blonde—start there and then move onto Magma.

High Water No Boundary IPA

Chico, California
ABV: 6.5%
Hops: Varies—typically from Southern Hemisphere

No Boundary IPA is a thrice-a-year release, which is always a little bit different and inspired by the best of the available ingredients. What stays the same is that it's always fermented with a Belgian yeast strain (which has varied between brews). It gets a low bittering hop addition that's bolstered by lemon verbena grown by High Water's Steve Altimari, some star anise is thrown in late, and hops have so far all been southern hemisphere (plus some American Citra). Whatever you get, you should look forward to drinking it. Beneath the fragrant grapefruit, grape, and orange of the hops is the yeast, which makes the fruitiness fruitier; it gives a tannic, grape-skin dryness, mirrors the peppery and earthy hops, and leaves a little citrus pith at the end as a reminder of the lemon verbena.

Deschutes Chainbreaker IPA

Deschutes, Oregon
ABV: 5.6%
Hops: Bravo, Citra, Centennial, Cascade

Let me introduce you to White IPA. It's IPA meets Wheat beer, sometimes a supersized and American-hopped Belgian Wit and other times a pumped-up American Wheat. Pale straw in color with a white, wispy foam, Chainbreaker is one of the first White IPAs to go into year-round production and it takes a Belgian Wit, complete with ground coriander and orange, and goes big with American hops. The aroma is a wicked mix of lemon, spice, orange, and grapefruit. It's smooth and slick, making it satisfying and refreshing, then comes bitterness and yeast, leaving a dry finish along with pith and pepper at the back of your tongue. It's a great style, a spring kind of beer, which has a uniquely zesty freshness—I hope more breweries try out this style and, if they do, then have it with some lemon-and-herb-roasted chicken.

Hardknott Queboid

Millom, England
ABV: 8.0%
Hops: Centennial, Cascade, Amarillo

I like Dave Bailey, the man behind Hardknott. He's definitely got the right temperament to be a brewer: he's hardworking, full of ideas, willing to do things differently, and he's bonkers. That craziness transfers to the beers with a range of styles, including Infra Red, a fantastic Red IPA; Granite, a once-a-year Barley Wine; and Æther Blæc, a barrel-aged strong Stout; plus some regular specials. Then there's Queboid, a wild ride of a beer with unexpected twists and flips. Queboid pours a hazy bronze, and the aroma throws out all kinds of surprises with festively baked apples, strawberries, peppercorns, roasted citrus pith, and fruity coffee. There's some sweet bready malt in the middle, more roasted fruit, citrus, and loads of yeast depth clinging on with pepper and clove. Every mouthful is different, unexpected, fun, and it makes you think. This beer is Dave's personality in a glass.

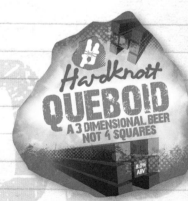

BLACK IPA (AKA AMERICAN BLACK ALE)

BLACK INDIA PALE ALE? STUFF THE SEMANTICS; IT'S BETTER TO THINK OF THE INITIALIZATION AND THE IDEA OF AN IPA, JUST TURNED BLACK. IN OTHER WORDS, IPA HAS NOTHING TO DO WITH INDIA AND PALENESS; IT'S A BEER MADE WITH LOTS OF HOPS AND HAS A STRONG BASE OF MALT. OTHER NAMES EXIST, INCLUDING CASCADIAN DARK (NAMED AFTER THE MOUNTAINS IN THE PACIFIC NORTHWEST), INDIA BLACK, OR AMERICAN BLACK ALE, BUT BLACK IPA IS THE ONE THAT HAS STUCK AROUND AND LABELED THIS INCREASINGLY POPULAR STYLE. PERSONALLY, I RECKON AMERICAN BLACK ALE WILL BE THE NAME WE ALL COME TO USE BECAUSE BLACK IPA STILL FEELS A BIT LIKE AN IN-JOKE THAT HAS GOTTEN OUT OF HAND—WHAT DO YOU MEAN, A BLACK PALE ALE? THAT'S SO SILLY AND OUTRAGEOUS; WHAT A CRAZY BREWMASTER YOU ARE!

What you'll get in these beers are aromatic hops (citrus, floral, herbal, tropical, and pine) and a big bash of bitterness at the end. The better versions, I think, don't let the roast bitterness interfere with the sharp citrus hops and they play a trick between your eyes and tongue: it tastes like the pale caramel base of an IPA, smooth, rounded, and full-bodied, only it looks dark. That's what I want from a Black IPA because, if it's going to be called an IPA, then I want it to taste like one. You might get a hint of chocolate, which is nice, but if your Black IPA tastes like breakfast gone wrong (bitter coffee, grapefruit juice, and burnt toast), then you are probably drinking an American Stout or a hoppy Porter rebadged to try to make it trendier.

Deschutes Hop in the Dark

Bend, Oregon
ABV: 6.5%
Hops: Northern Brewer, Nugget, Centennial, Amarillo, Cascade, Citra

Until I had Hop in the Dark, I didn't understand all the fuss about Black IPAs. Most of them prior to this were harsh in their dark malt flavor and acrid with roast bitterness before the grapefruit came in—and that's not a good combo. Hop in the Dark is different. Close your eyes and it's an IPA, open them and it looks like a Stout. That's the trick and fun in this style, and that's what the best examples achieve. Caramel, bread, and toasty malt make it smooth to drink (aided by oats in the mash), with a full body, all lifted to be juicy with tropical fruit and sweetly citrusy hops also giving pith, pine, and herbs (mint and sage). There's also a hint of darkness in the aroma but that might be a trick of its appearance.

Uinta Dubhe Imperial Black IPA

Salt Lake City, Utah
ABV: 9.2%
Hops: Bravo

Dubhe, pronounced "doo-bee," is the second brightest star in the Ursa Major; it's part of the Big Dipper and it's the official star of the state of Utah (yeah, apparently states have official stars...). The beer is also brewed with hemp seeds, rolling the name up to give a dual meaning. Thick and rich with malt, but not like crap coffee, there's caramel and some sweet chocolate with vanilla and a woody depth, with the roast a distant hint of a bonfire in a forest. With 100 IBUs, the bitterness is bold, herbal, and clinging, and the whole thing is kept bright by the juicy citrus, orchard fruit, and grassy hops which don't dominate but make it interesting. A star-gazing kind of beer, it's one to drink outside, late at night, while lying on the ground staring up into the sky wondering: "What's out there?" "How did we get here?" "What is a Black IPA?"

Odell Mountain Standard

Fort Collins, Colorado
ABV: 9.5%
Hops: Chinook, Cascade

Which Odell beer to choose... There's St Lupulin or Myrcenary, both pale hop-forward beers reverentially named after the hop oils that give them their fantastic flavor; there's the IPA, one of my favorites of the style, so smooth and juicily fruity; or the harder-to-find barrel-aged masterpieces where the use of wood and wild yeast adds wonderful complexity to beautiful beers... One defining feature links all the Odell beers: a masterful interplay and balance between all the elements. Mountain Standard shows this off in a big way, with so much balance and an impossible lightness to the elevated ABV. A not-quite-black Double Black IPA, the beer's body is smooth and full with hints of chocolate, sweet wood, and cherry, and then the hops, which are grown in Colorado and picked by the brewers, give fresh citrus and a spicy, floral background with a lasting pithy bitterness that's beguilingly brilliant.

Pacific Brewing Laboratory Squid Ink

San Francisco, California
ABV: 7.0%
Hops: Cascade, Nugget, Summit, Cluster

I met Patrick, one of the two guys behind Pac Brew Lab, by chance. I was in San Francisco to drink beer. I got introduced to Richard Brewer-Hall, an Englishman living in the city who (home)brews and has a pub in his basement. He invited me to watch the Superbowl at his place, so I went for the free beer and food. Patrick was there, pouring his incredible DIPA homebrew, and it was one of the best beers I drank during a week in California. He has since gone on to open Pac Brew Lab, and Squid Ink and Nautilus, a hibiscus Saison, are the frontline beers. Squid Ink is filled with cocoa, coffee, toffee, orange, pine, and grapefruit, all deftly done with a rich body and herbal bitterness. Now where can I get more of that incredible homebrewed DIPA?

Magic Rock Magic 8 Ball

Huddersfield, England
ABV: 7.0%
Hops: Apollo, Cascade, Columbus,
Nelson Sauvin

In 2001, an experiment was done on schooled wine experts at the University of Bordeaux. They were given a white wine and a red wine and asked to give their impressions of them, describing them very differently. However, they were actually drinking the same white wine in both glasses; the "red" one had been dyed with a flavorless coloring. Black IPA is a bit like that and this one does a better job than most of gazumping the gray matter. Mango, peach, apricot, and thyme in the aroma, plus a hint of cocoa and vanilla, this one is slick and smooth with a caramel sweetness in the middle, some chocolate-covered tropical fruit, and a potent bitterness, all finishing with another round of tropical fruit. A trick on the tongue, is it black and pale? The Magic 8 Ball says... Reply hazy, try again.

AleBrowar Black Hope

Lebork, Poland
ABV: 6.2%
Hops: Simcoe, Chinook, Citra,
Cascade, Palisade

In May 2012, AleBrowar opened and launched three beers with the attitude of pushing forward Polish craft-brewing. Brewed under contract at Poland's oldest family brewery, Gościszewo Browar, AleBrowar make a Witbier, an IPA, and a Black IPA. Both IPAs use the same hops, the same yeast, and are the same ABV. The difference comes with the addition of dark malts to turn one black. Some coffee roast is there with berries, smoke, and dark chocolate giving a hint of acidity; there's earthy, herbal hops plus some pithy citrus, some caramel fills out the middle, and it all folds together into an interesting and unusual interpretation of the style. It's exciting to see a new brewery jump into the craft-beer market—let's hope they manage to start a small Polish movement of bars and breweries, tempting Poles away from the Tsykie.

Yeastie Boys Pot Kettle Black

Wellington, New Zealand
ABV: 6.0%
Hops: NZ Styrian Golding, NZ Cascade, Nelson Sauvin

This one could be put into a Pacific Black IPA category, or perhaps a Nelsonian Dark to America's Cascadian Dark, or just as a hoppy Porter. Whatever way you want to badge it, it's another one of those beers that plays with your mind, only this one does it a little differently. At the beginning it's an IPA. Fruit fires out of the glass with grape skin, blackcurrant (the sort of cross-beverage blackcurrant you get in wine, coffee, and beer), resiny pine, floral, and grapefruit pith. In the middle, it's a Porter: luscious, licorice, chocolate, and caramel. Then, at the end, it goes back to being an IPA with grassy, earthy hops, herbs, citrus pith, and tropical-fruit juice, leaving a lingering, fruity bitterness. Pot and kettle can call each other whatever the hell they want to; all that matters is that it tastes damn good.

AMERICAN AMBER AND RED ALE

AMBERS ARE CARAMEL-COLORED ALES WHICH DEVELOPED ALONGSIDE PALE ALE AS THE TWO TRAIL-BLAZING STYLES OF THE EMERGING AMERICAN CRAFT-BEER MOVEMENT IN THE 1980S—IN MANY WAYS PALE ALE CAME TO BE THE BIG STAR BEER AROUND THE WORLD, WHILE AMBER STAYED AT HOME AND DID THE HARD WORK IN THE BARS AROUND AMERICA, WHERE IT IS, BY VOLUME CONSUMED, IN THE TOP FIVE CRAFT-BEER STYLES. OVER THE LAST DECADE, AS STYLES HAVE DANCED AROUND AND HUDDLED TOGETHER DIFFERENTLY, AMBER HAS TAKEN ON TWO FORMS: A LIGHTLY HOPPED, GATEWAY KIND OF AMBER (WHICH CAN BE ALE OR LAGER WITH SOME CROSSOVER TO ALTS OR MINI-MÄRZENS) AND AMERICAN AMBER, A HIGHLY-HOPPED BEER CLOSER TO PALE ALE. AMERICAN RED STEPS UP THE AMBER INTO A BIGGER, MALTIER, AND HOPPIER BEER—IT'S WHAT YOU'D EXPECT IF YOU SAW THE WORDS "RED IPA."

Look at the inside bands on a rainbow; that's what colors you'll get here. From dark yellow, through orange, and up to deep red, perhaps with a violet streak, the use of darker (crystal) malts gives these beers the appearance their names suggest. A chewy toffee or caramel profile might be present in the middle with a sweet nuttiness in Reds. The American prefix tells us that the styles are hop-dominated with a moderate to high bitterness (30–80 IBUs) and a vibrant use of late and dry hops for flavor and aroma. Alcohol will likely be 5.0–8.0% ABV, but, as with most styles, Imperial versions exist, particularly with Reds.

Half Acre Ginger Twin

Chicago, Illinois
ABV: 6.5%
Hops: Chinook, Simcoe

I have this thing about beer labels. It's sort of an obsession and a mindset: if a beer looks bad on the shelf, then in my mind it'll taste bad as well, whereas a beautiful-looking beer is something I imagine will taste delicious. This isn't always accurate, of course, but I'll always buy a beer that looks good over one that doesn't. The Half Acre beers are some of the best-looking and most appealing in the world, with their whole range being a visual treat. The great thing is that they taste as good as they look. Ginger Twin is an India-style Red Ale, which is a wordy way of saying Red IPA. It pours a rusty copper and the malt gives it a nutty, brown-bread depth that's subtle beneath the earthy, floral, grapefruit, and herbal hop aroma, which gives a lingering, resinous bitterness. The balance is beautiful, interesting, and striking—just like the label.

8 Wired Tall Poppy

Blenheim, New Zealand
ABV: 7.0%
Hops: Warrior,
Columbus, Simcoe,
Amarillo

This is what a Red IPA should be like.
It's got all that wonderful, fragrant,
"in-your-face" American hop
character and builds it up upon a
base beer that's fuller than regular
IPAs: nuttier, darker, and a little
chocolaty with berry fruit in the
background. There's just something
about that malt base that brings out
different qualities in the hops, too: it
gives darker berry fruits instead of
juicy orchard fruit; roasted citrus
instead of freshly squeezed; floral
honey instead of freshly picked
flowers; woody bark instead of pine
resin. It's as if all the flavors mature,
get bigger, and evolve, which I guess
makes Tall Poppy an appropriate name.
This one is great with jerk chicken and can handle a
little spicing, although nothing fierce, to fight the hops.
Coconut-based curries are also excellent with the cooling
effect of the coconut like a lupulin lullaby.

Swan Lake Amber Swan Ale

Kanaya City, Japan
ABV: 5.0%
Hops: Cascade, Nugget,
Columbus

This is one of Japan's most highly
regarded craft beers, winning loads
of awards around the world since
the brewery opened in 1997. It's
made by Hyouko Yashiki No Mori
Brewery (which can be translated as
"Swan Lake") and this one sits right
between the Alt-like Ambers and
the American-hopped versions.
A toasty malt base loads up the
glass, and the citrus, floral, and
peachy American hops hang
suggestively from it, giving a
delicate yet still inviting hop flavor
and a quenching kind of bitterness.
You'll also get a grassy, earthy,
spicy depth that plays around with
the darker malts in the mash. This all points it toward
grilled meats like yakitori or to a plate overflowing with
plump gyoza parcels, preferably the ones that have been
fried so that you get that wonderful, crisp coating which
sweetens the nutty notes in the ale.

Pizza Port Ocean Beach Chronic

San Diego, California
ABV: 4.7%
Hops: Liberty

There are four Pizza Port brewpubs, plus a production brewery, all along the
Pacific Ocean on California's coast. Each one brews and also makes amazing
pizzas. The first opened in 1987 in Solana Beach. They sold their own beers for
the first time in 1992 and then they opened Carlsbad, San Clemente, and then
Ocean Beach. In 2013, a production brewery opened in Bressi Ranch to support
the pubs and add a canning line for their beers. If you're near any of them, then go:
they make some of the best beers in America, I reckon. Ocean Beach's Chronic is a
smooth, nutty, clean kind of Amber. Not hop-heavy; instead, it's clean and balanced, and the
ideal beer to gulp after a few hours spent watching the waves.

Brodie's Hackney Red IPA

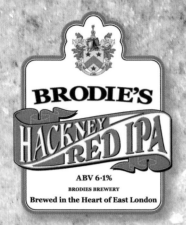

London, England
ABV: 6.1%
Hops: Amarillo, Citra

In a small, garage-like space behind the King William IV pub in Leyton, East London, is Brodie's Brewery. London's (and possibly Britain's) most experimental brewery, they knock out an unbelievable range of different beers, while still maintaining a large core base. Go to the King William IV for a proper East London, pub-drinking experience complete with crappy old carpets and colorful characters, plus a snaking bar lined with Brodie's beers. The Red IPA is a massive hop bomb, brutal in a brilliant way, with a huge aroma of American hops, bitter grapefruit, roasted citrus, a smooth body of toasty caramel, and then a big smack of bitterness at the end. Also look out for Dalston Black IPA, which is another seriously good, explosive kind of beer, plus a range of low-ABV Sour Ales which are tart and quenching.

Szot Amber Ale

Santiago, Chile
ABV: 6.0%
Hops: Cascade

Started by American Kevin Szot and his Chilean wife Astrid, Szot Microbrewery is one of around 50 craft breweries in Chile. What's exciting is that Chile, along with its neighboring Argentina, has begun to grow hops, so we'll soon start seeing beers made with South American hop varieties. With a range of beers including an American Pale Ale, a California Common and Imperial Stout, Szot's inspiration is clear. Amber Ale is similar to the Pale Ale, only it's made with more crystal malt (which gives it a darker color), leaving more unfermentable sugars, meaning more residual, caramel-like sweetness, which suits the Chilean palate but isn't too sweet for everyone else. A light citrus and floral aroma, some delicate stone fruits, a smooth body, and crisp finish; it's great with fresh fish (especially fish stews) caught along Chile's huge coastline.

Ithaca Cascazilla

Ithaca, New York
ABV: 7.0%
Hops: Cascade, Chinook, Crystal, Amarillo

I don't know about you, but I can't resist a beer that's called Cascazilla, especially having had Ithaca's Flower Power IPA, a beer for which I don't know enough superlatives. Cascazilla isn't just named after a hop monster; near the brewery is the Cascadilla Gorge, a serene spot with bridges, creeks, and waterfalls. Cascazilla the Beer is as serene as a city under attack from a giant beast. This bold Red IPA has an aroma that screams citrus, floral, and pine, with a kind of marmalade background that mixes with the juicy, nutty, toffee malt. The bitterness is earthy and resinous, clinging remorselessly at the end, giving a monstrous roar, the same sort of roar you give as you order another, a guttural growl that pushes the "zilla" part from the back of the throat. Want something tamer? They make root beer, too.

NOT A BEER STYLE, BUT AN INGREDIENT THAT ADDS A DISTINCT FLAVOR TO THE BREW. RYE WAS USED IN OLD EUROPEAN STYLES OF BEER, SUCH AS ROGGENBIER, BUT IT GREW TO BE MORE POPULAR FOR BAKING THAN BREWING. RYE IS A GRAIN USED IN MAKING WHISKY AND GIN, AND IT'S ONLY RECENTLY THAT IT'S HAD A RESURGENCE IN THE BREWHOUSE. IT'S NOT AN EASY GRAIN TO BREW WITH: IT DOESN'T HAVE A HUSK AND SO TAKES UP BREWING LIQUOR EASILY AND CAUSES A STICKY MASH, GIVING BREWERS POTENTIAL PROBLEMS. REGARDLESS OF THIS, RYE IS USED FOR ITS DISTINCTIVELY SPICY, NUTTY, MINTY FLAVOR, FOR THE RED COLOR IT GIVES TO A BEER, AND BECAUSE IT ADDS A DEPTH AND TEXTURE TO BEERS THAT CAN'T BE ACHIEVED WITH ANY OTHER INGREDIENT.

RYE BEER

Rye can be used in any beer style. Sometimes it's there as a background note whereas other brews make it the dominant feature. Many rye beers emphasize the spicy flavor by going for a clean body and an aromatic hop flourish where floral American hops can be particularly complementary to rye's herbal earthiness. Also good is the spiciness and berry fruit of some British or American hop varieties, again used to accentuate the grain's flavor. ABV and IBU are as wide as the grin on a rye-beer lover's face when they see the style on tap.

Upright Six

Portland, Oregon
ABV: 6.7%
Hops: Tettnang, Magnum

Along with Four, Five, and Seven, Six is one of Upright's four year-round beers. Each of them uses the same Saison yeast strain, grain grown and malted locally, and hops from the Annen Brothers farm in Mt. Angel, south of Portland. All are very different and show the vast potential that can be achieved when brewers put together a few ingredients to make very different beers. Six is a Rye American Saison, although categories tend to elude these Upright beers. It pours a deep mahogany, the kind of color that makes you look a little longer before taking a gulp. The aromas are unusual and intoxicating, as you chase them around your glass: rye bread, chocolate, fig, cherry, tobacco, pepper, banana, bubble gum, roasted apple, grass. The rye makes it dry and spicy, which the yeast amplifies, giving a peppery, almost-acidic tang at the end.

Half Acre Baumé

Chicago, Illinois
ABV: 7.0%
Hops: Chinook

Half Acre was started in 2006, though they didn't get their own brewery until 2009. Before then it was brewed by Sand Creek in Wisconsin and then driven into Chicago to sell. When Ska Brewing upscaled, Half Acre drove to Durango, Colorado, and returned with four trailers stacked with stainless steel. In 2012, they opened a taproom on the side of their brewery, ready to pour all their many beers—if you're in Chicago, then it's a must-visit place. Baumé is a special, limited-release American chocolate rye stout. A dark brown pour, it's luscious like thick chocolate and sweet coffee; there's lots of rye spice adding bread and minty herb, which goes so well with the mocha depth, and then the hops give an unexpected freshness with a grassy green depth of pepper and spice. The rye is never overpowered, nor overpowering, and adds its unique depth to this magnificent brew.

Summer Wine Cohort

Holmfirth, England
ABV: 7.5%
Hops: Summit, Citra, Chinook, Simcoe, Amarillo

If you like a lot of hops in your beer, then you'll like Summer Wine. They are not shy when it comes to opening up the hop sack and pouring them all in, going for big bitterness and outrageous aromas on all of their beers, most of which follow a modern American influence, such as Diablo IPA, a hop explosion that'll leave your tongue tingling. Cohort is a little different and a lot special. It's a Double Black Belgian Rye IPA. What could be a crazy collision of influences turns out to be a brilliant display of brewing bravado and skill: full-bodied, there's chocolate and rye, mint and orange, berries and smoke, and the hops give floral and citrus. Peppery yeast and hops combine with the rye spice and make this miraculous mix of different things into a damn good beer.

Sixpoint Righteous Ale

Brooklyn, New York
ABV: 6.3%
Hops: Cascade, Columbus, Chinook

If American rye ale was a beer found in the style guides, then you'd expect it to be described like an American Pale Ale or IPA made with rye in the mash, and brewed with hops which complement the grain's spicy, herbal depth, while spiking them with citrus. Righteous would be the textbook example of an American rye: amber-red, peppery, really dry and quenching, so dry it almost makes you think there's a citrus tartness to it, the type you get from the chewiest rye bread. The hops push forward the herbal side of rye by bringing an earthiness that is then kept from being overpowering by the pithy, floral, citrus lift of C-hops. Here's some beer trivia: a six-pointed star is a brewing icon: it's symbolic of purity as it represents the ingredients needed to brew (water, grain, malt, hops, yeast, and the brewer), as well as being the alchemic reconciliation of fire and water.

Haymarket Angry Birds Belgian Rye IPA

Chicago, Illinois
ABV: 7.5%
Hop: Amarillo, Cascade

Hearing our British accents, the bartender started talking to us, "Where you from?" "How'd you like Chicago?" "Oh, you're here to drink beer? Do you want to see the brewery?" We jumped off our bar stools and followed him to where the neat set-up knocks out a range of superb beers. Then we see the "cellar": a line of kegs backed by a bank of serving tanks. That's how fresh the beer is—it's coming straight from the tank. We'd already commented on how fresh the beer tasted and now we knew why. Angry Birds Belgian Rye shows off Haymarket's barely rivaled ability to combine Belgian yeast and American hops as spicy yeast and rye mix sensationally well with the peach and apricot of Amarillo and the floral side of Cascade. Oscar's Pardon is a dry-hopped Belgian Pale Ale, which is another brilliant coming together of Belgium and America. If you're in Chicago, you must visit Haymarket.

Tempest RyePA

Kelso, Scotland
ABV: 5.5%
Hops: Summit, Centennial, Columbus

Tempest started brewing in 2010 and they've become a leading Scottish name by making beers that are a little different—lavish hop users, happy to brew strong beers, and experimental with unusual ingredients. Red Eye Flight (7.4% ABV) is a lusciously smooth and heartily roasty Porter brewed with cocoa, demerara sugar, and coffee; Chipotle Porter (5.6% ABV) infuses the earthy, smoky dried jalapeños into a rich dark beer, which tempers the fruit's fiery side; Long White Cloud (5.6% ABV) is filled with the tropical-fruit flavors of New Zealand hops. RyePA is Tempest's take on an American Rye IPA where the rye is nutty and spicy with a brown-bread background, the malty middle peeks at a caramel sweetness before the grassy, pithy, herbal hops come out, finishing with a squeeze of citrus.

Deep Ellum Rye Pils

Dallas, Texas
ABV: 4.6%
Hops: Liberty, Mt Hood, Sterling

Adding rye to the base of a Pilsner gives us the chance to see what kind of depth a different grain can bring to a subtle style. In this golden brew, with that hint of red at the edges, it's the hops which dominate before we reach the rye—brewed with American-grown hops of German descent, they give a grassy, floral, pithy citrus fruit that's fresh and delicate and not like an IPA line-drive. The body is smooth and clean, and then comes the rye-cracker spiciness at the end, which dries it all out and finishes it with a citrusy tag team of grain and hops—altogether the rye adds a whole new complexity and depth to a Pilsner. Made in Texas, this one is a dream with a barbecue on the side: the rye is so good at complementing the dry-rub spices, while the delicate citrus in the hops cut through the richness.

As time passes, beer styles evolve and yet the stories attached to them tend to root them in a specific moment. Mild suggests that this beer is low in flavor and, in a beer world that seeks maximum impact, who wants that? But this isn't necessarily the case... Mild has been around for over 300 years and the name was originally used to indicate freshness, not a particular style (it had a milder taste compared with aged beers). It's shifted around a lot since then, being stronger than India Pale Ale at one time (and bitter by today's standards), before dropping to be a "milder" flavor. That's when grain restrictions during the First World War had an impact: breweries had to reduce the strength of their beers and Mild took a big hit. Post-war and ABV levels rose but new taxes in the 1930s slashed the strength again, before the Second World War reduced the alcohol content further, taking the hops with it. And from there it stuck as the beer we're more familiar with now— low in alcohol and lightly hopped.

Mild is an anomaly of an idea that has been bullied into the boring corner of the room by bigger, louder styles. But Mild is in transition. Influenced by a move toward low-ABV drinkability, Mild is gaining a new identity. It can be gold to black in color, though red-brown is most common, ABV will range from 3.0 to 6.0%, and IBU might get into the 30s, where English hops give a delicate fragrance. Some Milds are dull, but others can be wonderfully full of flavor and depth with a rasp of quenching bitterness to please the modern palate. While there are no real rules for a Mild now, its key characteristic is an easy-drinking balance of malt and hops. Mild is modernizing again and has become a style that's modest in ABV, but big in character—the name might be the only thing holding it back.

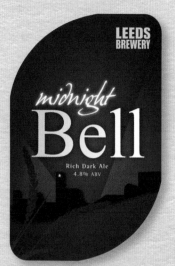

Leeds Midnight Bells

Leeds, England
ABV: 4.8%
Hops: First Gold, Bobek, Willamette

In the United Kingdom, you'll find Dark Mild, Golden Mild, and stronger Ruby Milds, showing the style's versatility. Leeds Brewery's Midnight Bells is a great example of a Dark Mild. A deep red-brown with a tight tan foam (pulled in the northern style through a "sparkler" which gives a thick, creamy crown), it's smooth and clean with a chestnut kind of background, a faint hint of chocolate, but mostly just a fantastic, easy-drinking depth. The hops give an elegant, English, floral quality in the aroma, bolstered by the blackcurrant of Willamette hops and leaving a little peppery Bobek tickle on the way down—it's balanced beautifully. If you go to Leeds, then the brewery has a couple of pubs where you can try the full range of mostly modern Yorkshire styles—Best Bitters, English Pale Ales, and hoppy Bitters, all done superbly well and perfect with classic pub food.

Pizza Port Ocean Beach Skidmark Brown

San Diego, California
ABV: 4.1%
Hops: Phoenix, Brewers Gold, Sterling

You don't expect one of the best beers you have during a week in San Diego—home of West Coast IPAs—to be a Mild, do you? Well, Ocean Beach's Skidmark surprised and delighted me in so many ways, mostly because I wasn't expecting its big flavor. At 4.1% ABV you get the body and texture of a bulkier brown ale; it's full-bodied, super clean (in that you can precisely taste the simplicity of the malt base), and nutty with a slight hint of good coffee. The hops are earthy and balanced but still taste fresh and inviting, and there's just so much going on in the glass that it left me sitting back in my bar seat and wondering why other brewers can't do this. Freshness, flavor, balance, and drinkability: it defines what a modern Mild is.

Tap East East End Mild

London, England
ABV: 3.5%
Hops: Fuggles

This is one for the guys. You know what it's like to get dragged shopping when you'd rather just sit in the pub? Well, things just got a little better in London. Tap East is a brewbar in Europe's biggest shopping center. Feign interest in shopping, then tell her you're just going to look in the "electronics shops at plugs and stuff." At which point you sprint as fast as possible, get to Tap East, and relax until you get the "where are you, babe?" text. East End Mild is a chestnut color with chewy English malt bulking out the core. The aroma is all earthy, grassy, and hedgerow fruit with a lasting bitterness in which the Fuggles flavor comes to dominate. If America tastes like IPA, then this is England in a glass. And it's made in a mall to help make shopping for clothes bearable.

Little Creatures Rogers Beer

Freemantle, Australia
ABV: 3.8%
Hops: East Kent Goldings, Galaxy, Cascade

Australia's premier craft brewery, Little Creatures, was built on the foundation of their Pale Ale, a juicy, fresh, American-inspired beer, which uses hops from America and Australia to get the orange, grapefruit, and floral flavors into the country's ultimate refrigerator beer. Amber in color, Rogers Beer is a bit different. At only 3.8% ABV, it rams way more flavor into your glass than you might have been expecting. The aroma lets you know first that they use some juicy southern hemisphere hops, giving a little floral and fresh berries. The body is clean and dry, while subtle malt presence gives some toasted nuts and far-away caramel. It's simple in a way that makes it wonderful to drink—in a world where brewers are trying to stuff as much flavor into beer glasses as possible, this one is the epitome of skillful restraint.

BROWN ALE IS A LONDON-BORN STYLE, ALTHOUGH ONE THAT DIDN'T GET NAMED UNTIL YEARS AFTER IT WAS FIRST BREWED. ORIGINALLY JUST THE STANDARD BREW OF THE CITY, IT LED TO THE DRIER, STRONGER, MORE HOPPED PORTER. A SECOND WAVE, THIS TIME USING THE NAME, CAME IN THE 20TH CENTURY WITH TWO VERSIONS DEVELOPING: SWEET BROWN ALE (THINK MANN'S) AND DRY, NUTTY NORTHERN BROWN (THINK NEWCASTLE). WHILE THE SWEET BROWN STYLE VIRTUALLY DISAPPEARED, NORTHERN NEWCASTLE BECAME A FLAGSHIP WORLD BEER, THOUGH FEW OTHERS TEND TO REPLICATE THE SAME STYLE. BROWN ALE HAS PERPETUALLY BEEN ON THE MOVE, ALWAYS GETTING REPLACED BY SOMETHING MORE POPULAR. BUT THE STORY GETS INTERESTING AGAIN THANKS TO AMERICAN CRAFT BREWERS, WHO TOOK THE IDEA OF BROWN ALE AND MADE IT INTO SOMETHING NEW, EXCITING, AND (HOPEFULLY) HERE TO STAY.

BROWN ALE

Today there's British Brown Ale and American Brown Ale. British versions (4.0–5.5% ABV) are nutty, toasty, and roasty, medium-bodied, and have an earthy bitterness (25–35 IBUs), with English hop varieties giving floral, earthy, hedgerow fruit. American Browns tend toward more alcohol (5.0–6.5% ABV), more body with roast and chocolate depth, and a feisty floral and citrus hop flavor from American varieties giving a dry, hefty bitterness (up to 50 IBUs). Some old relic Browns still exist, but modern versions are more popular, especially the American-style ones—in fact, Brown Ales are quite rare in Britain now, unfashionable, and in a wasteland (which is ready for development) between Bitter, Pale Ale and Stout. In America, you might find India Brown Ale, Brown IPA, or Imperial Brown, which are, of course, bigger.

Baird Angry Boy Brown Ale

Shizuoka, Japan
ABV: 6.8%
Hops: Nelson Sauvin, Glacier, Cascade

Angry Boy Brown is one of those unexpected treats of a beer. Brown Ale is a little like saying, "let's go to the furnishings store to look at lampshades." It just sounds like a boring thing. Brown. Brown. Brown. Not exciting, is it? Well, it is if you're drinking Baird's Angry Boy. A hazy dark copper in the glass, the aroma makes you do the equivalent of a double take at a pretty passer-by as you quickly press your nose back inside the rim of the glass: peach, pineapple, mandarin, and some dried herbs, all subtle and yet so fresh. It's got a great, clean body of malt, gentle roast, and mainly toffee, nuts, and toast, and some dark chocolate before the bitterness dries it out and makes it refreshing, all while the fine hop flavor permeates everything. Drinking Angry Boy makes me a happy boy.

Surly Bender

Brooklyn Center, Minnesota
ABV: 5.5%
Hops: Columbus, Willamette

Bender is brewed with some oats in the mash, making this an Oatmeal Brown Ale. The oats give the beer a smooth, rich creaminess in the body and a rounded mouthfeel. That's good. Mouthfeel is something that generally makes the difference between a good beer and a great one. Body is particularly important in darker beers where the roasted grains have an acrid acidity that can make it thin and astringent. Bender is brilliant because it's got that richness in the body, which can carry all the roast, toffee, vanilla, and chocolate. Hops hang back, giving a tobacco and leafy depth with a little pithy drag at the end—it's supremely well balanced. Surly also make Coffee Bender—they cold-press Bender with Guatemalan beans to give a mighty mocha flavor to the already delicious beer. If you're a hop-head (rather than a malt monster), then go for Furious, as it's a marvellous IPA.

Pretty Things St Botolph's Town

Cambridge, Massachusetts
ABV: 5.7%
Hops: Fuggles

Pale ale malt, malted oats, torrified wheat, crystal malt, brown malt, and black malt go into the mash for St. Botolph's along with four small doses of sugar to give color and flavor. Then, two yeast strains are used: a typical English strain and an untypically German strain. And what all this creates is an astonishing malt masterpiece. Pretty Things consistently make me raise my already stellar opinion of them (my notebook scribbles for this beer say, "It's like a normal beer but a million times tastier—how do PT do it?"). So, so smooth and richly malty in the most elegant of ways, an outrageously pronounced flavor as if you're drinking in 4D, complex yet subtle, you could drink three bottles in a row and still be excited about it. Fuggles give a grassy, fresh aroma of forests and the most perfectly balanced bitterness you might ever taste. It's sensational.

Runa Agullons

Mediona, Spain
ABV: 5.0%
Hops: Fuggles, Northern Brewer

The Ales Agullons brewery is just outside Barcelona and has been making beer since 2009 in a farmhouse surrounded by barley and vineyards. With a depth of roasted nuts, cocoa, and brown bread, Runa is built up with a floral, woodland, and minty hop aroma and a lingering earthy bitterness, making Runa a Catalan take on a British Brown. Really easy drinking but still interesting, it's the little extra burst of hop freshness that makes this great. Agullons make a range of English-style beers (some with an American hop edge), plus regular specials—look out for Septembre, a blend of Pura Pale (Cascade- and Fuggles-hopped Pale Ale) and Lambic, which is aged for two years before release. With fruit, oak, and funk, it's a taste closer to the winemaking that used to happen in the farmhouse where the beer is now brewed.

Cigar City

Tampa, Florida
ABV: 5.5–9.0%
Hops: Varies per beer

Not many breweries make a Brown Ale (it's just not as fashionable as IPA, is it?), so to find one that makes five through the year, plus some on the side, is rare. But then Cigar City aren't like everyone else. Maduro Brown has a hearty malt depth and a sweet tobacco edge; Cubano-Style Espresso Brown Ale, made with coffee, gives earthy roast and vanilla before malt, hop, and coffee bitterness combine; Bolita Double Nut Brown Ale is a 9.0% ABV monster loaded with roasted nuts, toffee, and earthy hops; with Improv Oatmeal Rye India-Style Brown Ale the name says it all, but doesn't prepare you for the resinous hop hit; and Sugar Plus, a spiced Christmas Brown Ale. There is something about all of these beers that tastes a bit like the liquid interpretation of different cigars.

Nøgne Ø
Imperial Brown Ale

Grimstad, Norway
ABV: 7.5%
Hops: Columbus, Chinook,
East Kent Goldings

I once spent an evening drinking Nøgne Ø beers at the Norwegian embassy in London, which is definitely the fanciest place I've been invited for a pint. The Imperial Brown feels very Scandinavian as it sits right between a British and American beer. Deep red-brown, the body is substantial and rich, giving toffee, nuts, rye bread, a bit of chocolate, and a tangy English kind of depth. The hops are balanced, earthy, and floral with a lingering bitterness that signs off as "C-hops." It's not an explosive Brown; instead, it's one that shows what happens when you go bigger on the malt, while keeping everything balanced and restrained. Nøgne Ø are Norway's craft-beer ambassador and one of Scandinavia's top craft breweries.

8 Wired Rewired Brown Ale

Blenheim, New Zealand
ABV: 5.7%
Hops: Pacific Jade, Pacifica, Cascade

Rewired is definitely the right name for this beer and you can feel the brain synapses snapping, firing, pausing, and rechecking before moving around and reconfiguring themselves. What I like most about Rewired is that it's a joy to drink, while also being able to shift preconceptions of what a Brown Ale is: an uplift of freshness comes first with juicy blackcurrant and a spring-day grassiness; the body is bready and toasty with a spoonful of treacle and a lingering, roast-malt bitterness; the hop flavor flows through as you drink with hedgerow, roasted tropical fruit, and floral pithiness. To me, Brown Ale means one thing: a summer necking Newcastle's version straight from the bottle in a dark, sweaty rock club, trying to look cool while attempting—and failing—to chat to girls. Old memories get the halcyon glow while Brown Ale is re-imagined.

SYNONYMOUS WITH ORDERING A PINT OF ALE IN AN ENGLISH PUB, BITTER IS THE WORKHORSE OF THE BRITISH BEER INDUSTRY AND THE EVERYDAY BEER CHOICE OF MANY. THE NAME DEVELOPED AS A PRE-PUMP CLIP COLLOQUIALISM TO DIFFERENTIATE BETWEEN THE "SWEET" MILDS AND THE MORE BITTER PALE ALES; THE NAME THEN CAME INTO POPULAR USE. PALE ALE AND BITTER (WHICH STARTED AS THE SAME THING) GREW IN POPULARITY IN THE 19TH AND 20TH CENTURIES, BUT LIKE MANY OTHER GREAT BRITISH ICONS (THE BEATLES, MINIS, JAMES BOND), IT CAME INTO ITS OWN IN THE 1960S AND FROM THERE WE CAN TRACE A MORE RECENT HISTORY AS THE STYLE EVOLVED SEPARATELY FROM PALE ALES.

BITTER

Bitter is more of a category of beers than a precise thing; the defining qualities are a sessionable ABV ranging from 3.5 to 4.5%, and a dry, well-hopped finish, making them highly drinkable. It could be anywhere between gold and russet brown in color; earthy and floral English hops are classic, though American hops have evolved the style; bitterness could be a teasing 20 IBUs up to a feisty 50 IBUs. A Bitter is a pub beer: some belong in grumpy old pubs with curtains and carpet from the 1950s, while others light up the taps in cosmopolitan beer bars. A style on the move, Bitter might be in danger of being crowded out, pushed from all around by Golden Ale, Pale Ale, and dark ales. Fear not, the style won't go away, but a new moniker might develop, perhaps a more open and generic British ale or session beer: the name "Bitter" is the fashion equivalent of a flat cap and pipe (which are, in some hipster hangouts, cool again...).

ADNAMS SOUTHWOLD BITTER

SOUTHWOLD, ENGLAND
ABV: 3.7%
HOPS: FUGGLES

CLASSIC

I like Adnams a lot. I think their range of beers is excellent, the quality is exceptionally high, they experiment with new styles, they regularly bring out new beers, and they are a brewery that you can always rely on for a good pint. Southwold Bitter is their bread-and-butter brew. Made with malt grown close to the brewery and English Fuggles hops, it was first brewed in 1967. It has the completely classic taste of English malt, that full flavor, a hard-to-describe chewiness, and toasty notes. Then the distinctive Fuggles hops come in, pungently earthy and a little floral, while the hardness of the water emphasizes the hop bitterness—drink it from cask to fully appreciate its depth and subtlety. Also look for Adnams Innovation, a brilliant, modern European IPA hopped with Bodicea, Columbus, and Styrian Goldings—there's citrus, spring-morning freshness, and a spicy, earthy finish.

Oakham Asylum

Peterborough, England

ABV: 4.5%

Hops: Amarillo, Chinook, Cascade, Bramling Cross, Willamette

Asylum is where British Bitters are going. Getting lighter and brighter than the brown beers served in a handled mug which we imagine when talking about the style, the whole flavor profile is evolving. Golden in color, there's a hint of pleasing sweetness first, then grapefruit, grapes, and grass above a crisp body of malt which leads into a pithy, clawing bitterness that makes your tongue seek asylum in that first burst of sweetness. There's big flavor, particularly from the American hops, but it's all so well balanced. Oakham have brewed themselves into a position as one of Britain's top breweries simply by making consistently excellent beers with full flavor profiles (look out for Citra and Green Devil IPA). They have a brewery tap in Peterborough—a regular train goes from London and it's definitely worth the trip.

Toccalmatto Stray Dog No Rules Bitter

Fidenza, Italy

ABV: 4.2%

Hops: East Kent Goldings, Styrian Goldings, Citra

This Italian twist on the British style is made incredible by the punchy use of English hops plus the juiciness of Citra, taking the classic base and making it something entirely new. I drank this one in Bir & Fud, Rome. My girlfriend, Lauren, and I went to the city for a long weekend, seeing the sights by day and the beer bars by night. Bir & Fud, with their amazing pizzas and long beer list, was top of my beer tourist must-visit list. I had a violet-amber Stray Dog to start and was as blown away by that as I was by seeing the Trevi Fountain earlier in the day. The aroma was roasted citrus and mango, pepper, peach, and apricot, so fresh I could hardly believe it, and a biting, lasting, spicy bitterness. A great mate for one of the best pizzas I've had.

Kent Brewery KGB

West Malling, Kent

ABV: 4.1%

Hops: East Kent Goldings, Fuggles

Kent is the garden of England. More appropriately, it's the hop garden of England, and Kent Brewery's KGB makes great use of the county's most famous variety. East Kent Goldings got their name when hop grower Tony Redsell suggested to the Hop Marketing Board that the Goldings he grows in East Kent are different from the ones grown around the country. At that time, in the 1970s, the Board made all the decisions and they said "yes" to this one. Now Tony, who in 2012 oversaw his 63rd hop harvest, is trying to get PGI (Protected Geographical Indication) status for the hop that takes up most of his gardens. Making full use of East Kent Goldings, plus the famous Fuggle, Kent Brewery throw in lots of the earthy, pungently fruity, citrus-edged hops to give a rough, unforgiving bitterness, sappy tree bark, and woodland flowers in a light, quaffing kind of pale, dry, bitter beer—a definitive, modern Kentish ale.

KENT BREWERY

KGB

4.1%

Kent Golding Bitter

A full-on dose of Golding and Fuggles hops, with a rich variety of local malts, to make you proud of Kent's heritage.

www.kentbrewery.com

Mont Salève Special Bitter

Neydens, France
ABV: 4.2%

They might be close neighbors of England, Belgium, and Germany, but the French aren't yet known for their beer, despite a few new breweries making interesting things. Brasserie du Mont Salève are one of the classiest of the French craft breweries with a range of styles that shows their world outlook: a British Stout, Belgian Blonde, American IPA, and German Weizen. There's also this Special Bitter, a very English type of golden beer. The malt hangs in the background while the hops do the hard work, giving perfumy peach, candied citrus peel, a fresh earthy grassiness, and a bracing botanic bitterness. Inviting with the aroma, exciting with that bitterness. If you see their Sorachi Ace Bitter, then get it: bursting with lemon, grapefruit, bubble gum, and a herbal edge—it's a powerful hit for a short-swinging 2.5% ABV.

21st Amendment Bitter American

San Francisco, California
ABV: 4.4%
Hops: Warrior, Cascade, Simcoe, Centennial

I love the way the 21st Amendment cans look, and I lust after the way they taste. I went to the brewpub once and my only memories are of drinking a lot of strong beer and getting a photo of me holding two watermelons and looking far too excited (they famously make a wheat beer with watermelons, you see). Bitter American is an extra pale session ale—which is the sexy way of saying "Best Bitter." I first drank this beer at 3 a.m. on the roof of our New York hotel, overlooking the skyline. Amazing experience—the beer and the moment: caramel and bread in the body, skyscrapers all around, citrus pith, pine, floral, orange, yellow cabs speeding by below us, bitter to finish but light and fresh, a fresh breeze in the dark sky carrying the distant buzz of the city. Beautiful, flavorful, and memorable in so many ways.

Social Kitchen & Brewery SF Session

San Francisco, California
ABV: 4.4%
Hops: East Kent Goldings, Bramling Cross

The best Bitters have a neck-back drinkability which means you can sip them all night without getting bored. It takes a lot of skill to make an amazing Bitter that keeps drinkers interested, but SKB's head-brewer Kim Sturdavant has nailed the style, something he learned while traveling and working in different British breweries. SF Session is a summer ale and typifies the modern evolution of a British Bitter by combining delicate English hop flavors with a golden body of beer, where the malt mingles in the background, and the spicy, fragrant, biting hop bitterness quenches. It's utterly English, yet somehow tastes of San Francisco. Grab a menu and also check out the kitchen side of Social. While deciding what to eat, try the SKB Pilsner, an elegant lager that's dry and delicious.

THIS IS EXTRA SPECIAL BITTER—ONE OF THE ORIGINALS AND STILL ONE OF THE BEST. FULLER'S ESB WAS FIRST BREWED IN 1971 AND STARTED THE STYLE. ESB IS NOW MADE IN LONDON, ROME, TOKYO, SYDNEY, LOS ANGELES, AND NEW YORK (AND EVERYWHERE IN BETWEEN). THE FULLER'S VERSION SITS RIGHT IN THE MIDDLE OF THE STYLE, WHICH HAS EVOLVED AROUND IT LIKE A TOWN GROWING AROUND A CHURCH (OR A PUB).

Sometimes also called strong bitter, the style is a larger version of a Bitter, one with more malt and hops but keeping that bracingly dry bitterness. The malt in an ESB is substantial but not dominant; you should get a chewy, English kind of maltiness with cookies, cereal, and caramel and a satisfying full-ish body. That malt base is balanced by lots of hops, giving an earthy bitterness (30–60 IBUs) and an English hop aroma: floral, grassy, hedgerow, earthy (you'll get pine, flowers, or pith if American hops are used, not the freshness of citrus juice). It'll often look on the amber color scale, from deep gold up to red-brown, and have an ABV of around 5.0–6.5%. The best ESBs bring together a deep, yet not overpowering, malt base with a hefty hop bitterness and perfumey, fruity aroma. Not all ESBs will taste like Fuller's ESB, but all of them will likely, and rightly, be inspired by it.

FULLER'S ESB

LONDON, ENGLAND
ABV: 5.9%
HOPS: CHALLENGER, GOLDINGS, NORTHDOWN, TARGET

CLASSIC

This beer tastes like England. It makes me want to sing the national anthem while eating a roast dinner beside a village cricket pitch where the tonk of leather on willow is backed by polite applause from the resilient spectators who don't mind the drizzle because they've got tea and cakes. There's just something so deeply English about it. It's the way the English malt is bigger and bulkier than usual, showing more of its mouth-filling depth. It's how the hops have a stick-in-the-gums bitterness and give a glorious mix of spicy earthiness, a roast orange depth, strawberry fields, and woodland aroma (which all together smells like you're walking through the countryside on a warm summer day while carrying a hop sack over your shoulder and eating a marmalade sandwich). This one is 5.5% ABV on cask and 5.9% in the bottle. Both share a generous depth of malt, yet have a lightness of body and an intoxicating aroma. An evocatively special beer.

Central City Red Racer ESB

Surrey, Canada
ABV: 5.5%
Hops: Horizon, Cascade, Centennial

Central City is a brewpub in British Columbia, making a canned and draft range of Red Racer beers. The ESB is a spin on the classic flavor of the style: brewed using British Maris Otter malt and crystal malts, they give the beer a red tinge at the edges and a depth of caramel, roasted nuts, and toast. Surrounding the malt base comes a mix of American hops bringing a floral side with elderflower and orange blossom, then there's a peppery and earthy bitterness and a citrus-pith fruitiness. Red Racer IPA is the beer which gets around the most and that's also excellent. The best place to drink them is the brewpub—order a pulled pork sandwich with the ESB, as the richness in the beer, plus the fragrant hops, are perfect with the pork's succulence and sauce.

Jämtlands Postiljon

Pilgrimstad, Sweden
ABV: 5.8%

Pilgrimstad, the town where Postiljon is brewed, gets its name from a well that was a resting point for pilgrims traveling to Trondheim, an important old Norwegian town. People stopped at the well because the water was said to have healing powers. The small number of current Pilgrimstad inhabitants still take water from the well, as does Jämtlands Bryggeri, one of Sweden's most bedazzling breweries, wearing a coat covered in medals won at beer competitions. Postiljon pours a deep red color with the sort of foam that clings to the glass for the whole pint. It tastes majestically English: chewy malt gives a toasty, nutty depth surrounded by a hint of chocolate and roasted fruit, while the hops give a floral earthiness and a lingering bitterness, all in a beer with a wonderfully clean depth of flavor thanks to that magic well water.

Tallgrass Oasis

Manhattan, Kansas
ABV: 7.2%
Hops: Northern Brewer, Columbus, Cascade

Oasis is a dry-hopped Imperial ESB. A ballsy 7.2% ABV, it isn't like many other beers. It's got spicy, grassy, orangey hops in the aroma, the malt character has a juiciness to it, and a satisfying lip-smacking kind of depth with an earthy, berry-fruit flavor before 93 IBUs of bitterness beats its way through dressed in an IPA costume. It's powerful but incredibly well balanced with everything just bigger than usual and more tasty. Tallgrass have the classic homebrewer-turned-pro story when, in 2007, Jeff Gill made his pro-brewing dream into a reality. Now Tallgrass make a range of great-looking and great-tasting beers packaged in 16 fl oz (500ml) cans. Push-start with the 8-Bit Pale Ale, chill out with a Halcyon Wheat, jump on the Velvet Rooster Tripel, lick the Buffalo Sweat (it tastes like Milk Stout), and then end up in the hop-filled Oasis.

A SCOTCH ALE, OR 'WEE HEAVY," IS A MALTY, FULL-BODIED STRONG ALE ORIGINATING IN SCOTLAND IN THE 18TH CENTURY. SCOTTISH BARLEY WAS PLENTIFUL, USED BY BREWERS AND DISTILLERS, BUT HOPS WEREN'T SO EASILY AVAILABLE (ALTHOUGH SOMETHING CHANGED, BECAUSE EDINBURGH BECAME FAMOUS FOR ITS INDIA PALE ALE IN THE 19TH CENTURY). THIS MEANT INDIGENOUS SCOTTISH BEERS WERE MALT-FORWARD AND LIGHTLY HOPPED (OR THEY USED HERBS OR HEATHER FOR FLAVOR). DEVELOPING FROM THERE AS A BROADER CATEGORY OF "SCOTTISH ALES," AT SOME POINT IN THE 19TH CENTURY BEERS BECAME KNOWN BY THEIR SHILLING PRICE PER BARREL; THE STYLE NAME STUCK WHILE THE PRICE DIDN'T: LIGHT WAS 60/-, HEAVY WAS 70/-, AND EXPORT 80/-, WHILE BEERS OVER 100/- WOULD'VE BEEN CALLED "WEE HEAVY." ALL SHARE A SIMILAR MALT PROFILE AND LOW BITTERNESS. SOME EXAMPLES OF THESE SCOTTISH BEERS STILL EXIST, ALTHOUGH AROUND THE WORLD THE WORDS SCOTCH ALE ON TAP MOST LIKELY INDICATE THE STRONGER BEER.

SCOTCH ALE

Scotch Ale is mashed at high temperatures to give a caramelized flavor; classic examples are sparingly hopped; it's fermented cooler than traditional ales (a nod to the chilly Scottish temperatures), meaning it's low on fruity yeast esters. It might be made with peated or smoked malt, an idea linking up beer and whisky production, giving bonfire or the peaty aroma of Islay whisky. Red-brown in color, ABV from 6.0 to 9.0%, bitterness might hit the 30s, with hops adding balance and flavor but not much aroma. It's a surprisingly popular style; a malt-forward counterpoint to the screaming citrus of American hops.

Black Isle Scotch Ale

Munlochy, Scotland
ABV: 6.2%
Hops: Pilgrim, Cascade

The Black Isle beers keep a close link to the planet and local environment: they are brewed using only organic ingredients, they take water from a well beneath the Black Isle peninsula in the Scottish Highlands, and they feed their farm stock (because the brewery has cows and sheep) on spent grain. Their Scotch Ale takes the old style of beer and gives the brew a new form, though keeping the same basic shape. Ruby to look at, the beer's aroma is full of inviting caramel, dried fruit, toast, and a woody, vanilla quality. Its smooth maltiness is met by a herbal, grassy edge, which keeps it interesting—there's also a 7.9% ABV Export version which is a malt monster of a beer, bigger in every direction with more hops stuffed in. Lamb raised on the brewery's organic farm and fed on spent grain would be perfect with the beer.

Oskar Blues Old Chub

Longmont, Colorado
ABV: 8.0%
Hops: Columbus or Summit (bittering only)

Oskar Blues started as a restaurant, then came the brewery, and then in 2002 they hand-canned their delicious Dale's Pale Ale and started a revolution (the "Canned Beer Apocalypse"). Since 2002 they've continually been expanding, upgrading to a big canning line and adding more beers to the range, including a Double IPA and Imperial Stout, plus a far lighter Pilsner. Old Chub aggressively packs the can full of malt yet unleashing it gives the equivalent of a comforting olfactory hug: apple crumble, vanilla, brown sugar, and caramelized nuts, plus a background hint reminiscent of heather or parma violets. The ruby-brown body is so smooth with cocoa, caramelized apples, and just a waft of smoke. Lush, but never sweet, it finishes dry, which makes it wonderfully light and refreshing, even for such a big, malt-driven beer. It tastes like a glorious fall day and one to warm the cool Colorado winters.

Renaissance Stonecutter Scotch Ale

Blenheim, New Zealand
ABV: 7.0%
Hops: Southern Cross, Pacific Jade

Brewed in Blenheim, in Marlborough wine country, Renaissance's beer range ticks all the boxes: Pilsner, Pale Ale, IPA, Porter, Scotch, and Barley Wine. In those beers, they only use New Zealand hops, giving a distinctive Kiwi accent to everything they brew. The delicious Elemental Porter is richly chocolaty with leather, coffee, a floral perfume, and cigarette smoke which combine to remind me of a night I was trying to forget (though it's a beer I definitely won't forget). The Stonecutter Scotch is a malt monolog, while hops hum a complementary backing track: toffee apple, caramel, cocoa, toasty malts, raisins, roasted almonds, and licorice; the hops are floral and peppery, giving aromas of grassy fields and plump berries. It's a very modern kind of Scotch ale, giving a fresh lift from the hops alongside the malt, while remaining light and easy drinking.

S:t Eriks 80/-

Stockholm, Sweden
ABV: 5.7%
Hops: East Kent Goldings

Opening in 1859, in its first 22 years as a brewery it had two names—Brusells Brewing Company and the Stockholm Brewing Company—before settling on S:t Eriks in 1881, taking its new name from their most popular beer: S:t Eriks Lager Öl. It grew to be Stockholm's biggest beer brand, but they found times hard in the 1930s, having to move premises and fight temperance and takeovers. In 1959, their centenary year, they emptied the tanks and closed. The new story begins 50 years later when Galatea, the leading Swedish beer importer, get the rights to the S:t Eriks brand, with the dream of reviving the historic name. "Flying Brewmaster" Jessica Heidrich made the dream a reality and in 2010 the modern range of S:t Eriks beers was launched, including a wonderful revision of the famous old Pilsner. There's also this 80/-, a respectful update on the old 80-shilling style; it's ruby-brown and smoothly malt-forward with caramel and chocolate, roast and raisins, with a clean peppery hop finish.

A STRONG ALE TYPICALLY PULLS TOGETHER ANYTHING BETWEEN A BARLEY WINE, STOUT, ESB, AND IPA THAT DOESN'T FIT NEATLY UNDER THOSE STYLE HEADERS. STRONG ALES GENERALLY SHARE A HIGH ALCOHOLIC STRENGTH (7.0–11.0% ABV) AND WILL USUALLY HAVE A HIGH HOP CONTENT, BUT NO OTHER CHARACTERISTICS CAN EASILY DEFINE THEM. SOMETIMES THEY'RE BREWED TO BE AGED AND MATURED FOR A FEW YEARS (SOME CAN LAST OVER A DECADE IF WELL CARED FOR); SOMETIMES THEY ARE DESIGNED TO BE DRUNK FRESH; SOME ARE GOOD FOR BOTH, SHOWING OFF HOP QUALITY WHEN FRESH AND MALT WHEN AGED. AMERICAN STRONG ALE IS THE AGGRESSIVELY HOPPED CRAFT-BEER EVOLUTION. A SIDELINE OF THESE BEERS DATES BACK A FEW CENTURIES TO BRITAIN'S OLD ALES, NAMED THAT WAY BECAUSE THEY WERE LITERALLY OLD WHEN THEY REACHED THE DRINKER, HAVING BEEN AGED AT THE BREWERY, TAKING ON A MELLOW DEPTH BUT ALSO SHERRY-LIKE OXIDIZED FLAVORS, A SOURNESS, AND A NEW COMPLEXITY. "OLD ALE" DIDN'T START AS A "STYLE" AND IT WAS NAMED AFTER ITS AGE—IF IT HAD BEEN SOLD FRESH, IT WOULD'VE BEEN CALLED A MILD.

If you see a beer described as a strong ale (or old ale), then you never quite know what to expect, which, like Russian Roulette, is either a good thing or a bad thing, depending on what your trigger finger goes for.

Fuller's Vintage Ale

London, England
ABV: 8.5%
Hops: Varies; always English

Every year I buy half a case of Fuller's Vintage. I drink a bottle fresh, then put the rest in the back of the beer cupboard, and leave them for a few years. This is beer for aging—in my experience they start great, get better after three to four years, and then get incredible after 10 (though only if you look after the bottles well). In 2011, I went to a 15-year vertical tasting of all the Vintages ever brewed and it was remarkable to see how beer changes with time, hitting highs but also suffering some lows (beer doesn't age in a straight line; it's more like a wave that goes up and down). The Vintage Ale is brewed to a similar recipe each year, though not exactly the same. When fresh, you'll get stone fruits and bitter, peppery hops; as it ages, cherry and almond notes tend to come through, followed by raisins and a cakey depth, plus sherry notes as it reaches its tenth birthday. Buy a few and see how well they age.

Thornbridge Bracia

Bakewell,
England
ABV: 10.0%
Hops: Target,
Pioneer,
Northern
Brewer,
Sorachi Ace

It pours a thick,
glugging, inky black,
the sort of pour that
billows out a mocha
foam and looks so good
you say, "Wow!" It's made with bittersweet Italian
chestnut honey, plus a long list of world hops and a
hefty malt bill, and it all combines to give one of
Britain's best beers. Cocoa, dark chocolate, fresh coffee,
red berries, fresh sweet bread, white chocolate, minty
herbs, chocolate muffins, toasted hazelnuts, licorice,
perfumy hops, sweet smoke... every joyful sip of this
beer gives something different. Slick and thick, the
bitterness is big, earthy, and dry, the sort of finish that
veers towards savory, but, in doing so, makes everything
else taste sweeter. It's almost a stout but that's too
simple a name for this extraordinary beer.

Stone Arrogant Bastard

Escondido,
California
ABV: 7.2%
Hops:
Arrogantly they
say this is
"Classified"

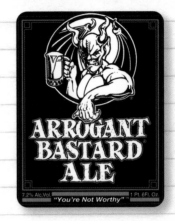

"You probably won't
like it," the bottle
tells you. It's
aggressive, strong,
loaded with malt,
hugely hoppy, and
defiantly self-assured. So self-assured, it created the
American Strong Ale category of beers (and it damn well
knows it). Born in 1997, it epitomizes the
uncompromising Stone Brewing ethos now, but at the
time it was a mistake: Steve Wagner and Greg Koch, the
men behind the grimacing gargoyles, were trying out the
recipe for Stone Pale Ale, but massively miscalculated
the ingredients and added far more of everything than
they needed. The mistake was so good that they brewed
it again a few years later and released it onto the
unwitting market. It's a mouthful of hops: resinous,
piney, citrus pith, and peppery. It's bitter. Very bitter.
The malt teases in the background, promising to help out
with a little sweetness, but it doesn't. You can get it in
6-US-pint (3-liter) magnums, which is about as arrogant
as beer gets.

Hair of the Dog Adam

Portland, Oregon
ABV: 10.0%
Hops: Locally grown hops

This is inspired by Adambier, a strong, well-hopped, well-aged Imperial Alt-
like brew from Dortmund which Hair of the Dog have resurrected and made
their own. It was the first beer made at the brewery and they brew it three to
five times a year, so get it when you see it (if you see Adam from the Wood, then
that's a version aged in American oak, giving a wonderful, toasty vanilla depth). It
pours a really dark brown and from within its depths comes a whole lot of malt and hop flavor: dark chocolate,
tobacco, dried fruit, roasted apples, caramel, freshly baked cinnamon buns, a distant waft of smoke, and then a big,
earthy, woody, and lingering bitterness. It's warming and rich, and so loaded with depth you can hardly believe it.
It's a winter kind of beer, best served with a strong cheddar.

DARK ISLAND
RESERVE
THE EXTRAORDINARY ORCADIAN ALE

Dark Island Reserve is a rich, robust Orcadian Ale. After a gentle fermentation at our brewery in Quoyloo, the beer is finished in old oak casks formerly used to Mature Fine Malt Whiskies. This unhurried process creates a timeless classic tasting of fruit, spice, oak & roast malt aromas. An Extraordinary ale.

Andrew Fulton
Head Brewer, The Orkney Brewery

75cl℮   BREWED IN SCOTLAND   Alc.
1pt 9.4fl oz   10%/vol
LIMITED EDITION
HAND CRAFTED IN SMALL BATCHES

Orkney Dark Island Reserve

Orkney, Scotland
ABV: 10.0%
Hops: East Kent Goldings, First Gold

Moon Dog Henry Ford's Girthsome Fjord

Melbourne, Australia
ABV: 8.0%
Hops: Summit, Horizon, Amarillo, Cascade, Glacier

The minds behind Moon Dog are brilliantly bonkers. You figure this out fast when you read the poem they named their brewery after: "Moon Dog, Moon Dog; Moon Dog chained; Moon Dog free; Moon Dog, Moon Dog." Their aim is to create the boldest, most unique beers in Australia and they're succeeding. The label of Henry Ford's Girthsome Fjord says it's a "Belgo-American India Brown Ale" and it gets there by using loads of American hops and a Trappist yeast, though it also uses an

American ale and an English ale yeast. The combination is as unusual as the name but it works in the weirdest, most wonderful way: think roasted bananas and oranges with chocolate syrup, sprinkled with brown sugar, pine needles, and black pepper. Great drink and also a brewery to make you smile.

The Orkney Islands are an archipelago (70 islands, around 20 inhabited) north of the Scottish mainland, which have been inhabited for thousands of years, despite their remoteness. Now you can visit old Viking cathedrals and castles, see the Standing Stones around the islands, and just before you reach the brewery, stop at Skara Brae, a well-preserved Neolithic village. Cattle farming and fishing are two of the main industries on the islands. Start with crab and an Orkney Northern Light, a zesty and refreshing Pale Ale, then enjoy the smoky depths of Dragonhead Stout with local steak, and then finish with Orkney cheeses and Dark Island Reserve. The beer is a 10.0% ABV Orcadian ale and it gets three months in whisky barrels before bottling. Think figs, chocolate, dried fruit, vanilla, caramel, and earthy, woody spices. It's interesting, complex, and warming, like reading an old, leather-bound copy of something by Robert Burns by a crackling fire.

Porterhouse An Brain Blásta

Dublin, Ireland
ABV: 7.0%
Hops: Galena, Nugget, East Kent Goldings

Go to Dublin, Bray (Ireland), London, and New York and you can drink in a Porterhouse pub. The New York one is attached to the Fraunces Tavern, a historic building in south Manhattan with a museum mixing beer with the birth and growth of a nation. The Porterhouse in London is where I learnt a lot about beer. We'd go for the Oyster Stout or choose random bottles from the refrigerator. There was also An Brain Blásta (the name means "tasty drop" in Gaelic) which, at a scary 7.0% ABV, no one dared to drink unless we'd already had a few (this was before we'd discovered really strong beers). Opening a bottle years later was a sensational surprise: there's a fresh and inviting earthy aroma of berries and flowers from the amber-red liquid. The body is smooth with more berries, almond, and dried fruit with depth and richness before a big, clinging bitterness. Complex and extraordinarily interesting, not the fearsome brain-blaster I remember.

ORIGINATING IN BRITAIN, BARLEY WINE'S NAME COMES FROM THE VINOUS TASTE AND HIGH ABV, WHICH WAS OFTEN THE STRONGEST BEER A BREWERY PRODUCED. THE BIG BOOZE IN THESE ALES WAS ORIGINALLY PRODUCED WITH THE FIRST RUNNINGS OF WORT IN A PARTI-GYLE BREW. THIS INVOLVED GETTING A COUPLE OF DIFFERENT BEERS OUT OF ONE MASH WITH THE STRONGER FIRST RUNNINGS OF WORT GOING INTO ONE KETTLE AND THE WEAKER SECOND RUNNINGS GOING INTO ANOTHER. THESE RUNNINGS WERE THEN BOILED AND HOPPED DIFFERENTLY BEFORE BEING FERMENTED SEPARATELY. BARLEY WINE CHANGED OVER TIME, LIKE SO MANY BEER STYLES, AND BECAME UNFASHIONABLY STRONG, WHEREUPON IT THREATENED TO BE LOST FROM BAR TOPS, BUT IT WAS GIVEN A NEW LIFE AS IT REACHED AMERICA'S WEST COAST IN THE 1970S AND 1980S, THANKS TO ANCHOR AND SIERRA NEVADA, WHO SPECIFICALLY WANTED IT FOR ITS ELEVATED ABV. THESE NEW BREWS, AND THEIR NEW FLAVOR PROFILE, HAVE ALLOWED BARLEY WINE TO SPREAD AROUND THE WORLD.

BARLEY WINE

Whatever the history, few old examples exist, so it's more pertinent to focus on the new wave of British and American Barley Wines, which share a similar base that's high in alcohol (8.0–12% ABV), rich with malt, caramel, brown sugar, nuts, plummy or dried fruit, some darker flavors, and a full-bodied smoothness. Where British versions have a berry-like hop flavor and a punchy, earthy bitterness (40–70 IBUs), American versions are closer to Double IPAs with huge bitterness (60–100 plus IBUs) and massive roast citrus and pine aroma from the gung-ho use of American hops. Both beers mature well, though the hops don't keep their vibrancy, mellowing into the beer.

ANCHOR OLD FOGHORN

SAN FRANCISCO, CALIFORNIA
ABV: 8.0–10.0%
HOPS: CASCADE

It's easy to look around now and see the many different beer styles brewed in America and assume that it's always been this way. But go back to 1975, when Old Foghorn was first brewed, and everything was very different. This pioneering beer—America's first Barley Wine—fueled the microbrewery renaissance and made something so completely different from all the other beers out there. It's brewed in the old parti-gyle way of taking the sweetest first runnings to create the strong beer—the second runnings then go to make Small Beer, Anchor's 3.3% ABV table beer. Old Foghorn is lavishly hopped and dry-hopped with grapefruity and floral Cascades, which are button-bright when fresh. The base beer is ruby-brown, there's dried fruits, cocoa, toast, molasses, and then resinous hops give a peppery bitterness. It ages wonderfully with the malt softening the zesty hops.

Nøgne Ø
100

Grimstad,
Norway
ABV: 10.0%
Hops:
Columbus,
Chinook,
Centennial

#100

The 100th brew at Nøgne Ø was so good that they decided to make it a permanent addition to the line-up. It pours a chestnut-brown and you get toast, caramel, fruit bread, chocolate, and even some smoke or spice. The aroma belies the hops hidden within, but take a sip and they come out with their resinous bitterness, herbal hit, and perfumey fragrance. Altogether this one evokes a cold fall night, and that's definitely when this beer is best enjoyed, especially if you've got a board of cheeses in front of you—the malt sweetness marries with the creaminess in the cheese before the hops cut off the richness and, while barley wines are perfect for almost all cheeses, blue-veined are especially good. Don't fancy cheese? Nøgne Ø also make sake (Europe's first sake brewery), so follow 100 with a Nama-Genshu chaser.

Marble Barley Wine

Manchester, England
ABV: 10.7%
Hops: Goldings, Green Bullet,
Pacific Gem, Motueka, Simcoe

The Marble beers used to be brewed in the back of the Marble Arch, a handsome street-corner pub in Manchester, but production outgrew the space and so they moved a few hundred yards down the hill to a bigger production unit. Marble are known for pale, hoppy, low-ABV beers such as Manchester Bitter (4.2% ABV), a modern take on classic British Bitters, which is brightly hopped to give citrus and tropical fruit above the clean, quaffing kind of body. Marble also make a wide range of special beers, including Saisons, Tripels, Imperial Stouts, and this Barley Wine, which is a beer that exemplifies what the brewery do best: a British base giving dried fruit, treacle, and chocolate before the barnstorming bitterness from New World hops comes in, hugely aromatic with citrus pith, sappy pine, pepper, and floral black tea. It's a very modern take on a classic style, and that's the Marble way.

Montegioco Draco

Montegioco, Italy
ABV: 11.0%
Hops: Fuggles, East Kent Goldings

Pouring a hazy plum color with a thick foam, there's an enticing, intoxicating freshness to the aroma, which is floral, grassy, and with a hint of nutty, figgy Amontillado sherry. Take a sip and there's dried fruit, a rich nutty depth, low sweetness, and a stone-fruit hop flavor giving creamy dried apricots, while the bitterness is elegant and makes this even more wonderfully complex. Blueberries are also added, though they only give a subtle floral, fruity note. There's a definite sherry flavor profile, which is fantastic, and would make this great served cold in small glasses for an aperitivo or with antipasto. Look for Montegioco's other beers: La Mummia is a sensational, sharp, and smooth barrel-aged Sour; Quarta Runa is brewed with peaches, giving an amaretto depth to the spicy, dry beer; or Bran, a strong Belgian ale, which is all molasses, dried fruit, spice, and chocolate.

À l'Abri de la Tempête Corps Mort

Îles-de-la-Madeleine,
Canada
ABV: 11.0%
Hops: Hersbrücker

Located by the beach on Îles-de-la-Madeleine, a small archipelago in the Gulf of St Lawrence, north of Nova Scotia (but part of Quebec), À l'Abri de la Tempête, which means "Shelter from the Storm," is the place to go after a day of walking and enjoying the picture-postcard islands. The brewery use local barley in their beers. Given their location, the grains are grown in ground that gets battered by salty sea winds, giving it a unique sense of terroir. For Corps Mort, some of the barley also goes to Le Fumoir d'Antan, which smokes mackerel and herring, so this is a smoked, salty Barley Wine. It pours a sunset-amber color; there's a woody smokiness and a saline sea breeze; sweet smoke leads the taste, backed by marmalade, brown sugar, and floral fruits; and that faint saltiness enhances everything, making it incredibly complex and interesting.

AleSmith Old Numbskull

San Diego, California
ABV: 11.0%
Hops: CTZ, Chinook, Cascade, Palisade, Amarillo, Simcoe, Summit

I can't not order AleSmith IPA if I see it—it's one of the world's best American IPAs: citrus, peach, and apricot and the cleanest hop bitterness you'll find. Speedway Stout is one of the world's best Imperial Stouts, rich and roasty yet impossibly smooth, only the bourbon-barrel-aged version beats it by adding caramel and vanilla. X is fruity, juicy, and incredibly drinkable—I just wish I could buy more of it. Lil Devil and Horny Devil flex their Belgian muscles and give brilliant interpretations of classics. Then there's Old Numbskull: ruby-colored, it's got a gem of an aroma with dried and fresh fruit mingling with candy, vanilla, dates, some background booze, and citrusy, resinous hops which leave a lasting grip of bitterness. The barrel-aged version is even better. I'm out of words, so here's the short version: I love all of the AleSmith beers.

Brouwerij 't IJ Struis

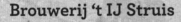

Amsterdam, Netherlands
ABV: 9.0%
Hops: NZ Hallertauer

The Netherlands is another of Europe's leading countries for great beers and with inspiration from Germany, Belgium, and America, the range of beers produced dwarfs most other brewing countries. If you're in Amsterdam (and you should go because it's a great beer-drinking city), then go to Brouwerij 't IJ, who have a taproom: you can't miss it, as it's beneath a windmill (you just have to find the right one of the city's eight windmills). Struis is red-brown in the glass, it's got dried fruit, orchard fruit, peppery hops, plums roasted in brown sugar, some estery fruit aroma, and a background of spiciness—it sits somewhere between a Barley Wine and Belgian Quad. A local farmer takes the spent grain to feed his sheep; their milk makes Skeapsrond cheese, which the brewer then takes as payment for his grain. Drink Struis with that cheese beneath the windmill.

SMOKED BEER AND RAUCHBIER

SMOKED MALT IS A FLAVOR THAT GOES BACK MANY CENTURIES WHEN GRAIN WOULD'VE HAD A WAFT OF SMOKINESS THANKS TO THE DRYING PROCESS THAT PUT IT OVER FIRE. NOW THE PROCESS IS CONTROLLED AND SMOKED GRAINS ARE COMMERCIALLY AVAILABLE. MALT THAT HAS BEEN SMOKED WILL GIVE A RANGE OF DIFFERENT SMOKY FLAVORS, FROM SCOTCH TO SCORCHED AND FLAVOR COMES FROM WHATEVER FUELS THE FIRE TO DRY OR SMOKE THE GRAIN. RAUCHBIER IS THE CLASSIC SMOKED STYLE FROM BAMBERG, GERMANY; MADE WITH MALT SMOKED OVER BEECHWOOD, IT TASTES UNMISTAKABLY LIKE SMOKED SAUSAGES. USING A PEATED MALT WILL GIVE THE EARTHY, POTENT, PHENOLIC FLAVOR OF ISLAY WHISKIES, WHILE A BURNING-BONFIRE QUALITY CAN COME FROM OTHER TYPES OF SMOKED GRAIN. INCIDENTALLY, ROASTED BARLEY, WHILE NOT SMOKED, CAN ALSO GIVE AN ASHEN, SMOKY QUALITY. MOST SMOKED GRAIN IS PALE IN COLOR AND CAN BE A POTENT ADDITION TO THE GRAIN BILL.

Any beer style can include smoked malt to change its flavor profile, though Bamberg-style Rauchbier generally stands as its own category. Smoked beers can range from weak to strong, from low to high bitterness, from pale Pilsners to sunlight-sucking Stouts. The best fold in the smoky flavors, adding an interesting, appetizing complexity to the beer. Barbecue and bacon-like smoke can mirror the smoky flavor of meat and trick you into experiencing an umami double-whammy, making these beers particularly good with food.

AECHT SCHLENKERLA RAUCHBIER MARZEN

CLASSIC

BAMBERG, GERMANY
ABV: 5.1%
HOPS: HALLERTAUER MAGNUM

It smells like bacon! That's the typical reaction to Rauchbier, a lager from Bamberg, Germany. Schlenkerla is an adulteration of the German for "not moving straight." It started as a nickname for one of the brewers who walked crookedly because of an accident, then eventually the brewery became named after his peculiar gait. Schlenkerla have their own malthouse and that's where the distinctive flavor comes from: after germination, the grain is kilned over beechwood and it sucks up all the smoky flavor. There's a range of Schlenkerla beers from the Urbock to Helles (not made with smoked malt but it's still faintly smoky), Wheat beer, and others. The Märzen is copper-brown, smells like smoked meat, and has a richness of malt which gives it a satisfying texture. Appetizing, unusual, and, as the brewery say, "Even if the brew tastes somewhat strange at the first swallow, do not stop, because soon you will realize that your thirst will not decrease and your pleasure will visibly increase." Presumably to the point when you schlenkern.

Beavertown Brewery Smog Rocket

London, England
ABV: 5.4%
Hops: Challenger,
East Kent Goldings

Brewing has to start very early in the morning at Beavertown because the mash tun and kettle are opposite the smoker and grill in Duke's Brew and Que, a brewpub-come-BBQ joint; the brewers need to mash in, dig it out, and transfer it to the tanks in the cellar before the chefs clock in. Started by buddies Byron and Logan, Duke's brings together beer and BBQ, and Smog Rocket is the hand-slapping high five between the two. Made with smoked malt (though not smoked in the kitchen—that's too busy doing incredible things to meat), this London Porter is reminiscent of charred wood, flame-licked meat, whisky, and cocoa. If ever food and beer were meant to go together, then it's Smog Rocket and a stack of ribs in Duke's. While you wait for the food, try 8 Ball Rye—it's a spicy, American-style rye IPA with loads of zesty citrus.

Fujizakura Kougen Rauch Beer

Yamanashi-ken, Japan
ABV: 5.5%
Hops: Perle

The first sip of Rauchbier is likely to be one of those beer moments you won't forget, mostly because it's the sort of drink which is unequivocal in what people think of it: it's either love or hate. Though, like both emotions, it's possible to grow to feel them and, while the first smoky gulp might be shocking, a few beers later comes the "a ha!" moment of realization, when you suddenly get what it's all about. It took me a few Rauchbiers to "get it," finally having my moment of realization when I drank it with salmon sashimi followed by a bowl of ramen. The savory soup is so good with the smoky beer, creating an umami explosion. Recreate that with Fujizakura's Rauch which has toasty grain, a little caramel like the char on grilled meat, before a flourish of floral hops finish it, adding a fresh grassiness which lightens the noodle broth.

Yeastie Boys Rex Attitude

Wellington, New Zealand
ABV: 7.0%
Hops: Willamette

Do you like the sort of peaty whiskies that are phenolic, peaty, and saline with a rush of boozy heat that rips through your head like a vicious Scottish gale? I love them. The whiskies get their flavor from the water and from peated malt—that malt is dried over peat fires and the lick of the flames spirals upward into the grain, giving their inimitable flavor. While this may be common in whisky, far less peated malt makes it into the brewhouse. Rex Attitude is the outrageous exception. It's not made with a small percentage, it's made with 100 per cent peated malt. The beer is gentle gold in color and the aroma is a fiery bog of peaty earth, wood smoke, charcoal, and bandaids (which your nose might need after inhaling this one). Utterly unique and outrageous, it drinks like a whisky with a hop freshness at the end to remind you it's still a beer.

Ölvisholt Brugghús Lava

Selfoss, Iceland
ABV: 9.4%
Hops: First Gold, Fuggles

The name "Lava" sums this one up nicely. Brewed on a farm with a view of Hekla, an Icelandic volcano, the fiery smoke from the beer lights up the glass like a night-time eruption. Smokehouse, molasses, mocha, and some alcohol warmth come out of the beer which pours the shining charcoal color of a dried lava flow. The smoke is filled out with the charred edges of roast malt, chocolate, treacle, and fruitcake with aniseed spices, all wrapped in a full, smooth body. The smoke in this one takes the beer to another level—it's not subtle, but it's so well integrated and interesting. If volcanoes are too much, then you could try Ölvisholt Brugghús's Skjálfti, a lager with a name that means earthquake. Away from the destruction of natural disasters, there's Freyja, a refreshing kiss-of-life Wit beer named after the Norse goddess of fertility.

Bamberg Rauchbier

Sao Paolo, Brazil
ABV: 5.2%
Hops: Magnum

Imagine maple-glazed smoked bacon because that's what this one smells like. Sounds good, right? It is. It's hard to ignore a Rauchbier made by a brewery that has named itself after the city famous for smoked beers. Cervejaria Bamberg's version is definitely authentic in its depth, though it's toned down compared with its German inspiration. That sweet-glazed smoke is intoxicating and inviting, just like the ember-red color and nicotine-yellow foam. Like a fairytale, this one comes in three parts: the beginning is a hint of sweet maple syrup, then comes a middle of stone fruit, charred chestnuts, and an earthy toastiness (plus a whispering "hello" of smoke), and then a little sweetness returns at the end, rounding it all up and wrapping it in a shroud of smoke. Great with Brazilian rice and beans, even better with smoked pork. Bamberg started brewing in 2005 and their consistent quality has made them one of Brazil's best and most respected craft breweries.

Brasserie des Franches-Montagnes The Tarry Suchong

Jura, Switzerland
ABV: 6.0%
Hops: East Kent Goldings

Inspiration for beers can come from many places but, curiously, this beer aims to re-create the smell of asphalt mines in Travers, Switzerland (asphalt is the potent-smelling stuff that goes on roads and roofs). Regardless, BFM did it and they've made a miraculous brew. Using the beechwood-smoked malt of Bamberg, they also add Lapsang Souchong, a black tea that's smoke-dried over pinewood fires to give a savory bonfire depth. Bacon and campfire combine in the brew and make The Tarry Suchong an unusual and interesting drink: the smell of the amber beer is sweet smoke, burning pine trees, and woody and floral tea, then there's a sharp fruitiness before the tea gives earthy smoke, tannin, and a herbal, dry finish. I've never been in an asphalt mine but this beer makes me want to visit one.

MILK AND OATMEAL STOUT

I FIND IT HARD TO RESIST MILK OR OATMEAL STOUTS. IT'S THE CREAMY, SLIGHTLY SWEET, NUTTY, CHOCOLATY FULLNESS OF THE BODY THAT I LOVE. MILK AND OATS COME TOGETHER BECAUSE THEY SHARE A SWEETER, CREAMIER FLAVOR THAN DRY STOUT AND A LESS AGGRESSIVE FLAVOR THAN AMERICAN STOUT. MILK STOUT (ALSO KNOWN AS SWEET STOUT) IS MADE WITH MILK SUGAR OR LACTOSE, WHICH IS UNFERMENTABLE, MEANING THAT THE LUSCIOUS RICHNESS REMAINS IN THE BEER. OATMEAL STOUTS ARE BREWED WITH OATS AS PART OF THE GRAIN BILL: OATS GIVE A SOFT, CREAMY, SMOOTH TEXTURE AND MOUTHFEEL. BOTH MILK AND OATMEAL STOUTS WERE SEEN AS NOURISHING DRINKS IN THE EARLY AND MID 20TH CENTURY, ESPECIALLY FOR CHILDREN AND THE INFIRM. INTERESTINGLY, WHILE STOUT STARTED AS A NAME FOR STRONG BEERS OF ANY COLOR IN THE 18TH CENTURY, BY THE TIME MILK STOUT WAS FIRST BREWED BY MACKESON'S IN 1907, STOUT SIMPLY MEANT A BLACK BEER AND NOT NECESSARILY A STRONG ONE.

Classic Stout flavors come through with dark chocolate and coffee, though it's softened in both styles. The beers shouldn't be sugary to taste; instead, you should get the impression of roundness in the body and a hint of pleasing sweetness. Bitterness will typically be low in both, with little or no hop aroma. ABV will be 3.0–7.0%, with Milk Stouts typically lower in alcohol (Double Oatmeal Stouts boost the booze and make a far bigger beer). Milk Stout rarely passes 25 IBUs, while Oatmeal Stouts might make it to 40 IBUs. The best versions of both have a mouth-filling smoothness and richness and no dark malt acidity.

Bristol Beer Factory Milk Stout

Bristol, England
ABV: 4.5%
Hops: Challenger, Fuggles

Bristol is the cosmopolitan center of West Country cider territory. As a city, it's developed into one of Britain's top spots for food and drink with an ever-growing beer contingent that is being led by the brilliant Bristol Beer Factory. The building they have been brewing in since 2005 has two centuries of beer history, as it used to be home to the Ashton Gate Brewing Company. BBF make a range of great beers, including American-inspired Southville Hop, a 6.5% ABV IPA, or Independence, a 4.6% ABV American Pale Ale loaded with Amarillo, Cascade, and Centennial. Being a Milk Stout fiend, that's the beer I go back for again and again. So smooth, there's a delicate kiss of sweetness and a creaminess to the body that makes it like a luxurious chocolate and hazelnut shake before a balanced berry bitterness rounds it off. It's great with chili.

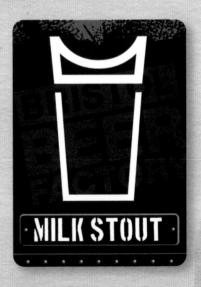

Portsmouth Oatmeal Stout

Portsmouth, New Hampshire
ABV: 6.0%

This beer is the reason I love Oatmeal Stouts. The Great British Beer Festival always has a selection of American beers and they tend to be brews we've never seen in the United Kingdom before, so I spend all day hanging around that stand. I ordered the Portsmouth Oatmeal Stout and a mate ordered their IPA, and then we spent the next few minutes completely engrossed with what we were drinking. Juicy tangerine and mango in the IPA made it stand out above all the others that day, but the Oatmeal Stout is something I can still taste now. Luscious like milk chocolate melting on the tongue, hazelnut sweetness, the most gentle finish with no hint of bitterness, and just a lingering taste of chocolate oats. Above it all was just a tiny trace of orange from the hops, adding something unexpectedly wonderful. I want all Oatmeal Stouts to taste just like this.

Elizabeth Street Brewery Daddy's Chocolate Milk

San Francisco, California
ABV: 5.0%
Hops: Cluster, Goldings

Richard Hay married a brewer—literally. His wife is Allie Brewer and they now use the double-barrel surname of Brewer-Hay. I'm sure that one day he'll open a brewery but until then Richard brews from his house in San Francisco, so this is a little different from all the other beers featured. Brewing upstairs, he then pours them from the British-style pub in his basement. It's not an official brewery or bar so he can't charge people to drink there; instead, he pours freely and the customers typically buy a $20 hat on the way out (or tip generously). Daddy's Chocolate Milk is a fantastic beer. Just the name makes me thirsty and I can taste the thick richness of chocolate milk laced with roast bitterness. Send Richard an email and see when the next keg is being tapped in the ultimate man-cave beneath his house.

DADDY'S CHOCOLATE MILK

NOE VALLEY - SAN FRANCISCO

Tiny Rebel Dirty Stop Out

Newport, Wales
ABV: 5.0%
Hops: Columbus, Styrian Goldings, Cascade

Tiny Rebel make some superior southern hemisphere-hopped brews, including Full Nelson, a "Maori Pale Ale," and Billabong, an all-Aussie-hopped Pale Ale—both are bursting with hop freshness, the sort of light, juicy, and elegant freshness that cask beer can be so good at pronouncing. There's also Cwtch, a Welsh word that is somewhere between a snuggle and a snug, a warm feeling from a safe place—the beer is a Welsh Red Ale made with love and attention, which is reminiscent of marmalade on toast (which itself is kind of cwtch). Dirty Stop Out is an Oatmeal Stout with the addition of sweetly smoked malt giving a smooth beer laced with mocha, a floral perfume, and a hint of bonfire. Or try Chocoholic, which is infused with Belgian chocolate. Watch out for the little rebellious bear with its hood up looking for trouble.

Bierwerk Aardwolf

Western Cape, South Africa
ABV: 8.5%

For a country that makes many fantastic wines, their beer culture is lagging behind, though emerging breweries like Bierwerk are changing things. Interestingly, Africa, along with the Caribbean, has a sweet tooth for Sweet Stouts, so it's good to see a craft version taking on the Guinness Goliath. Aardwolf is a strong Sweet Stout made with African coffee beans, and part of the beer is aged in French oak and then blended back in. Black with red edges, it's an oily-thick pour, which pushes out all of the chocolate, caramel, and vanilla oak notes.

Beneath that is a whole layer of roast and dark fruits, and then comes molasses. An innocent, indulgent sweetness mixes with the mature intensity of coffee and then combine magnificently. We can expect to see more South-African-hopped beers as the country's hop acreage is increasing—varieties include Southern Promise, Southern Star and Southern Brewer.

Le Brewery Odo

Joué-du-Bois, France
ABV: 6.6%
Hops: Challenger, Styrian Golding, Cobb

Mackeson's made the first Milk Stout. Originally brewed in 1907 in Hythe, Kent, though now brewed elsewhere, it's a fun little 3.0% ABV sweet treat that's smooth with creaminess and a little caramel-covered chocolate. Le Brewery was founded by Steve Skews in 2001 and his mission was to take good beer to cider-sipping Normandy—over a decade later we can say he succeeded. Steve even grows his own hops at the brewery, including Cobb, an old English variety that is rarely seen. Odo is a smoothly malty milk stout with dark, roasty depths; there's a bubble-gum and root-beer sweetness, a sharp roast note, and a lingering herbal spiciness, which adds a great complexity. It's fantastic with the camembert made nearby, especially if it's baked: smooth, melting cheese smothered by the beer's roasty richness.

Brewfist Fear

Codogno, Italy
ABV: 5.2%
Hops: Magnum

My friend Leo gave us a long list of places to visit when we were in Rome. For lunch, he said we couldn't miss Pizzarium, just outside the Vatican City walls. After a hot walk through the historic city and a few wrong lefts and rights, we found the tiny pizza place. The pizzas were so unbelievably good (on my list of top three pizzas ever) that we had to go back for another slice. This time it was a potato and cheese-topped pizza and I grabbed one of the boldly labeled beers from the fridge, flicked the cap off, and took a deep gulp from the bottle. The rich, oily, cheese-topped pizza, stodgy with potato, and yet light and crisp, was complete perfection with the slick, sweetly nutty, chocolaty richness of the milk chocolate Stout. We went back the next day but the beer was gone and so was the potato pizza. Beer and food serendipity.

UNLESS YOUR STOUT IS PREFIXED WITH MILK, SWEET, OATMEAL, AMERICAN OR IMPERIAL, THEN THAT ICONIC PINT OF BLACK BEER TOPPED WITH A CREAMY, WHITE FOAM WILL PROBABLY BE A DRY STOUT. AT THE BEGINNING OF THE 19TH CENTURY, ONE OF LONDON'S BIGGEST BREWERIES, BARCLAY PERKINS, MADE A PALE STOUT. AT THAT TIME "STOUT" SIMPLY MEANT A STRONG BEER AND HAD NO LINK TO COLOR; IT WAS A PREFIX WHICH TOLD THE DRINKER THEY WERE ORDERING A STRONGER-THAN-USUAL VERSION OF THEIR BEER. TO DIFFERENTIATE, ONE COULD BUY PALE STOUT, BROWN STOUT, OR STOUT PORTER. BY THE 1840S, STOUT HAD COME TO BE KNOWN AS A STRONG, DARK BEER AND NO LONGER PALE. FAST FORWARD ANOTHER 60 YEARS AND "STOUT" HAD LOST THE STRONG LINK AND SIMPLY MEANT A BLACK BEER. FROM LONDON, IT WAS MADE MORE FAMOUS IN IRELAND WHERE THE STYLES DEVELOPED SEPARATELY.

DRY STOUT

Dry stouts are dark brown to black in color. They may be pumped with nitrogen before packaging, in the style of Guinness: as nitrogen has smaller bubbles than carbon dioxide, the beer feels fuller and creamier to drink. There'll be roast bitterness in the beer, a bitterness that meets hop bitterness, which can be high (40–60 IBUs). Roast flavors of coffee and dark chocolate run through the beer, along with dark fruit, caramel, an earthiness, and sometimes some smoke. The finish will be dry with very little sweetness and may have some malt acidity. ABV is typically moderate: 4.0–5.5%. Born in London, it grew up in Dublin, and now it's traveling the world.

Dungarvan Black Rock Stout

Dungarvan, Ireland
ABV: 4.3%
Hops: Northern Brewer

There's more than one stout brewed in Ireland, and when you look away from the beer everyone else is drinking, you see a whole new group of beers. Take the Porterhouse, for example: superb Stouts, textured and rich, genuine, and full of flavor. O'Hara's Irish Stout is dry, dark, and luxurious, while others, such as Trouble Brewing, side step and make a Porter. Then there's Dungarvan's Black Rock Stout, named after the landmark rock that sailors see when they pass into or out of Dungarvan harbor on the south-east coast of the country. The beer first marks itself out as different with its hops: green, grassy, herbal, and there throughout the mouthful. Then you get the smooth chocolate and a hint of vanilla fudge before the roast comes in and leads to a long, dry bitterness where malt and hops meet again and play a resounding encore. The stout tradition gets a new timeline with these great craft Irish Stouts.

Brasserie Sainte Hélène Black Mamba

Virton, Belgium
ABV: 4.5%
Hops: Citra, Simcoe

Brasserie Sainte Hélène started selling beer commercially in 1999, gradually growing year-on-year until, in 2011, the business stepped forward by rebranding into their smart, bold, new design and adding a bottling facility to increase quality, speed, and consistency. The striking new labels make a real visual impact, while the beers inside make an impact on the tongue. La Grognarde (5.5% ABV) is a Belgian Blonde hopped with Brewers Gold and Saaz; it's got a grassy fresh aroma and a big bitterness that really clings to the tongue. Gypsy Rose, a Tripel, has an elegant lightness to its 9.0% ABV before berries, almonds, and a lingering, fruity bitterness finish it off. Black Mamba is an American-hopped Dry Stout, giving roast-citrus rind, sharp coffee, charred wood, dark cocoa, and subtle toffee before the hops bite at the end; it's a playful mix of hops and dark malt held together with a full, ABV-belying body.

Pelican Tsunami Stout

Pacific City, Oregon
ABV: 7.0%
Hops: Magnum, Willamette

There's more than just good beer and food at the Pelican Pub & Brewery in Pacific City—there's great beer, great food, and a brilliant view. Sitting on the seafront, banked by the Cape Kiwanda State Natural Area and looking out to the Haystock Rock that grows majestically from the sea a half-mile from the beach, you can sip a brew with the wow-inducing view of nature and the crashing waves around you. Get to Pacific City, walk the trail to build up your hunger and thirst, and then find the Pelican and take a seat out front because you can't beat a beer with a view. Tsunami Stout is a big dry stout: black, full of chocolate smoothness, hints of roast coffee, toffee, licorice, coconut, and dark fruits, and a real smooth finish, making it great paired with food. This is something Pelican specialize in—they suggest Tsunami Stout chili or pan-fried oysters.

Minoh Stout

Hokusetsu, Japan
ABV: 5.5%
Hops: Perle, East Kent Goldings

In 1997, Mayuko and Kaori Ohshita's father bought a brewery and put them in charge of it. Their first reaction might have sounded just like their surname, but since then they've made Minoh one of Japan's most interesting and awarded breweries. Located in a pretty part of northern Osaka, in an area famous for its waterfall and wild monkeys, the Minoh beers have that equal measure of beauty and playfulness: there's a Weizen brewed with local peaches or a Wit made with yuzu; W-IPA is a 9.0% ABV Double IPA overflowing with Cascades; Cabernet is brewed with Cabernet Sauvignon juice; while their Stouts are rightly famous. The Imperial Stout (8.5% ABV) is so deliciously smooth and rich like bitter-chocolate truffles, while the regular Stout has a drier, though still creamy, texture with thick foam, lots of coffee roast, vanilla-infused brown sugar, and herbal, spicy notes at the edges.

Darling Brew Black Mist

Cape Town, South Africa
ABV: 5.0%
Hops: Southern Promise, Cascade

This is "slow beer" brewed in South Africa. That is Darling Brew's mantra—not craft nor micro—these guys go slow. Darling is the name of the town and the idea of slow is good: beer takes time to make, it can't be rushed, it gets there in its own time, and you should enjoy it considerately. Darling Brew have a smart taproom which is the best place to taste all the beers (there's a lager, Brown Ale, and Wit alongside the Stout). Grab a flight, sip them slowly, and enjoy. Black Mist pours near-black, and the body has a refreshing lightness before the dark, dry finish. Everything combines to taste like the morning-after: coffee, cigarettes, burst toast, sweet perfume, nascent love, and a bitter kiss goodbye—only with Black Mist, when you promise to call and go out again sometime, you mean it.

Camden Ink

London,
England
ABV: 4.4%
Hops:
Northdown,
Pacific Gem

Why should Guinness have such a stranglehold over the Stout market around the world? Why aren't there any great alternatives, which still give that full texture but also have a load of flavor? The catalyst for Camden Town was to create a great-tasting Dry Stout to give London another option on the dark side of the bar. Stout started in London before moving to Dublin (and from there it took over the world); Camden Ink brings it back to London and makes it taste boldly new. Nitro'd in tank, it's got a creamy body and settles sexily as the foam forms on top. There's a whole lot of roast in here, dark and milk chocolate, but a soulful smoothness before a hop and roast bitterness. Pacific Gem adds a burst of blackberries at the end and a lift of grassy aroma.

Invercargill Pitch Black

Invercargill, New Zealand
ABV: 4.5%
Hops: Pacific Gem

Invercargill Brewery is run by the father-and-son duo of Gerry and Steve Nally. They started in 1999 and put their brewhouse in what used to be a dairy shed before outgrowing the space and moving into a new brewery in 2005. As well as beer, the Nallys have also made an eponymous cider since they started Invercargill—it's a 5.0% ABV blend of Granny Smith and Braeburn, which is sweet and juicy to begin with before finishing with a refreshing tartness. Back to beer and Pitch Black pours the color the name suggests. Screaming chocolate at first, there's earthy coffee beans, a sweet hint of vanilla toffee, a lush creaminess, and a finish that lets Pacific Gem's woody, berry flavor through with some plums and cherries. Invercargill is by Bluff Harbor, the home of the famous Bluff oyster, so there's the local food and beer match sorted.

GOING IMPERIAL

A style prefixed with Imperial or Double (the terms are inter-changable) tells you to limber up and do some tongue stretches in preparation for something BIG. The name is inherited from Russian Imperial Stout, a strong, dark beer known as 'extra stout porter', which was brewed in London at the end of the 18th century and exported east. The drink became popular at the Russian imperial court of Czarina Catherine the Great, hence the name.

As American craft beer kicked forward, brewers started taking styles and making bigger versions of them, searching for bolder flavors that were as far away as possible from the lackluster lagers that everyone else was drinking. As a bigger version of a standard style, these brewers knew the story of Imperial Stout and pinched the name for themselves.

Supersizing beers started with IPA, the king of craft beer. Brewers noted the 6% versions and raised the ABV by a couple of percent and threw a lot more hops into the pot. Since then it's spread to almost every style: Pale Ale, Hefeweizen, Brown Ale, Pilsner, Wit, Helles, Red... although many of the classic Belgian styles evaded the Imperial amplification (Double Dubbel? Imperial Lambic?).

"At best, one can hope for some echo of an established beer style, with some of its positive characteristics boosted along with the alcohol," writes a wary Garrett Oliver in the *Oxford Companion to Beer*. For many brewers, the intention is to keep the style familiar and just blow it up, showing off different qualities of malt, hops, or yeast by doing so, while challenging tastebuds and preconceptions and showing balls-out bravado. There's also an aspect of macho salesmanship in labeling a beer as Imperial. Think of it like a burger: would you rather the regular version or the imperial one?

To balance the bigger booze levels, which also bring bulkier bodies, the hops increase. When doing this, brewers often take the opportunity to tag-out classic varieties and tag-in New World varieties to add a different characteristic. With Double IPA as the modern hero of the Imperial beer world, it sometimes feels like many bigger beers are born by the brewer asking what the combination of a Double IPA and another chosen style would taste like. The bold use of American hops has defined many Imperial beer examples, but American hops aren't a prerequisite; sometimes the most interesting Imperial examples come from keeping the ingredients traditional and just doing everything bigger. Imagine if you drew a face onto a balloon and then blew it up, the same happens with the ingredients of beer. Even if classic ingredients go in, simply by making them bigger their flavors change.

The thing with beer styles is that they are fluid and open to interpretation, which makes this such an interesting and varied thing to look at. We know what a Pilsner tastes like, so what does an Imperial version taste like? What happens when you use a lot more of those classic Noble hops? What flavor profile do you end up with? And does the brew keep a quality of the style or does it drastically change it?

I like Imperial versions of beer styles. Not all of them are good—too boozy, too bitter, too sweet, too unbalanced—but they can be very interesting and seriously tasty, pushing palates and imaginations. And they are making the beer world a bigger place with more variety. Double high five to that.

AMERICAN STOUT

MILK AND OATMEAL STOUTS HAVE A LULLABY CALMNESS, AN UNCHALLENGING SWEETNESS, AND A CREAMY, SLEEPY TEXTURE; DRY STOUTS HAVE ROAST DEPTHS AND A DRY BITTERNESS REMINISCENT OF COAL FIRES ON COLD NIGHTS; IMPERIAL STOUTS ARE RICH, STRONG, SIPPING BEERS WITH DEPTH AND COMPLEXITY; AND AMERICAN STOUTS ARE DIFFERENT: THEY ARE HOLLERING IN YOUR EARS, JUMPING ON YOUR TOES, AND ELBOW-DROPPING YOUR TASTEBUDS.

It's what you'd expect from the Americanization of a beer style and it's surely inspired by the idea of an American Double IPA, only applied to Stout. A shoulder-dropping, swaggering kind of beer, this one mixes the uncompromising roast of dark malt with the aggressive use of American hops to give a double bang of bitterness. It's a tongue-thumping, fanfare-tooting kind of Americanized beer, not far away from a Black IPA where the hefty hop aroma generally gives fragrant floral, pine, or roasted citrus, and it's this aroma, along with the bitterness, that makes the style special. ABV will be 6.0–9.0% with IBUs as high as hop skyscrapers and they combine to give brutal, black flavor bombs of great intensity, though the best keep a smooth, full-bodied richness to hold all of the hops in place.

Green Flash Double Stout

San Diego, California
ABV: 8.8%
Hops: East Kent Goldings

I think this is the quintessential American Stout. An opaque black pour with a foam that settles handsomely dark on top, it's got a billowing aroma of hazelnuts and sweet coffee with some pine backing it up. The body is big, bold, and rich; it's sweet like toffee and bitter like coffee; there's berries and cherries, creamy roasted nuts, and a background of hop flavor which is fresh and invigorating— that juicy lightness belies the brutal darkness, while the bitterness is softened by sweetness, making it an outrageously drinkable beer which tastes so good that you nail the pint in no time. I've never seen a green flash sunset but I'd happily take a few bottles of Double Stout down to the Californian coast every night until I did see one.

Beachwood Kilgore Stout

Long Beach, California
ABV: 7.1%
Hops: Chinook, Columbus, Centennial, Cascade

I respect somewhere that has the tagline: "Where the fork meets the pork." I respect them even more when they also brew fantastic beers. The barbecue side of things looks great (I haven't been to eat... yet), the beer side *is* great. Knucklehead Red is a 5.7% ABV, all-American-hopped fruit bowl of peaches and orange wrapped in a woody, herbal spiciness. Foam Top is an American Cream ale that's grassy, clean, and easy-drinking. Kilgore is a ballsy American Stout: black, intensely roasty, laden with C-hops (grapefruit, orange pith, resinous herbs), and there's licorice, toast, coffee, dark cocoa, and caramel coming out from all directions before the bitterness lies down on your tongue and refuses to leave. Grapefruit, coffee, burnt toast, and booze-barbecued meat on the side... sounds like a Breakfast of Champions to me (which presumably ties in the Kurt Vonnegut reference to the beer's name...).

Sixpoint Diesel

Brooklyn, New York
ABV: 6.3%
Hops: Centennial, Columbus, Northern Brewer

Sixpoint's winter seasonal is Diesel. Sitting somewhere between an American Stout, a Black IPA, and a fiery dark hole of hop hell, this is a badass black brew with an epically big mouthfeel and the sort of finish that feels like your tongue has fought off a firing squad of heavies launching grenades at your tonsils. It's one of those exhilarating beers that's just so loaded with flavor you almost plead for mercy in the middle before you realize how damn great it tastes; at which point, you just want more of it. Bitter roast comes first like a cannonball, then herbal hops and licorice, and it's like a pine forest has caught fire in your glass and been extinguished with dark chocolate. I drank this in Barcade, Brooklyn, while playing arcade games—the dichotomy of darkness and light made both more fun.

Williams Bros Profanity Stout

Alloa, Scotland
ABV: 7.0%
Hops: Nelson Sauvin, First Gold, Centennial, Amarillo

From a beautiful-looking bottle, this beer pours a near-opaque black with a thick foam. The aroma hits first, giving a big bang of hop fruitiness with roasted grapes, citrus peel, and something distantly fragrant and floral—it's the sort of aroma you don't get in Stouts very often. It's full and smooth like a 7.0% ABV Stout should be, there's good chocolate, fruity coffee, a little booze pokes through, and it's roasty but never astringent before a second wave of hops crashes down on your tongue with a floral, resinous, and dry bitterness. The recipe was developed by two students on Heriot-Watt's brewing degree course. Those guys can be pretty pleased with their university work— the best I managed while studying was vodka jelly and, although that jelly was delicious, it just wasn't quite as good as Profanity Stout.

PORTER: CARRYING HISTORY

Porter is one of the original and most important beer styles in the world. It was one of the first to get a name, one of the first to travel (America, Australia, Baltic countries, India), and the first to be made on an industrial scale. Porter is also a vortex of historical "facts' and untruths and a beer that has shifted identity so many times it's hard to keep up.

Porter came after the undefined, shape-shifting Brown Ale and was a stronger, more hopped, and more aged version of that brown beer. It gets its name from London porters, a large group of people who earned their living by carrying things around the city. It first gained popularity with the porters who unloaded ships and moved the cargo; their hard work would need refreshment and sustenance throughout the day, so they'd put down their load when they came to a pub and grab a pot of beer before carrying on.

Porter was initially a slang term, but by the 1760s brewers were also using the name for the dark beer that the workers liked so much. The beer was originally aged, sometimes for up to two years, taking on tart and funky flavors; often, next to this on the bar, was a "mild" version, which was unaged. A popular story says that Porter was a beer made from "three threads": part fresh beer, part aged beer, part stale beer, giving smoky, roasty and tart dark ales, but at some point it was conceived as an "entire" ale and brewed instead of just blended in the glass. While that tends to be the most commonly used story to explain the origin of Porter, it's not necessarily the correct one.

Whatever its origin, by the end of the 18th century it's likely that most Porter was not blended and was served "mild." From there it ruled as Britain's most popular beer style for around 100 years, a dark brew, high in bitterness and rich in flavor, character, and depth, just like a Dickens novel.

The beer reached the Colonies in America and was a top tipple there for many years until the German lager brewers took over. Along with the Pale Ales, Porter was also sent to India for the generals to drink. It was popular around the Baltic States and shares some history with the Imperial Stouts made famous in the region. Back in Britain, the story crosses over into the arrival of Stout. These "Stout Porters" were stronger versions of Porter until Stout started breaking free on its own, eventually becoming the more popular of the two dark beers and, by the first decades of the 20th century, Mild, Pale Ale, and Stout left Porter behind, where it was fatally wounded during the two world wars as the style got weaker, thanks to malt shortages and tax rises. Even the huge London Porter breweries (it was made to such an awesome scale that some breweries had vast vats capable of holding over 5 million pints in each) dropped the style and it virtually died out for a few decades after the Second World War, becoming extinct at the same time as the street porters who gave the beer its name.

Now Porter is back and thriving as one of craft beer's most prominent beer styles and it's made around the world—British brewers got there first in the 1970s, then came American brewers in the 1980s. Now you might get Brown Porter, Baltic Porter, Robust Porter, Imperial Porter, American Porter... it's a style that's still evolving, something consistent with how it's changed over the last three centuries and will continue to change for many more years.

PORTER VS. STOUT

Stout arrived at the beginning of the 19th century, whereas Porter is a century older. Since Stout's beginning, the two styles have grown up side by side and individually changed many times. Working out the difference between Porter and Stout is like trying to hit an impossibly small bullseye on a fast-moving target.

When the word "Stout" was first used in relation to beer, it meant a strong beer and could refer to any style or color. To differentiate, brewers called their beers "Pale Stout," "Brown Stout," or "Stout Porter"—the latter being a stronger version of a regular Porter. By the middle of the 19th century, Stout meant a strong, dark beer, although Porter was still the darling beer of the day. They moved along together, recipes evolved and crossed over, and things started to change at the beginning of the 20th century. By then, Stout simply meant a dark beer and not necessarily a strong one. Sweet Stouts arrived, creating a sub-style away from the "dry" London and Dublin versions. At this time, Stouts also became more fashionable as drinks for giving health benefits, while Porter became a relic of past times. When war broke out and malt was rationed, it was Stout that stayed as close to its peacetime pint as possible, whereas Porter recipes were weakened, eventually leading to them dying out around the time that the Second World War ended, while Stout has been around ever since.

The style returned in the 1970s and started to spread in popularity once more, sitting besides Stout as the two most popular dark beers.

And "dark beers" is as close as we can squeeze them together now. No modern Porters are aged in huge vats for many months and pour with a sharp tang, as happened with the original ones, and while it's possible that some taste like the milder versions of the old beer, it's impossible to know for certain. So the recipes we have now must be seen as modern interpretations of the old style. Likewise, Stouts have changed so much in 200 years that their evolution is impossible to define in simple terms. Both styles have a long history, with complicated crossovers, and both have changed a lot during their years as prominent beer styles.

Is there a difference between Stout and Porter? No. Their "basic" brews (Dry Stout and Robust Porter) now tend to share similar ABVs and similar flavor profiles with only the sub-styles standing out as different. Even the style guidelines find it hard to differentiate, suggesting that the difference is more roast-barley bitterness in Stout, while Porters are higher in ABV, but the reality is that a brewer can call their black beer a Stout or a Porter and they are not wrong.

PORTER BREWED 250 YEARS AGO WOULD HAVE BEEN VERY DIFFERENT FROM THE PORTER OF 150 YEARS AGO OR OF TODAY. IT MAY ONCE HAVE BEEN DARK, SMOKY, AND SLIGHTLY SOUR (THANKS TO AN EXTENDED AGING BEFORE LEAVING THE BREWERY); IT WAS ALSO ONCE A WEAK, NON-SOUR, LIGHTLY HOPPED DARK BEER; AT ANOTHER STAGE IT WAS SERVED "MILD" AND WOULD'VE BEEN ROASTY AND DARK WITH A BIG HOP BITE. NOW IT'S A BEER RICH WITH DARK MALTS, COFFEE, CHOCOLATE, CARAMEL, AND SOMETIMES A WAFT OF SMOKE.

Robust Porter and Brown Porter are the most popular "standard" Porters—the difference is more roast in the Robust version. They are, however, very similar and a distinction is rarely necessary. ABV will be between 5.0 and 7.0% and IBU could get into the 40s, with English hops classically used to give an earthy, dark-fruit depth, though American hops are now common, typically ones with a blackcurrant and floral flavor profile. Hop and roast-barley bitterness are generally not forced down your throat, but exceptions exist, which are like chewing coffee beans—there may also be some malt acidity. You might see Baltic Porter, which is strong (6.0–9.0% ABV), classically cold-fermented with lager yeast (modern versions tend to go with a top-fermenting yeast), brewed with European hops, light on bitter roastiness and bitter hops, and slightly aged to give a vinous quality. Porter has been many things in the past and will continue to be a broad, interesting style brewed around the world. One simple description will never encapsulate its great history or breadth.

Meantime London Porter

London, England
ABV: 6.5%
Hops: Fuggles

London developed three of the most famous beer styles—Porter, Stout, and India Pale Ale—and Meantime make interpretations of all three. The India Pale Ale is an excellent version of the old British style: botanic, earthy, chewy, and yet light and fresh to drink. The London Porter is a wonderfully complex beer. The aroma swirls out dark chocolate, coffee roast, earthy fruits, nuts charred over fire, hints of smoke—it's an evocative aroma, which flicks an image of Hogarth's Beer Street into my head but adds some grubby Dickensian villains in the background. Its got roast depth, a slick mouthfeel, dark berry fruits, brown sugar, and bonfires before a malt and hop bitterness combine to give a dry finish. The London Brewers Alliance, the collective of the capital's brewers, are aiming to get London Porter a protection of origin, thanks to its historic nature and unique story—this will be one of the leading examples to support the case.

Bad Attitude Two Penny Porter

Stabio, Switzerland
ABV: 8.15%
Hops: Amarillo, Chinook, Willamette

As well as the stylish stubby bottles, Bad Attitude also put a couple of their beers in cans. Kurt is their Pale Ale brewed with New Zealand hops, and Dude is an "almost-Double" American IPA. What I love about Bad Attitude beers, as well as how terrific they taste, is that they look so damn good on the shelf. Two Penny is an American-style Porter with London inspiration and precise Swiss execution. A super-slick body of coffee, dark chocolate brownies, vanilla, and a savory-like edge is attacked from all around by the bold use of American hops, adding blackcurranty bitterness, pithy aroma, and a herbal kick at the end. To help hit the 76 IBUs, hops are added to the first runnings of wort. I'd happily pay a lot more than two pennies to fill my refrigerator with this beer.

8 Degrees Knockmealdown Porter

Mitchelstown, Ireland
ABV: 5.0%
Hops: Admiral, Fuggles

A thick black pour with a mountainous mocha foam (which is fitting because the beer is named after the Irish mountain range), Knockmealdown is a great-looking glassful. Intense dark chocolate, leather, cocoa-covered berries, caramel, and a clean complexity, there's no acrid notes of roasted malt and instead it stays deliciously smooth with a long-lasting finish of floral and earthy hops. Aussie Cam and Kiwi Scott, who started the brewery, offer a few possibilities for the name of their brewery: 8° West is the longitude running through Ireland; 8°C (46°F) is the perfect serving temperature for their beers; after God slept off his seven days of hard work, he made beer on the eighth day; or my favorite possibility, which is the 8° lean that drinkers get when relaxing with a pint of 8 Degree beer (which is best served at a cool 8°C while standing at 8° longitude, of course).

Marin Brewing Point Reyes Porter

Larkspur, California
ABV: 6.0%
Hops: East Kent Goldings, Challenger

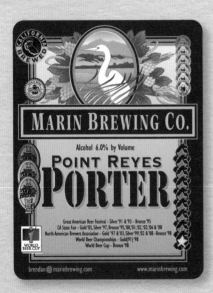

I don't know about you, but there are some beers that taste like the brewmaster could see into my brain and create my dream beer: I think that's what happened at Marin with their Point Reyes Porter. Across the Bay from San Francisco, a ferry takes you to Larkspur and a short walk gets you to Marin Brewery. The mash tun and kettle are on your left as you walk in and the whole place is filled with the sweet smell of beer brewing. A flight of beer and a burger later and there's time for one pint before we leave. I take the Porter because it's too good to leave without having another. It's bold, creamy (like the best mocha milkshake ever) and intensely roasty; there's a berry sweetness, a lactic edge, smoke, roasted nuts, and a dry finish, made amazing by the full richness of the body. It's my idea of a perfect Porter.

Holgate Temptress

Woodend, Australia
ABV: 6.0%
Hops: Topaz

A rich, lusciously dark Porter infused with Dutch cocoa and vanilla beans definitely deserves the name "Temptress." Dark brown with red at the edges and a thick, creamy foam, the cocoa and vanilla come out first (like you've just opened a good box of chocolates), then comes coffee and roast, a brown-sugar richness, some herbal and fragrant spice, chocolate brownies, and some roasted figs—it smells like dessert, and that's the way to treat this one: open it after dinner and serve on its own, with two glasses (it's best used as a means of seduction). The slick mouthfeel, the depth of cocoa and coffee (giving just a hint of bitterness) and dark fruits, plus the floral top notes of vanilla make this a real treat of a beer. The brewery has a restaurant and hotel on site, so, if things go extraordinarily well, then there are rooms upstairs. Grab an extra bottle on your way out for a decadent nightcap.

Narke Black Golding Starkporter

Örebro, Sweden
ABV: 7.2%
Hops: East Kent Goldings

Baltic Porter started as a stronger version of Porter, which was brewed in London and shipped through the Baltic ports. These powerful Porters were picked up and brewed in the region from the beginning of the 19th century, with breweries in Finland, Sweden, Russia, and Poland, among others, all making the style. The London versions would've been brewed with top-fermenting ale yeast, but, as bottom-fermenting yeasts reached the cold Baltic countries, they swapped to cool lager fermentation and a long maturation time. Narke is one of Sweden's most renowned breweries, mostly because of their barrel-aged Imperial Porter, Stormaktsporter, and their beers' rarity. Their Starkporter takes the Baltic tradition forward with a full body of dark malts, intense cocoa, coffee, caramel, and toasted nuts, with an earthy drag of bitterness and hints of berry sharpness at the edges. Wonderfully simple, remarkably complex, bloody rare.

Redemption Fellowship Porter

London, England
ABV: 5.1%
Hops: WGV, Liberty, Cascade

London's street and river porters were split into two divisions: ticket porters (like modern mailmen, they would've carried anything from letters to heavy boxes) and fellowship porters (who carried such things as malt and coal from large deliveries). Breweries were big employers of porters, needing them to deliver the raw ingredients and to help move barrels around the city. Famously thirsty, these porters sustained themselves through their hard day by regular stops at pubs, grabbing a pot of Porter before moving on. Redemption's Fellowship Porter is loaded with licorice, chocolate, and coffee; there are some hints of treacle, smoke, blackberries, and vanilla, before it ends with a looming dry bitterness—it's a Sunday lunch kind of beer, perfect with roast beef. Redemption are consistently excellent in their output. Also look for Trinity, a 3.0% ABV, highly hopped beer; Big Chief, a 5.5% hopped-up American Pale Ale; and Hopspur, a Pale Ale that sits somewhere in between.

Negev Porter Alon

Kiryat Gat, Israel
ABV: 5.0%
Hops: Magnum, Fuggles

What a handsome beer bottle this one is. The fact that it's brewed in Israel makes it doubly appealing. Named after the desert covering the south of the country, this beer glimmers like an oasis against the mass-made lagers. Porter Alon pours a midnight black with a creamy foam, it's laced with licorice bitterness, coffee roast, milk chocolate, plums, and a faint vanilla note, thanks to the oak chips that this gets aged on. Smooth to start, it ends desert-dry and quenching (incidentally, if you happen to be stuck in the Negev desert, then this beer is fine, but I'd rather have Negev's Passiflora, a light Golden Ale brewed with passion fruit). With no brewing heritage to guide them, the exciting new Israeli brewers are writing the history books as they progress the country's craft beer forward.

Yoho Tokyo Black

Karuizawa, Japan
ABV: 5.0%
Hops: Cascade, Perle

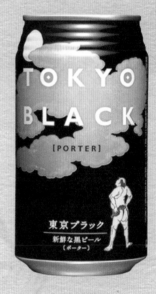

I find it hard to resist beer in cans. There's just something about drinking beer from a can that makes me feel like I'm in a movie from the 1980s, though I have no idea where that peculiar association comes from. The Yoho beers are made in one of Japan's top whisky-producing areas and both brewer and distiller use the excellent local water source in their mash tuns. With dark beers increasing in popularity in Japan, Tokyo Black jumped into the market as a great craft Porter, modeled on the London style, via a recipe from America and some tweaks for the local tastes. What you get is a near-black beer, just peeking through red at the edges. Cocoa and caramel in the aroma, then a clean body with a smooth, chocolaty middle, low roast bitterness, a fragrantly floral hop depth, and a hint of lemon peel—similar to a Schwarzbier.

Mayflower Porter

Plymouth, Massachusetts
ABV: 6.0%
Hops: Pilgrim, Glacier

Seasick and, after 66 days, running low on beer, the pilgrims on the *Mayflower*, which was aiming for Virginia, finally lowered anchor after finding a suitable place to stop in Plymouth Bay, Massachusetts. Barely surviving the winter, the pilgrims held a communal thanksgiving feast a year later, and, at this, a cask of beer was tapped—dark and cloudy, it was safer (and more intoxicating) than drinking the dark, cloudy water. While Porter isn't in America from day one, beer is, and a century later Porter is shipped over from London and becomes the most-mentioned and storied beer in American history. Mayflower's Porter is near black, intensely roasty, loaded with chocolate and dark fruits, with a bittersweet lingering malt and hop finish (appropriately using Pilgrim hops). And, to add to the history, the brewery was started by the tenth great-grandson of John Alden, a cooper (or barrel-maker) on board the *Mayflower*.

IMPERIAL STOUT AND PORTER

CZARINA CATHERINE THE GREAT'S DRINK OF CHOICE IN THE RUSSIAN IMPERIAL COURT WAS "EXTRA STOUT PORTER," A STRONG, DARK BEER BREWED IN LONDON AND SHIPPED EAST. JUST LIKE INDIA PALE ALE, THE STORIES AND IDEAS NOW ATTACHED TO IMPERIAL STOUT HAVE ROMANTICIZED THE STYLE FOR MODERN DRINKERS. IN THE 18TH CENTURY, LONDON BREWERS HAD A GOOD MARKET IN THE BALTIC STATES—THE MYTHOLOGY BEHIND THE STYLE SAYS THAT THEY WERE BREWED STRONG AND HIGHLY HOPPED TO SURVIVE THE LONG JOURNEY, BUT IT'S MORE LIKELY THAT THE MARKET THEY WERE GOING TO JUST WANTED STRONG, RICH STOUTS (ALTHOUGH THERE'S PROBABLY A CHICKEN VS. EGG DEBATE SOMEWHERE). THE WORD IMPERIAL TOLD THE DRINKER THAT THIS WAS THE BIGGEST BEER MADE BY A BREWERY AND, AT THAT TIME, IT COULD BE APPLIED TO ANY TYPE OF BEER. NOW IMPERIAL STOUT IS ONE OF THE WORLD'S MOST POPULAR STYLES.

Big, strong, and rich, like a wrestling Russian oligarch, these beers will be dark brown to opaque black, and their bodies will be medium to full. Malt leads the way with roast, caramel, coffee, chocolate, sometimes a smokiness, and dark-fruit depth. Some will finish very dry, whereas others will be sweet. Hops give lots of bitterness (50–100 IBUs) and even some variety-dependent flavor, though hop aroma isn't common. ABV can start at 8.0% and keep on going upward indefinitely, but these beers shouldn't taste boozy; instead, the alcohol should be well integrated and smooth. Imperial Stouts often find themselves in bourbon barrels and at the top of "favorite beer" lists.

Kernel Imperial Brown Stout

London, England
ABV: 10.1%
Hops: Fuggles

With their Imperial Brown Stout, Kernel have brought back a beer from Barclay Perkins's archives (this one is from 1856), meaning this is an interpretation of what the original strong London Stouts would've been like. The ingredient list is simple: Maris Otter, Amber Brown, and Black make up the grain bill and only Fuggles go into the kettle. Those four things create a phenomenal beer. Imperial Brown Stout pours a thick black, not the color of its name—that's a hangover from the times when "Stout" meant strong and so was prefixed with "Pale" or "Brown" or called "Stout Porter" to differentiate between them. There's chocolate, toast, and caramel but not much big roast, making it velvet-smooth. Hops give earthiness and even a hint of the hedgerow, which is emphasized by blackberries and plums. Old London beer wonderfully re-created by one of London's top new breweries.

Hornbeer Black Magic Woman

Kirke Hyllinge, Denmark
ABV: 9.9%
Hops: Columbus, Centennial, Amarillo

It's late at night in Brussels. Very late. I've no idea how late. One of the guys with us is asleep at the table, another has just spent €20 on a very old beer that tastes like soy sauce. Drinking buddy John has bought a bottle of Black Magic Woman because we couldn't resist the name or the way the bottle looked in the refrigerator. Despite (or maybe because of) our advanced refreshment, this beer grabbed our attention right away with slick dark chocolate, gentle roast, a full body, cocoa-dusted cranberries, a weave of charred wood smoke, and a lingering bitterness. Loaded with flavor and depth, it was one of those beers where your expectations are well exceeded and you're stunned by the magic that's in your glass. Trying a bottle a year later showed me just how spellbinding this beer really is.

Jester King Black Metal

Austin, Texas
ABV: 9.3%
Hops: Millennium, East Kent Goldings

Jester King are a farmhouse brewery in Texas who fully embrace their terroir, whether it's by using their own well water or cultivating yeast strains from around them—look for Das Wunderkind, a sour Saison brewed with that yeast. Their beer range also cheers on the farmhouse inspiration from years ago: Noble King is a riff of hops and spicy yeast, giving hop sack, floral, orange, and a bold grassiness that all linger intensely on the tongue. Le Petit Prince is a table beer, something rarely seen in craft beer, and it's a 2.9% ABV glugger that elegantly balances hops and farmhouse yeast. Black Metal is a Farmhouse Imperial Stout. It takes that peppery, spicy, dry-finishing yeast and lets it power through the sweetness of a big dark beer. There's big roast depth, loads of intense dark chocolate, tobacco, and licorice before it gets drier and drier, leading into a peppery finish.

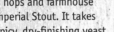

Dugges Idjit!

Landvetter, Sweden
ABV: 9.5%
Hops: Brewers Gold, Chinook

Dugges Ale & Porterbryggeri is their full name, and the bright, pastel-colored labels present a soft side in contrast to the powerful beers within them. Brewing just outside Gothenburg, Dugges increased their capacity in 2012 to keep up with the ever-growing demand for their beers, some of which are distributed internationally. The best-known beers are part of their "express yourself" series of American-inspired beers: Holy Cow!, Bollox!, High Five! (all American IPAs), and Idjit! You'd have to be an idjit not to like Idjit!, which is a hell yeah!, hollering Imperial Stout that's oily with espresso, molasses, and dark cocoa; it's rich and full-bodied with a floral-fruity fig flavor giving a vinous depth. Perfect Idjit! is a barrel-aged version, giving vanilla and toffee on top of the base brew. There's also ½ Idjit!, a 7.0% ABV Robust Porter with more licorice, figs, and anise notes and less on the roast, finishing with a sharp coffee fruitiness.

Fritz Ale Imperial Stout

Bonn, Germany

ABV: 9.7%

Hops: Simcoe

Inspired by American craft beer, Fritz Ale produce a range that includes an American IPA, Imperial IPA, and Imperial Stout, all lavishly hopped with American varieties. Their Belgian IPA takes an American base and spices it up with Belgian yeast, giving tropical fruit and bananas, roasted apples, and citrus before a kicking peppery finish. The Imperial Stout is a big beer. With loads of roast depth and intense espresso, it's got the sharpness of very dark chocolate, some roasted plums, and then the huge American hops, giving pine, leather, and a suggestion of a fall bonfire that burned through the flower garden. Also look out for another German Imperial Stout: Propeller's Nachtflug (Night Flight), a 9.1% ABV German Imperial Stout with a lightness to the body and an alluring roast, vanilla, and floral depth like blackberries drowned in espresso.

Antares Imperial Stout

Mar del Plata, Argentina

ABV: 8.5%

Hops: Apollo, Goldings, Fuggles

Named after the supergiant star in the Scorpius constellation, Antares has been brewing in Argentina since 1998 and was set up by three friends who wanted to drink better beer. Starting the brewery in Mar del Playa, the company has grown to have a group of brewpubs around the country. With a Kölsch, Cream Stout, Barley Wine, and regular specials, Antares has a range of beers throughout the set-up—if you visit, grab a tasting tray of all those available on tap. The Imperial Stout is near-black with a bouldering tan foam. You get the mocha roast and dark fruits you expect, then come cigar boxes, cherries, and spicy, earthy hops. There's a lightness to the body, which makes it very drinkable and also highlights a complex acidity at the end that is closer to an Argentinian Malbec.

Nail Clout Stout

Perth, Australia

ABV: 10.6%

Hops: Goldings, Pride of Ringwood

Nail Brewing was launched in 2000 by John Stallwood who, like so many others, started on a small homebrew kit. But the brewery's history isn't quite as smooth as Nail's super Oatmeal Stout—John was forced to halt brewing after being attacked in April 2004, trying to stop strangers fighting in the street. Lucky to be alive, but unable to work, John sold the brewery and concentrated on recovering. In May 2006, Nail Ale is back on the bar and a year later it's back in full production. Packaged in a beautiful 750ml bottle, Clout Stout is a once-a-year special release. Unlike the hugely nailable Nail Ale, an Australian Pale Ale made with Aussie Pride of Ringwood hops, Clout Stout demands a little more time and consideration. Full-bodied and rich with chocolate and coffee, there's sweet plums, roasted nuts, and vanilla—it's complex, superb, and special, a fine reflection of John's life motto: never give up.

Driftwood Singularity

Victoria, Canada
ABV: 14.0%
Hops: Bittering hops only

Imperial Stout is the style that most often slumbers in bourbon barrels. When you think about the chocolate and caramel richness of the beer and the vanilla, toffee, and spice in the bourbon, the combination just makes sense. Driftwood Singularity gets a few months in bourbon barrels and has become a Blockbuster beer that is released once a year to pandemonium as drinkers wrestle over the few available bottles. Black and bold, it pours like treacle and immediately yells "bourbon" with the boozy vanilla aroma from the wood, but then the base beer takes over with just a whisper of spirit in the background. Loads of thick dark chocolate, molasses, vanilla, aniseed, and spice and a finish like a bourbon-spiked ristretto. While you wait for its release, try Driftwood's Fat Tug IPA, a fresh mandarin, grapefruit, and pine explosion of a beer, or there's Farmhouse, a spicy, refreshing Saison.

Durham Temptation

Durham, England
ABV: 10.0%
Hops: Target, Goldings

"Innovation with tradition" is Durham's tagline and they focus on reimagining great British beer styles. Bombay 106 is an English-style IPA that's deep with earthy, pungent hops, while Evensong is a glorious Bitter, richly malty and yet bracingly hoppy. Then there's Temptation, a Stout that starts bready, then goes toasty, then moves into nutty, roasty, and chocolaty. There's some vanilla and vinous fruit, a boozy punch, a kiss of sweetness, lots of dark chocolate, a bitter and earthy finish, and a woody dryness to end it all. Durham also try a few different things: Diabolus is a 9.5% ABV Sour Stout, which is like intensely acidic dark chocolate but a million times more complex and interesting; and their White Stout looks back to the origins of the name. It is a pale, strong beer made modern with hefty handfuls of Columbus hops.

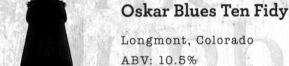

Oskar Blues Ten Fidy

Longmont, Colorado
ABV: 10.5%
Hops: Columbus

I went to the Oskar Blues brewery once. They have a basketball court in the corner, opposite the long canning line and in front of the huge silver tanks, which look like massive beer cans—it's a cool place, especially the tasting room. Crunch your thumb through the Ten Fidy ring-pull and you get cake shop, dark chocolate, vanilla, and roasted berries in the aroma; the body is so satisfyingly full that drinking it is a treat for the tongue; there's a brownie sweetness; the roast at the end doesn't overpower and instead you get rich chocolate balanced by a hop freshness, which lifts and lightens it. There's something wonderful about the combination of an Imperial Stout and a can; it makes me want to drink it on trains where everyone else thinks I'm sipping a soft drink when, in fact, I'm gulping one of the world's best Stouts—a bit like eating a lobster sandwich on the bus.

BARREL-AGED BEERS

WOODEN BARRELS WERE BEER'S CONTAINER OF CHOICE FOR MANY YEARS UNTIL THE CHEAPER AND MORE PRACTICAL STAINLESS STEEL TOOK OVER. WHERE WOOD WAS USED, IT WAS MERELY THERE AS THE MATURATION VESSEL OR MEANS OF GETTING IT TO THE BAR; BREWERS DIDN'T WANT THE BARRELS TO GIVE ANY FLAVOR TO THE BEER, SO THEY WERE TREATED TO PREVENT THE PASSING OF QUALITIES FROM WOOD TO LIQUID. NOW BREWERS SPECIFICALLY WANT BARRELS FOR THE FLAVORS THEY CAN PUSH INTO A BEER, RANGING FROM TANNIC TEXTURE, SWEET VANILLA, PHENOLIC SPICE, SMOKE, AND THE SPIRIT OF WHATEVER WAS IN THE BARREL BEFORE THE BEER.

Most, but not all, barrels will have previously held something else—bourbon, whisky, and wine are the most common, though rum, port, sherry, calvados, cognac, and tequila have all made it into breweries. The beer going into these barrels picks up the previous inhabitant's flavor, plus a depth from the wood, adding a new complexity to the beer—some will also add sourness, although whether this is good or not is dependent on the brewer's intention. Strong beers are most common because they can handle more maturation and pull in more flavor, but barrels are not used just for big and strong brews (Lambic and Gueuze, for example). The barrel-aged category is vast, going from light, soured wheat beers all the way to massive Imperial Stouts. Oak is the most common wood (French or American), though not the exclusive choice. The best barrel-aging adds extra depth, flavor, and texture to the base beer without overpowering it.

BrewDog Paradox

Fraserburgh, Scotland
ABV: Varies between 10% and 15%
Hops: Galena, Bramling Cross

The Paradox series uses different barrels from different distilleries for each release. The beer starts as an Imperial Stout, moves to whisky casks, and comes out with an expression of whatever whisky was in the barrel before it. Given BrewDog's remote Scottish location, they are closer to the many whisky distilleries than most breweries, making this a great Scottish project. The fun is seeing what different whiskies give to the same base beer: Islay casks sear the beer with smoke, earth, and sea; Jura gives stone, fruit and toffee; Isle of Arran gives ginger, spice, and vanilla. The base beer is smooth and richly chocolaty with a balanced bitterness: it's a big black canvas for barrel flavor. The beer is best enjoyed along with a dram of whisky from the barrel that it was aged in. Also try it with cranachan, a Scottish dessert of oats, cream, raspberries, honey, and whisky.

Cupacá Tequila

Mexicali, Mexico
ABV: 10.0%
Hops: Centennial

Whisky barrels tend to get one or two uses—bourbon is fresh barrel, used once and then done. Bourbon barrels are often sent to Scotland where they're filled again for one use. Tequila, however, can be used again and again, meaning that tequila producers are reluctant to give away their wood. In Mexico, tequila barrels are surely the ones craft brewers most want to put strong beer into, so the guys at Cupacá worked hard to get themselves some casks. Into these goes their barley wine and, five months later, you get a dark brown beer with a wonderful and unique wood character: brown sugar, caramel, and oak come from the beer and wood, there's a floral freshness, tropical fruit, and a sharp botanic lift from the spirit, and it's not shy on the tequila—which also brings citrus, mirroring the squeeze of lime, mixed with the smooth depths of aged tequila. It's an amazing transfer of flavor.

De Struise Pannepot Reserva

Oostvleteren, Belgium
ABV: 10.0%
Hops:Challenger, Magnum

Pannepot is an incredible beer of almost-unrivaled complexity, reminiscent of a bulked-up Belgian Quadrupel, only better. Its winning hand is the body of malt: dried fruit, figs, vanilla, roasted plums, cola, cocoa, a grassy freshness, and the malty and floral notes of black tea, all livened up by the spices that go into the brew, giving licorice, nutmeg, cinnamon, and cracked pepper. The complexity is astonishing, but the mouthfeel is what makes it so good, being so rich and satisfying to drink. Even better, if you can find it, is the Pannepot Reserva, which is oak-aged and that adds vanilla, caramel sweetness, and a drier, lingering herbal finish which is so good with the base flavor in the beer. They come with their vintage on the label; look after them well and they'll get better for around five years if you can manage to last that long without opening them.

Hallertau Porter Noir Pinot Noir

Auckland, New Zealand
ABV: 6.6%
Hops: Southern Cross

As part of their Heroic Series of beers, each showing a bodacious, hard-bodied Adonis, Hallertau's Porter Noir is a Porter aged in Pinot Noir barrels along with Brettanomyces. Wine barrels and wild yeast are popular around the world as brewers seek that tart, vinous, funky quality in their beer, and where some take it all the way to cheek-puckeringly sour, others just give it enough time to develop an edge of extra depth. Porter Noir pours near-noir and immediately you get barrel and brett—it's like berries, earth, and lemon followed by oak (this could be reminiscent of the early London Porters with their tart edges). Take a gulp and it's a wild ride between beer and wine, emphasized by the light texture: there's dark fruits, chocolate, cherries, spice, sweet barrel, earthy grape-skin dryness, and a sour finish like an exclamation at the end of a bold statement. Serious stuff, superbly done.

Dogfish Head Palo Santo Marron

Milton, Delaware
ABV: 12.0%
Hops: Warrior, Palisade

What makes Palo Santo Marron special, apart from the ambrosial taste, is the barrel it is aged in. In 2006, John Gasparine, who owns a floor company in Baltimore, was looking for sustainable wood in Paraguay when he saw that the local woodcutters were using palo santo, or "holy wood." When Gasparine told Dogfish Head's Sam Calagione about the wood, Sam set out to build "the biggest wooden barrel since the days of Prohibition." (The whole story is in a famous *New Yorker* article: look it up.) That big barrel has been joined by two others, each holding enough to fill over 100,000 12 fl oz (355ml) bottles per batch—it's one of the most ambitious year-round American craft beers. The wood, used only by Dogfish Head, gives a uniquely wonderful flavor to the strong brown ale: cherry, caramel, brown sugar, earthy spice, cocoa, juicy berries, and dried fruit. It's great with blueberry pancakes and maple syrup.

Kross 5

Santiago, Chile
ABV: 7.2%
Hops: Glacier, Horizon, Mt Hood, Cascade, Goldings

This copper-colored beer was Chile's first to get barrel-aged. Considering the wine influence all around, it took a while for beer to follow the same path and package a product in a way that makes it really stand out on the shelves. As a fifth birthday brew, Kross 5 came out in 2008 in the stunning 750ml bottle. Made in a region ringed by some of Chile's best-known white wine producers, this one swaggers about like the rebel kid in town. Lush malts give caramel, cognac, raisins, almonds, brown sugar, and cola; the oak gives a little but doesn't overpower, poking vanilla and wood in the gaps and adding a subtle background to everything. It finishes with a peppery, woody bitterness that adds more balance to the whole thing. It's a sharing with friends and food kind of beer.

Firestone Walker Anniversary Ale

Paso Robles, California
ABV: Varies—around 12.5%

London's old Porter brewers, and the old and new Belgian Lambic, Red, and Brown brewers, had to learn the skill of blending beer. Now many modern brewers have had to add it to their arsenal of skills. The practice of barrel-aging beers has become so complex and deeply explored that some breweries have cellars loaded with hundreds of casks of different ages and filled with different beers; as barrels mature individually, blending is necessary to get the right balance. Firestone Walker's Anniversary Ale (released once a year—2013's will be Sixteen) is a superior blend of the best stuff in their barrel room and it comes out with a list of the specific blend, meaning each year's is different. In the glass, it's oak, vanilla, bourbon, booze, chocolate, caramel, and dried fruit and then distant citrus hops and fresh beer. Stunningly complex and an ode to oak-aging.

Wild Beer Co. Modus Operandi

Bristol, England
ABV: 7.0%
Hops: Magnum, Fuggles

Wild Beer Co. started in a rural retreat in England's West Country in 2012. Their name comes from their modern English farmhouse-style, which is focusing on barrels and wild yeast (including a British Lambic). There will also be Fresh, a Pale Ale, and Epic Saison, spicy with yeast and fruity from Sorachi Ace hops. Modus Operandi is the flagship beer: it starts as an old ale inspired by the British beers of a century or two ago with a nascent, wild-yeast character. It's brewed and fermented in the classic way and then it's transferred into either red wine or bourbon barrels along with Brettanomyces. After 90 days, the beer is blended, bottled (bottle-conditioned), and then left for another month to mature at the brewery. Early batches were astonishing: cherry cola, caramel, a supreme lightness of body, a hint of sharp berries, and an earthy, bracing bitterness. Watch out for Wild Beer Co. in 2013.

Cidre Dupont Reserve

Victot-Pontfol, France
ABV: 7.5%
Hops: None

No, this isn't beer. But it is barrel-aged and does taste extraordinary. Craft-beer drinkers looking for more variety in their glasses are turning toward cider with more regularity, where the sprightly, bright, sharp-sweet flavor shares similarities with the wild and sour beers now brewed around the world. Domaine Dupont make cider, calvados, and pommeau (a blend of cider and calvados) in Normandy, northwest France. Cidre Dupont Reserve is aged in calvados barrels for six months before release and that gives a cider with elegance and complexity: there's green apple, fragrant citrus, tart tropical fruit, cellar-like funk, and a round depth of toffee and spice from the aging. As well as the smart bottles, you can also find this on draft and it's exported to the United States. Drinking this makes me wonder how a beer—a Bière de Garde, perhaps—aged in those barrels would taste...

Avery Rumpkin

Boulder, Colorado
ABV: 10-15%
Hops: Magnum, Sterling

This one makes me want to fly to Denver, drive to Avery's barrel-room, unbung a Rumpkin, and drink it straight from the wood— it's an Imperial Pumpkin Ale, spiced with nutmeg, cinnamon, and ginger, and aged in dark rum barrels for six months. I know there's a lot of other exciting stuff in the barrel-room, from Wild Ales to Imperial Stouts, in a mix of wine, port, rum, and bourbon barrels. Rumpkin, released once a year, is as close to a cocktail or dessert as it is to beer. It pours pumpkin-flesh amber, and the rum, oak, spices, and brown sugar come out first (like spiced rum and coke). Take a sip and it gets better, with marshmallows, toasted nuts, sweet pumpkin, molasses, and a lovely boozy coconut creaminess. Drink it with pumpkin pie.

HISTORIC RE-CREATIONS

AS BREWERS MOVE THINGS IN THEIR MASH TUNS FORWARD WITH NEW IDEAS AND INSPIRATIONS, THERE'S A GROWING INTEREST IN BEERS OF THE PAST.

BEER HAS BEEN MADE AND DRUNK FOR THOUSANDS OF YEARS, AND CIVILIZATION HAS GROWN BY HAVING A BREW AT THE END OF A HARD DAY HUNTING/BUILDING THINGS/FARMING/SITTING AT A DESK WAITING FOR I.T. TO FIX THAT PROBLEM WITH YOUR COMPUTER. LOOKING BACKWARD RAISES A LOT OF QUESTIONS: HOW DID AMERICAN LAGER TASTE BEFORE PROHIBITION? WHAT WAS PORTER LIKE IN 1900? HOW ABOUT IN 1800? HOW DID THE ORIGINAL INDIA PALE ALES TASTE? WHAT DID BEER BREWED 1,000 YEARS AGO TASTE LIKE? WHAT ABOUT 6,000 YEARS AGO? WOULD EARLY COLONIAL AMERICANS ENJOY A DOUBLE IPA? WOULD AN EGYPTIAN BUILDING THE PYRAMIDS PREFER A COLD PILSNER TO THE BEER HE WAS PAID IN?

Brewing records, particularly in Britain, have been well preserved with recipes and processes neatly written down, as if Victorian brewmasters had the thoughts of future brewers in their mind. We can see what was made, what ingredients were used, and the processes they went through—and this means that we can see a recipe and re-create it. Other beers have been brought back from ancient tradition, verse, or even analysis of old drinking vessels. History is reflected in a glass, providing a fascinating look back at what drinkers would've enjoyed many years ago.

Professor Fritz Briem 13th Century Gruit Beer

Friesing, Germany
ABV: 4.6%
Hops: Wild hops

To say that beer needs a bitter ingredient to balance the sweetness is not technically true: most beers have the majority of the sugars fermented out, meaning that they wouldn't be sweet. Instead, the real purpose of hops is to add seasoning, flavor, and balance (plus, historically, a preservative quality). Those elements have been necessary to make a palatable drink, of which you would want more than one medicinal gulp, for millennia. Before hops took over the primary flavoring role between the 15th and 17th centuries, Gruit (a herb, spice, and botanic mix) was added to give beer its defining depth. Professor Fritz Briem's 13th-century version contains bay leaves, ginger, caraway, anise, rosemary, and gentian plus wild hops (hops would've been used in a Gruit mix). It's a hazy, pale peach color and the aroma is immediately unlike a beer you've had before: ginger, hard herbs, licorice, lemon, and a savory side. It's sharp and botanic, slight of body; ginger pushes through the most, but it's seasoned with the other herbs, ending with a dry herbal depth. There's a reason hops took over the beer world, but it's fascinating to try a relic of centuries ago.

Dogfish Head

Milton, Delaware

As beer time travelers go, Dogfish Head have gone the furthest, both in time and place. With the help of Dr. Patrick McGovern, a molecular archaeologist specializing in booze, they've found recipes or decoded analyses of ancient brewing vessels and turned them into modern recipes. Chateau Jiahu (10.0% ABV) goes back 9,000 years to China and unravels a drink preserved in old pottery; the re-creation contains brown rice syrup, orange blossom honey, Muscat grapes, and hawthorn berries, and it's fermented with sake yeast. Midas Touch (9.0% ABV) resurrects a taste of King Midas's tomb with a golden beer including Muscat grapes, honey, and saffron. Theobroma (9.0% ABV) recalls an ancient alcoholic chocolate drink from Honduras and is brewed with Aztec cocoa powder, cocoa nibs, honey, chilies, and annatto seeds. Sah'tea (9.0% ABV) reimagines sahti, a Finnish brew made with rye and juniper. Dogfish's version contains juniper, a bunch of spices, and black tea, and is fermented with Weizen yeast. Ta Henket (4.5% ABV) translates Egyptian hieroglyphics and makes a beer from hearth-baked bread flavored with camomile, doum-palm fruit (similar to dates), and Middle Eastern herbs, plus a native Egyptian yeast. All interesting beers to experience and, while they are no doubt modern tastes, the stories and processes that come with the beers make the Ancient Ales series a fascinating project.

Fuller's Past Masters

London, England

This is a range of Fuller's beers that looks back into their old brewing archives and revives beers from the past. Fuller's began brewing in 1845 and every brew has been recorded between then and now, meaning that they've got recipes dating to day one and brewing books annotated with notes and scribbles like tiny snapshots into the life of a brewer many years ago. Past Masters is an ongoing project to re-create those old recipes. To make them as authentic as possible, the current brewers also try to source the exact ingredients that would've been used, even if this means looking for rare types of barley or hops. Just a single batch is brewed each time, so get them when you see them and store them away—most will age well. XX, a strong ale (7.5% ABV), was first brewed on September 2, 1891. Deeply malty, it has a peppery, earthy bitterness that lingers forever.

Double Stout (7.4% ABV) brings back a beer brewed on August 4, 1893, strong, smoky, and deep with dark malt. The third release was Old Burton Extra, resurrecting the brew of Thursday, September 10, 1931, a (7.3% ABV) Burton ale hopped with Fuggles and Goldings, as bittersweet as the knowledge that this style is now extinct. Maybe, in the 22nd century, Fuller's brewmasters might look back into the books and re-create Bengal Lancer or ESB. I wonder how close they'd get to how it tastes today?

SPECIALTY INGREDIENTS

WATER, GRAIN, HOPS, AND YEAST (PLUS TIME AND BREWERS) MAKE BEER. ON TOP OF THAT BASE, THE BREWERS CAN ADD ANYTHING THEY WANT TO THE BREW: FRUIT, SPICES, HERBS, FLOWERS, CHOCOLATE, COFFEE, VANILLA, VEGETABLES, TEA, NUTS, GINGER, AND A WHOLE SHOPPING BASKET OF OTHER THINGS. WHILE SOME INGREDIENTS ARE VERY UNUSUAL—BACON, FOR EXAMPLE—OTHERS, SUCH AS COFFEE, ARE VERY COMMON AND ADD AN EXTRA FLAVOR OR SENSATION TO THE BREW, EITHER EMPHASIZING AN EXISTING QUALITY (CHOCOLATE IN A MILK STOUT, HERBS IN A SAISON) OR GIVING A COMPLETELY DIFFERENT EXPERIENCE (CHILI IN AN IPA, GINGER IN AN ESB).

Before hops became beer's seasoning, a mix of wild-growing ingredients would've been used to add bitterness: wormwood, broom, dandelion, heather, juniper, pepper, and spices. As ingredients evolved, some brewers have looked back to those early days. A popular ingredient is pumpkin, basedona colonial brews and brought back by craft brewers who use the fruit to get a nutty sweetness into their beer, often accentuating it with pumpkin-pie spices.

Untypical ingredients can be added to any brew of any style. Open, varied, rule-free, and sometimes highly unusual, they expand the brewing and flavor possibilities of beer and can create interesting and excellent drinks. The best show a sleight of hand to make the ingredient integrate but not overpower. But beware of novelty beer: using something silly for the sake of some attention is not cool.

5 Rabbit Huitzi

Chicago, Illinois
ABV: 9.0%
Hops: Glacier
Ingredients: Hibiscus flowers, ginger, Thai palm sugar, Chicago honey

5 Rabbit is a Latin-inspired cerveceria based in Chicago, and most of the beers go beyond the four main ingredients. There's 5 Lizard, an American wheat with passion-fruit pulp, or 5 Vulture, a dark ale brewed with Piloncillo (Latin cane sugar) and Ancho chilies. Huitzi is a Belgian strong ale brewed with hibiscus flowers, ginger, Thai palm sugar, and Chicago honey. It's delightfully unusual and unexpected in the way it tastes: floral and orangey, there's a sweetness and a sharpness. The balance of flavors moves throughout the beer, going one way and then another; the ginger sneaks in, the honey brings an added floral character, the hops give citrus, there's spice from the yeast, and more hibiscus at the end. Fragrant, elegant, and surprisingly refreshing—drink with enchiladas.

Elysian The Great Pumpkin

Seattle, Washington
ABV: 8.1%
Hops: Magnum
Ingredients: Pumpkin (plus cinnamon, nutmeg, clove, allspice)

In colonial America, brewers took whatever starch they could to make beers. Barley hadn't yet spread and wasn't grown in enough volume, while the imports from Britain were slow to arrive and expensive. Pumpkin, with its American abundance and starchy middle, made for a good brewing option and became one of the country's indigenous beer styles. Fast-forward a few hundred years and pumpkins are back in breweries, typically released around the harvest time. Elysian are pumpkin specialists, even holding a pumpkin beer festival every October. The Great Pumpkin Ale adds pumpkin flesh and seeds to the mash, then more flesh goes into the kettle and fermenter—it's also spiced with cinnamon, nutmeg, clove, and allspice. It's smooth and comforting like pumpkin pie; there's a hint of pie-crust, brown sugar, sweet pumpkin, tingling fall spice, and an astonishing depth of flavor.

Three Boys Oyster Stout

Christchurch, New Zealand
ABV: 6.5%
Hops: Green Bullet, Fuggles
Ingredients: Oysters

This makes sense if you know that putting a pinch of salt into dark chocolate makes it taste sweeter and more chocolaty. Stout and Porter were the beers of choice in London in the late 19th century and, at that time, oysters weren't the luxury shuck they are today. Instead, they were plentiful, cheap, and plucked freely from the sea. Originally, oysters didn't go into the Stout; they were just served on the side, like Victorian sliders. Then one day the bivalves slid their way into the brew (it's thought that a Kiwi brewery in 1929 was the first to do this). For Three Boys' Oyster Stout, Bluff oysters are added midway through the boil. It pours inky black with a mocha foam; the aroma is chocolate, vanilla, hazelnut, and sweet berries. Take a gulp and a gush of saline brininess bursts forward, adding lemon and a peppery depth wrapped in all that lush chocolate—the beer's got body, depth, texture, fruit, and subtlety. It's a pearl of a pint and great with Tabasco-spiked oysters.

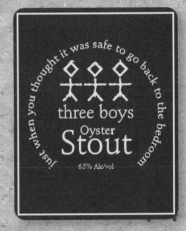

Williams Bros Nollaig

Alloa, Scotland
ABV: 7.0%
Hops: Centennial, Bobek, Southern Cross
Ingredients: Christmas trees

As well as a modern set of styles, Williams Bros make a range of traditional-style Scottish brews with Old World brewing ingredients found locally. Fraoch is the famous one: it's a hopless Heather Ale, one of Scotland's original beer styles, which also contains bog myrtle and is a resinous yet fragrantly floral beer. Kelpie puts seaweed into the mash tun for a fresh, seaside-air feel—this harks back to the time when Scottish coastal brewers fertilized their fields with seaweed. Nollaig is the most fun of these beers: it's made with Christmas trees. There are lots of faux-festive brews but this one is Santa-approved. Sappy with pine but somehow as bright as the lights that flicker above the presents, there's a fresh floral flavor, dried herbs, and some zesty citrus with a jammy kind of marmalade sweetness. No novelty value in the Williams Bros beers—they're all excellent.

Ballast Point Indra Kunindra

San Diego, California
ABV: 7.0%
Hops: Fuggles
Ingredients: Madras curry power, cayenne pepper, cumin, toasted coconut, kaffir lime leaf

This is unlike any beer I've ever had before. It's an "India-Style Export Stout," although that doesn't mean it's an IPA-style beer (if you're looking for that, then drink Ballast Point's Sculpin and Big Eye, two superb American IPAs). What you get with Indra Kunindra is a hugely aromatic, spiced strong Stout. It started as a collaboration with homebrewer Alex Tweet; they liked each other so much that Alex started working for the brewery full time. The phenomenal thing about Indra Kunindra is how you can taste each spice individually. Cayenne and cumin give an earthy, peppery warmth to the nostril, the toasted coconut complements the chocolaty roast, the curry powder gives all the flavor and depth, and the lime leaf lightens it at the end, mixing with the fragrant hop and cayenne heat. Outrageously unusual, spiced in a superior way, but potent—it's not for delicate tongues.

Dogfish Head Noble Rot

Milton, Delaware
ABV: 9.0%
Hops: CTZ, Willamette
Ingredients: Grape must

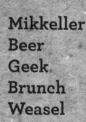

A number of wineries brew beer and breweries mature beers in old wine barrels, but there aren't many drinks that combine grape and grain so completely in the brewing process as Noble Rot. For this beer, Dogfish Head work with Alexandria Nicole Cellars in Washington. A huge volume of Viognier grapes must is mixed into the hopped wort. The must has been intentionally infected with *Botrytis cinerea*, or noble rot (a fungal infection that dehydrates grapes), concentrating sugars and acidity, and giving a dried apricot or marmalade depth. A Saison yeast flies through the malt and grape sugars before Pinot Gris must is added. The base beer is gold, the yeast and fruit shine through with grape skin, apple juice, peach, dried apricot, flowers, pepper, and banana. With apple skin and grapes mixing with the mellow malt depth and spice of Saison yeast, two worlds combine and give a fascinating drink.

Mikkeller Beer Geek Brunch Weasel

Copenhagen, Denmark
ABV: 10.9%
Hops: Centennial, Chinook, Cascade
Ingredients: Kopi luwak coffee

Coffee isn't an unusual ingredient of beer, and has gone into many styles—Stout, Porter, IPA, Bock. It's the coffee used in this one that makes it different: it takes beans that have been eaten by civet cats in Indonesia. These civets, or weasels, aren't able to digest the bean, which they excrete. Those beans are collected, roasted, and sold around the world. Mikkeller's Beer Geek Brunch Weasel is a coffee and oatmeal Imperial Stout. If possible, this is the beer I drink on Christmas morning—a luxurious breakfast treat for my favorite day of the year. It pours a thick, oily black, the aroma is coffee and dark chocolate, with some floral and fruity hops emphasizing the coffee's sweet acidity. The body is so mouthfilling and full, rich and roasty, and intense with a hint of caramel and vanilla. I love this beer.

Redwillow Smokeless

Macclesfield, England
ABV: 5.7%
Hops: Target
Ingredients: Chipotle chili

In 2010, homebrewer Toby McKenzie decided to quit his day job in I.T. and start brewing professionally—it was a good move because Redwillow almost immediately became a brewery that knowledgeable British drinkers wanted to find. Smokeless is a misnomer considering it's made with smoked malt and chipotle chili. Chilies can make beer taste like fire water, but they also have a sweet fruitiness when fresh, or take on an earthy, leathery warmth when dried. Porter, with its smothering chocolate depth, is great against chili heat, and they combine skillfully in Smokeless. The chipotle (added into the mash and kettle) gives smoked paprika and a red fruitiness, which is emphasized by floral, spicy hops, and then it goes into the roasty depths of Porter, giving subtle sweet smoke and ending with a lingering hint of roasted fruit. The brewery name comes from Toby's kids: his daughter is called Sophie Willow, his son is Jake Red.

Brasseurs
San Gluten
American Pale Ale

Montreal, Canada
ABV: 5.0%
Hops: Chinook, Cascade,
Centennial, Willamette
Ingredients: Millet,
buckwheat, corn, quinoa

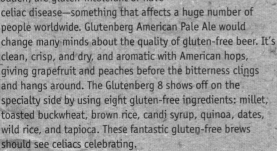

Canada's first specialist gluten-free microbrewery, Brasseurs San Gluten make four year-round beers without the typical barley, oats, rye, and wheat, instead brewing from a base of millet and other specialty grains. The brewery was started by Julien Niquet and David Cayer in 2010 to give beer options to those who, like Julien, are gluten-intolerant or have celiac disease—something that affects a huge number of people worldwide. Glutenberg American Pale Ale would change many minds about the quality of gluten-free beer. It's clean, crisp, and dry, and aromatic with American hops, giving grapefruit and peaches before the bitterness clings and hangs around. The Glutenberg 8 shows off on the specialty side by using eight gluten-free ingredients: millet, toasted buckwheat, brown rice, candi syrup, quinoa, dates, wild rice, and tapioca. These fantastic gluten-free brews should see celiacs celebrating.

Haandbryggeriet
Norwegian Wood

Drammen, Norway
ABV: 6.5%
Hops: Northern Brewer,
Centennial, Cluster
Ingredients: Juniper berries and twigs

Norway is too far north for hops to grow, but juniper is abundant and is a traditional flavoring and bittering ingredient. Norwegian Wood re-creates an old farmhouse beer that was brewed with juniper berries, twigs, and malt dried over fire, giving a smoky flavor. Fragrant and bitter, juniper also has an antiseptic quality that helped to preserve the beer, while the berries contain dextrose, a fermentable sugar. The classic beer put hay and juniper branches at the bottom of the brewing vessel, to act as a strainer, and added berries in the boil. The beer is evocative of walking through a pine forest with campfires crackling around you. The juniper gives botanic notes, peppery and fruity, plus woody pine. The body is soft with treacle and herbs, while the smoke swirls in the background.

EXTREME BEER

A MUTANT FORM OF BREWING AIMING TO
PUSH POSSIBILITIES, TASTEBUDS, AND THE MINDS OF
DRINKERS. ULTRA-STRONG, OUTRAGEOUSLY BITTER, MADE WITH UNUSUAL INGREDIENTS,
OR UNDERGOING AN UNTYPICAL BREWING PROCESS, EXTREME BEERS ARE AT THE OUTER LIMITS OF
WHAT'S POSSIBLE IN A MASH TUN, FERMENTATION TANK, OR A BREWER'S IMAGINATION.

The strongest beers in the world have passed 50.0% ABV, but they are controversial: brewed as normal beers, they then undergo an ice distillation by being partially frozen; the water freezes before the alcohol does and chunks of ice are removed, increasing the alcohol in the beer. Does that still count as beer? I say yes. The freezing is just another process in the production of the beer, like barrel-aging or dry-hopping, to get the finished product. The strongest beers produced with normal fermentation have reached around 28.0% ABV. Other processes or ingredients add an extreme element, perhaps it's the use of hot chili, meat, vegetables, or things usually found behind drugstore counters. And then there are incredibly bitter beers. Smart scientists don't think we can detect much above 120 IBU, just getting bitter noise on the tongue beyond that. Yet some beers have hit theoretical IBU levels of over 1,000. Not for everyday drinking, some extreme beers fall into the category of "mine's-bigger-than-yours willy-waving," while others are genuinely interesting and exciting concepts for beers, and the best come with great stories about how and why they were made.

BrewDog Tactical Nuclear Penguin

Fraserburgh, Scotland
ABV: 32.0%
Hops: Galena, Bramling Cross

Years ago, this started as a whisky-barrel-aged Imperial Stout, then BrewDog took it to their local ice-cream factory... They partially froze the 10.0% ABV beer, took out the ice (which leaves behind the alcohol), and then repeated it over three weeks, gradually increasing the strength until the beer got to 32.0% ABV, similar to the whiskies made by their Scottish brewing brothers. Boozy like bourbon, a background depth from the whisky barrel gives sweetness and smoke, and it's richly roasty like eating bitter chocolate by a bonfire. Most importantly, it still tastes like beer. You can go to the BrewDog bars around the United Kingdom and order a nip of it. Or you could try Sink the Bismarck!, a 41.0% quadruple IPA, which smells like hop oil and tastes like thick, boozy, bitter caramel. You've probably missed The End of History—that one was 55.0% ABV. These three beers have each, at their time of release, been the strongest beers in the world, only to be overtaken by something else.

Twisted Pine Ghost Face Killah

Boulder, Colorado
ABV: 5.0%
Hops: Willamette, Northern Brewer

This is as hardcore as hardcore beer gets. Approach with the caution of a man about to walk on fire: this beer is ferociously hot. The fuse leading to the bomb—the base beer—is a delicate 10 IBU. Made with six chilis—Anaheim, Fresno, Jalapeño, Serrano, Habanero, and Bhut Jolokia (aka the 1 million Scoville Ghost chili, which is so hot it's used as a military weapon)—you get sweet, smoked, and fruity green chili in the aroma, whispering a warning of what's coming, which is soon replaced by flares exploding at the back of your throat and up your nose while thrash metal bands scream "Fire!" in your ears. This is not for the delicate-tongued. Heat overpowers flavor, there's a hint of smoke, which makes you worry your mouth has combusted, your eyes water, your lips smart; you take another sip, wipe your tears, and breathe out some fire. Calling it the "hottest beer this side of hell," the brewery suggest milk or ice cream as a cooling accompaniment—you'll probably need it.

Mikkeller 1000 IBU

Copenhagen, Denmark
ABV: 9.6%
Hops: Magnum (extract), Simcoe

This is like crack for hop-heads in need of the ultimate fix, with its theoretical 1,000 IBUs of bitterness. Brash, brutal, extreme, and yet dangerously addictive, it's like you know it's probably bad for you but you can't stop sipping, loving the fierce hop-kick and the challenge to drink without wincing. Your brain probably thinks it's being poisoned and goes into high alert, ready to fight the toxins, all while your tongue is being ripped to pieces by extraordinary levels of bitterness. Yet... somehow... it remains incredibly drinkable—there's a lot of soothing, pleasing sweetness to temper the hops and you taste the hops in the same way that you can hear the music at a concert when you stand with an ear to the speaker: it fills your head with noise, but you can still sing along (picking out pine and citrus pith). The 9.6% ABV version is a Double IPA, while the 4.9% "Light" version is even more brutal as it rips around your mouth. Drink fresh for the full-on lupulin lash.

MEASURING IBU

Here's one for hop-obsessed math geeks: IBUs = U% x A% x W / V x C

U is hop utilization in percentage; A is the alpha acid content of the hop; W is the weight of hops in grams; V is the volume of beer in liters; and C is the gravity (the sugar content). The U is the important variable here: if the hops go in late, then they will score low on the utilization scale because they are there for aroma and not bitterness. The C is also a variable: low gravity will leave a higher perceptible bitterness, whereas a high gravity (and therefore more sweetness in the beer) will cover up some bitterness.

BLOCKBUSTER BEERS

SUPERSTAR BEERS ARE LIKE THOSE MUCH-ANTICIPATED MOVIE BLOCKBUSTERS THAT GET PEOPLE TALKING AND EXCITED WITH THE EXPECTATION OF SEEING THEM. RARE BEERS, BEERS WITH STORIES— THEIR NAMES BOUNCE AROUND BEER BARS, THEIR STORIES STICK DRY IN THE THROATS OF DRINKERS WHO HAVEN'T TASTED THEM YET, WHILE THOSE WHO HAVE TRIED THEM SIT UP A LITTLE TALLER AND TELL OF THEIR EXPERIENCE. "TOP OF MY MUST-DRINK LIST," "THE BEST BEER IN THE WORLD," "HAVE YOU HAD IT?" AND "HOW CAN I GET IT?"

If you read the beer-rating websites, take note of the beers that stay at or near the top. They aren't easy to get and their rarity raises their profile. The stories, and the things you need to do to get a taste, lift them to an elevated status. There they sit, surrounded by hype and expectation, raising your anticipation and desire for experience of them. Whether released once a year or available more often—but always incredibly difficult to get hold of—these beers are chased, craved, and sought after, justifying a bold tick next to their names in the "I've drunk that" column. Being rare and difficult to find, the best thing about them is that you need to go to the beer to drink it—it's the experience that matters.

Westvleteren 12

Westvleteren, Belgium
ABV: 10.2%
Hops: Locally grown hops from Poperinge

For years, Westvleteren 12 has been at the top of the best beer in the world lists on RateBeer.com and BeerAdvocate.com. It's a Belgian Quadrupel made in the smallest Trappist brewery—Sint Sixtus. It's made regularly but in small volumes and you need to go to the brewery to pick up a case if you want to drink it, and you must order in advance—one order per month per person, assuming the brewery even has the beer available. It's not expensive to buy but it's difficult to obtain. You can sometimes drink it in the café across from the monastery, but not always.

Once you have a glass of it in front of you, expect something excellent: tea, chocolate, sweetly bready, vanilla, toasted nuts, dates, and raisins. It has a rich, smooth, and light body and is a joy to drink. There's no doubt that it's a great beer, and it's impossible to drink without discussing the idea of the best beer in the world, which really adds to the drinking experience. Is this the best beer in the world? What is the best beer? Does it exist? This is a beer to get you thinking, sharing, and talking. In 2012, a packaged shipment was sent to America to sell in gift packs. Will this increased availability make the beer more popular, or will its hard-to-get allure gradually disappear?

Three Floyds Dark Lord

Munster, Indiana
ABV: 15.0%
Hops: Warrior

Dark Lord is so special that it has a whole day dedicated to it at the brewery. Once a year, on the last Saturday in April, the brewery opens up to thousands of people who are all there to grab a four-pack. I booked a trip to Chicago with mates and then realized Dark Lord Day coincided with it. We managed to get tickets (you have to buy them in advance), so we took a train and then a cab to Munster, and joined a three-hour line. The standing in line sucks, only made better by the bars selling other Three Floyds beers (and they make some incredible beer). All around, people drink Dark Lord or share special bottles that they've brought along; live bands provide entertainment, and there's lots of food, and a tangible, genuine excitement in the air: "We're at Dark Lord Day, dude!" But it's extraordinarily busy.

Finally, we get the beer and decide to leave soon after, avoiding more standing in line. On the train back, we share a bottle. It's an Imperial Stout made with Intelligentsia coffee, Mexican vanilla, and Indian sugar: thick like treacle, sweet like syrup, rich like chocolate, there are bursts of berries, ice cream, and even something floral in the aroma. It's hulking, brash, and outrageous. I don't love it, to be honest—give me a Gumballhead or Alpha King any day—but Dark Lord Day is an insane beer experience: go if you can.

Russian River Pliny the Younger

Santa Rosa, California
ABV: 10.5%
Hops: CTZ, Simcoe, Centennial, Amarillo, Chinook, CO2 extract

Brewed once a year, Pliny the Younger is a Triple IPA—a bigger version of Pliny the Elder, Russian River's kick-ass Double IPA. The day Younger's release (at the beginning of February), a line from the brewpub snakes all the way through Santa Rosa as people gather to get an elusive taste. The best place to find it is in the brewpub, but a few kegs will get to other bars; wherever it goes, the lines follow. It's available on tap only; the brewery used to do growler fills for takeout but they ended up all over the world or all over ebay, so they stopped it—this is a beer to drink local and fresh. I was in San Francisco the day it was released in 2010 and I met a Swedish guy who'd flown there to fill a growler and take it home with him to share with friends. Others had flown from all over America to get a taste. As a Triple IPA, the aroma is massive: sticky citrus, a pine forest, a cannabis factory. With a slick body of caramel and toffee-like malt, it's smooth to drink, adding balance to the massive wallop of bitterness at the end. It has an addictive extremity to it: sweet but brutal, a kiss and a punch. When you find it, it's hard to avoid the excitement of drinking it. I really like that.

Other blockbuster beers to look out for:

Bells Hopslam (beginning of the year), Foothills Sexual Chocolate (January), Portsmouth Kate the Great (first Monday in March), Cigar City Hunahpu's Imperial Stout (March), and The Bruery Black Tuesday.

LEARN MORE

BLOGS

Go online to find thousands of people talking and writing about beer. There are fascinating conversations taking place, interesting content, new beer reviews, and news posted. Almost all countries are home to someone writing about beer online—in fact, in 2012, Sweden had more beer bloggers than actual breweries, and there were over 1,000 American beer blogs. The Internet has made the beer world a far smaller place. Here are some of the best places to go to read about what's happening around the world:

EUROPE

Adrian Tierney-Jones—Called to the bar http://maltworms.blogspot.co.uk/
Andrea Turco (Italy)—Cronache di Birra http://www.cronachedibirra.it/
Andy Mogg—Beer Reviews http://www.beerreviews.co.uk/
Barry Masterson (Germany)—The Bitten Bullet
    http://thebittenbullet.blogspot.co.uk/
Boak & Bailey—Boak & Bailey's Beer Blog http://boakandbailey.com/
Chris Thompson—Beer and Life Matching
    http://www.beerandlifematching.com/
Darren Packman (Sweden)—Beer Sweden http://www.beerssweden.se/
Des de Moor—Beer Culture http://www.beerculture.org.uk/
Will—Ghost Drinker
    http://ghostdrinker.blogspot.co.uk/
Gianni, Alberto, and Vanessa (Italy)—In Birrerya
    http://www.inbirrerya.com/
Jeff Evans—Inside Beer
    http://www.insidebeer.com/
Joe Stange—Thirsty Pilgrim http://www.thirstypilgrim.com/
John Duffy (Ireland)—The Beer Nut http://thebeernut.blogspot.co.uk/
Leigh Linley—The Good Stuff http://goodfoodgoodbeer.wordpress.com/
Mark Charlwood—Beer.Birra.Bier http://www.beerbirrabier.com/
*Mark Dredge—Pencil&Spoon (That's me!)
    http://www.pencilandspoon.com/
Mark Fletcher (and others)—Real Ale Reviews http://real-ale-reviews.com/
Martyn Cornell—Zythophile http://zythophile.wordpress.com/
Maurizio Maestrelli (Italy)—Birragenda http://birragenda.blogspot.co.uk/
Matt Stokes—Beer & Food & Stuff
    http://www.beerandfoodandstuff.blogspot.co.uk/
Max Bahnson (Czech Republic)—Pivni Filosof http://www.pivni-filosof.com/
Neil—Eating Isn't Cheating http://eatingisntcheating.blogspot.co.uk/
Pete Brown—Pete Brown's Beer Blog http://petebrown.blogspot.co.uk/
Peter Alexander—Tandleman's Beer Blog
    http://tandlemanbeerblog.blogspot.co.uk/
Ron Pattinson—Shut up about Barclay Perkins
    http://barclayperkins.blogspot.co.uk/
Zak Avery—Are you tasting the pith? http://thebeerboy.blogspot.co.uk/

NORTH AMERICA

Alan McLeod—A Good Beer Blog http://beerblog.genx40.com/
Andy Crouch—Beer Scribe http://www.beerscribe.com/
Brewpublic http://brewpublic.com/
Ashley Routson—The Beer Wench http://drinkwiththewench.com/
Jay Brooks—Brookston Beer Bulletin http://brookstonbeerbulletin.com/
Jeff Alworth—Beervana http://beervana.blogspot.co.uk/
Lew Bryson—Seen Through a Glass http://lewbryson.blogspot.co.uk/
Mario Rubio—Brewed for Thought http://www.brewedforthought.com/
Pints and Panels http://www.pintsandpanels.com/
Stephen Beaumont—World of Beer http://worldofbeer.wordpress.com/
Stan Hieronymus—Appellation Beer http://appellationbeer.com/blog/
The Brewing Network http://www.thebrewingnetwork.com/
Velky Al—Fuggled http://www.fuggled.net/

REST OF THE WORLD

Ale of a Time (Australia)
    http://aleofatime.com/
Alice Galletly (New Zealand)—Beer for a Year
    http://beerforayear.wordpress.com/
Brews News (Australia)—http://www.brewsnews.com.au/
Japan Beer Times
    http://japanbeertimes.com
Logia Cervecera (Argentina) http://www.logiacervecera.com/
Phil Cook (New Zealand)—Beer Diary http://philcook.net/beerdiary/
Rafael Patricio—Cervesas Brasil Blog http://cervejasbrasil.wordpress.com/
The Crafty Pint (Australia)
    http://craftypint.com/

Ratebeer.com and Beeradvocate.com are also great places to check out if you want to talk about beer—the forums are very active.

BOOKS

So many great books have been written about beer, and I return to my favorites again and again. These are the ones that helped me during the writing of this book:

Amber, Black and Gold, Martyn Cornell
Ambitious Brew, Maureen Ogle
Beer Companion, Michael Jackson
Beer Craft, William Bostwick and Jessi Rymill
Brew Like a Monk, Stan Hieronymus
Brewed Awakening, Joshua Bernstein
Brewing with Wheat, Stan Hieronymus
The Brewmaster's Table, Garrett Oliver
The Flavour Thesaurus, Niki Segnit
For The Love of Hops, Stan Hieronymus
Good Beer Guide Prague, Evan Rail
Great American Craft Beer, Andy Crouch
Great British Pubs, Adrian Tierney-Jones
Hops and Glory, Pete Brown
The Northern California Craft Beer Guide, Ken Weaver
The Oxford Companion to Beer edited by Garrett Oliver
Tasting Beer, Randy Mosher
Three Sheets to the Wind, Pete Brown
The World Atlas of Beer, Tim Webb and Stephen Beaumont
The World Guide to Beer, Michael Jackson
World's Best Beers, Ben McFarland
1001 Beers, edited by Adrian Tierney-Jones
500 Beers, Zak Avery

GET THE CERTIFICATE

You can sign up for one of a number of recognized courses around the world to learn more about beer. Here are the best:

Cicerone—https://cicerone.org/
Beer Judge Certification Program—http://www.bjcp.org/index.php
Beer Academy—http://www.beeracademy.co.uk/
Siebel Institute—http://www.siebelinstitute.com/

INDEX

ACKNOWLEDGMENTS

Beer is a sharing kind of thing and it's always better with others. To make this book happen took a lot of input from a lot of different people, whether it was helping me understand complicated brewing techniques or pointing me toward a good bar or beer. First, a thank-you to the breweries: most replied very quickly to questions, showed interest in the book, and provided the images that brighten these pages. I hope I've done your great work justice. (And if I have got anything wrong, then I apologize; I tried hard to make this as accurate as possible.)

People from around the world have helped me out and while I want to go into more details, I simply don't have the space to be able to, so in no particular order, my thanks to: Adrian Tierney-Jones, Alessio Leone, Ken Weaver, Mark Fletcher, Andy Mogg, Leigh Linley, Simon Johnson, Darren Packman, Pelle Stridh, Fredrik Broberg, John Duffy, Barry Masterson, Kim Sturdavant, Evan Rail, Alexandre Bazzo, Bryan Harrell, Mark Melia, John Keeling, Stephen Beaumont, Tim Webb—I owe you all a beer or two. For having written great books or websites which provided insight or inspiration: Niki Segnit (I love The Flavour Thesaurus—everyone should own it), Ben McFarland, Ron Pattinson, Martyn Cornell, Joshua Bernstein, Andy Crouch, Jeff Alworth, Melissa Cole, Pete Brown, Tim Hampson, Garrett Oliver, Randy Mosher, Stan Heironymus, and, of course, Michael Jackson. The team at Camden Town Brewery deserve big high fives for having to answer my questions every day (for full transparency: I worked at the brewery while writing this book; I started working there because I love the beers). And special thanks to Kelly Ryan: he rounded up some of New Zealand's finest beers and also helped make sure my brewing knowledge didn't suck. Go to Good George Brewing in Hamilton and you'll find some of New Zealand's best beer in those tanks.

The team at Dog 'n' Bone deserve a lot of credit. Mark Latter made my words look good through the design, as did Paul Tilby. Caroline West edited out all of the typos and silly mistakes (any factual errors are definitely my fault, though!) and cheers to Pete Jorgensen for guidance, patience, and getting the book started (and finished)—let's go for a beer sometime.

To my mates (and drinking partners)—Matt Stokes, Lee Bacon, Mark Charlwood, Chris Perrin, Sean Mason, Pete Brissenden. When I needed to drink 20 Imperial Stouts, strong ales, and Barley Wines on the hottest day of the year, they were still willing to help out. Matt got me into beer in the first place so this is all his fault.

Mum and Dad: always supportive, always there when I need them, and always cheering me on (and Dad's always willing to share beer with me—thanks for helping out on the Brussels leg of the research!). Thank you so much for everything you have done and continue to do. Thanks to Vicki and Daryl: I hope that in 2027 some of these beers will still be around and I can share some with Frankie. To Sue and Nick: thanks for welcoming me into your family, for all the good food and drink, and for the good times (and Nick for also always being happy to share a beer with me).

And to Lauren. Thank you for not complaining at the 5 a.m. alarm, thank you for listening (and remembering), for caring, for your love, and for making me want to try harder and be better. This book is for you (even though you don't like beer).